The Feminist Companion to the Bible

5

Editor
Athalya Brenner

Sheffield Academic Press

a
$\mathcal{F}$eminist $\mathcal{C}$ompanion
to
Samuel and Kings

edited by Athalya Brenner

Copyright © 1994 Sheffield Academic Press

Sheffield Academic Press Ltd
343 Fulwood Road
Sheffield S10 3BP
England

Typeset by Sheffield Academic Press
and
Printed on acid-free paper in Great Britain
by The Cromwell Press
Melksham, Wiltshire

British Library Cataloguing in Publication Data

A catalogue record for this book is available
from the British Library

ISBN 1-85075-480-2

To the memory of

Fokkelien van Dijk-Hemmes

תּ·נ·צ·ב·ה·

CONTENTS

Epilogue
WOMEN IN LATER HISTORIOGRAPHY AND HISTORY

Abbreviations

AB	Anchor Bible
ANET	J.B. Pritchard (ed.), *Ancient Near Eastern Texts*
AOAT	Alter Orient und Altes Testament
AOS	American Oriental Series
ATANT	Abhandlungen zur Theologie des Alten und Neuen Testaments
BA	*Biblical Archaeologist*
BARev	*Biblical Archaeology Review*
BASOR	*Bulletin of the American Schools of Oriental Research*
BHK	R. Kittel (ed.), *Biblia hebraica*
BJS	Brown Judaic Studies
BR	*Biblical Research*
BWANT	Beiträge zur Wissenschaft vom Alten und Neuen Testament
BZAW	Beihefte zur *ZAW*
CBQ	*Catholic Biblical Quarterly*
CQR	*Church Quarterly Review*
CTA	A. Herdner, *Corpus des tablettes en cunéiformes alphabétiques découvertes à Ras Shamra-Ugarit de 1929 à 1939* (Paris: Imprimerie Nationale, 1963)
EHAT	Exegetisches Handbuch zum Alten Testament
EI	*Eretz Israel*
FOTL	The Forms of the Old Testament Literature
FRLANT	Forschungen zur Religion und Literatur des Alten und Neuen Testaments
HALAT	W. Baumgartner *et al.*, *Hebräisches und aramäisches Lexikon zum Alten Testament*
HKAT	Handkommentar zum Alten Testament
HSM	Harvard Semitic Monographs
HTR	*Harvard Theological Review*
HUCA	*Hebrew Union College Annual*
IB	*Interpreter's Bible*
ICC	International Critical Commentary
IDB	G.A. Buttrick (ed.), *Interpreter's Dictionary of the Bible*
IEJ	*Israel Exploration Journal*
Int	*Interpretation*

JANESCU	*Journal of the Ancient Near Eastern Society of Columbia University*
JBL	*Journal of Biblical Literature*
JEOL	*Jaarbericht...ex oriente lux*
JNES	*Journal of Near Eastern Studies*
JPSV	*Jewish Publication Society Version*
JSOT	*Journal for the Study of the Old Testament*
JSOTSup	*Journal for the Study of the Old Testament*, Supplement Series
JTS	*Journal of Theological Studies*
NICOT	New International Commentary on the Old Testament
NLH	*New Literary History*
OBO	Orbis biblicus et orientalis
OLP	Orientalia lovaniensia periodica
OTG	Old Testament Guides
OTL	Old Testament Library
OTS	*Oudtestamentische Studiën*
PRU	*Le Palais royal d'Ugarit*
RA	*Revue d'assyriologie et d'archéologie orientale*
REg	*Revue d'égyptologie*
RSR	*Recherches de science religieuse*
SBLDS	SBL Dissertation Series
SBLMS	SBL Monograph Series
SBT	Studies in Biblical Theology
SEL	*Studi epigrafici e linguistici*
ST	*Studia theologica*
StudOr	Studia orientalia
TLZ	*Theologische Literaturzeitung*
TOTC	Tyndale Old Testament Commentaries
TZ	*Theologische Zeitschrift*
USQR	*Union Seminary Quarterly Review*
VT	*Vetus Testamentum*
VTSup	*Vetus Testamentum*, Supplements
WBC	Word Biblical Commentary
WMANT	Wissenschaftliche Monographien zum Alten und Neuen Testament
WO	*Die Welt des Orients*
ZAH	*Zeitschrift für Althebraistik*
ZAW	*Zeitschrift für die alttestamentliche Wissenschaft*
ZDPV	*Zeitschrift des deutschen Palästina-Vereins*
ZTK	*Zeitschrift für Theologie und Kirche*

INTRODUCTION

Athalya Brenner

At the beginning of 1 Samuel 1, a woman (Hannah) is praying for a child. Her prayer is granted by YHWH. Maternal difficulties of childlessness, be they biological or social, regularly attend the birth of a biblical male hero and/or his evolvement into his vocation. So the woman becomes mother to a son: Samuel is born. Eventually he grows up to embody a wide range of religious and political functions. He is variously depicted as cultic official, prophet, judge, military and community leader—at least according to the story line we have in front of us.[1] He is also a figure of transition, a leader-mediator of premonarchic style who becomes a controller of kings. The narrative conceives him as a reluctant initiator of Israelite monarchy. He makes two kings (Saul and David) and breaks one (Saul).

At the beginning of 1 Kings 1, a woman (Bath Sheba) fights for her son's (Solomon's) physical and political survival. That son's birth is attended by difficulties too, this time not biological difficulties but social ones: his father David commits adultery with the mother while she is still married to Uriah. Eventually Solomon the son becomes king due to his mother's machinations and to the efforts of another king-maker, the prophet Nathan. Solomon too epitomizes a transition—from the personal charisma of leaders and kings to the institutionalized charisma of the Davidic dynasty.

Towards the end of 2 Kings a royal mother and her son, King

---

1. The text of Samuel, like many other biblical texts, is composite, as witnessed by the text-traditions now available. While I do not wish to quarrel with this fact, I also do not intend to re-present it. I believe that readers should first consider the end product, the text itself, before or apart from engaging in its developmental history.

Jehoiachin, are exiled to Babylon (2 Kgs 24.8-17).[1] This event, which prefigures the fall of Jerusalem to the Babylonians some ten years later, was apparently interpreted by contemporaries and later biblical authors as a political turning point of magnitude[2] and, therefore, a religiously significant occurrence. Indeed, that event was the beginning of the end of the Davidic monarchy, the biblical claim for which is that it was instituted by Samuel on behalf of God. No wonder that this transition from illusionary independence to acknowledged political dependence generated literary responses which, whatever their religio-political ideology, assumed the features of lament in both form and content.

One would expect the figure of the deported king to serve as the symbolic focal point of such lament, since the king personifies the institutions of Davidic kingship, political autonomy and divine grace. At the end of Kings, an optimistic ending of sorts is afforded by Jehoiachin's elevation in the Babylonian Court (2 Kgs 25.27-30); this change in his personal circumstances is a ray of future hope, analogous to the reference to Cyrus's edict at the end of Chronicles (2 Chron. 36.22-23). This answers our expectations: the monarch(y) is symbolic of land and political group. And yet two passages attributed to prophets lament the event not in terms of the king's fate, but in terms of the royal mother's fate (Jer. 13.18-20; Ezek. 19). This royal mother (be her identity as it may[3]), rather than the deposed king, symbolizes the collapse and imminent surrender of city (Jerusalem), territory, monarchy and political organization. In short, the historiographical text block which narrates monarchic Israel and Judah is framed at both its ends by female figures and/or figurations.[4] More specifically, this cycle of biblical historiography is enclosed

---

1. The parallel in 2 Chron. 36.9-10 is much shorter than the Kings passage. It omits all details of the king's retinue, including his mother.

2. Cf., for instance, the reference in Ezek. 17.12-14 (again without any mention of the king's entourage or his mother).

3. Cf. Ben-Barak's essay in this volume and the literature cited there.

4. The book of Proverbs is similarly framed: both its beginning (chs. 1–9) and end (ch. 31) deal with female figurations and discourse. Cf. C.V. Camp, *Wisdom and the Feminine in the Book of Proverbs* (Bible and Literature Series, 11; Sheffield: Almond Press, 1985).

by, embedded in, the figuration of the *leader's mother*.

Outside motherhood and family politics, women appear to have had almost no role open to them in ancient Israel's and Judah's political and religious life. The few prominent female figures encountered in biblical historiography are exceptions which underscore the rule. Is it surprising, then, that the historiographical narrative from Samuel to the fall of Jerusalem is thus enclosed? Should feminists, while pointing out the phenomenon, rejoice at its possibly deconstructive properties?

Perhaps not. The framing of biblical units by women stories[1] is fairly common. For instance, let us look at the book of Isaiah. It is widely recognized that, compositionally, Isaiah falls into at least three chief, separate, units: chs. 1–39, 40–55 and 56–66. Sawyer demonstrates that images of women and the female life cycle frame the whole book at its beginning (ch. 1) and end (ch. 66) and also recur in its middle sections (for instance, in chs. 47 and 49).[2] Ostensibly, this arrangement too may be read as a unifying element which underscores the significance of the female element in biblical culture. However, Sawyer shows how the image progresses from that of a 'daughter' to 'wife', sometimes an adulterous wife, to 'abandoned daughter/wife'; from 'mother' to 'bereaved/childless mother' to 'reinstated mother'. All these images are traditional, biologically-specific as well as socially relational (male-dependent) portraits of womanhood in an androcentric society. Even when they seem to foreground a female principle, they actually express and reinforce an established, male-oriented social order. The often-observed link between women and nature, women and land (and, by contiguity, women and the concept of territoriality, 'country') probably determines the female image of 'city' or political organization.[3]

1. That is, stories in which women have a central or at least significant role. This loose definition does not imply that the story is motivated by a concern for or love of femaleness. Such stories often serve a purpose extrinsic to their surface content; and see below.

2. J.F.A. Sawyer, 'Daughter of Zion and the Servant of the Lord in Isaiah: A Comparison', *JSOT* 44 (1989), pp. 89-107.

3. 'Town/city' as well as 'country' and 'land' are grammatically feminine in Hebrew. I am tempted to speculate that the grammatical categorization of those terms may have been derived from the cultural imaging

Sawyer reads the female imagery in Isaiah as a linear if circuitous 'story', from wayward 'daughter' (ch. 1) to fulfilled
'mother' (ch. 66, especially vv. 7-9). But this persuasive reading
reveals, not unexpectedly, a portrait of the ideal biblical woman:
mother of a male child or, better still, male children (vv. 7-8, 13).

It is therefore neither surprising nor particularly liberating for
womanly readers to find that the editorial framework of
Samuel–Kings presents figurations of motherhood at its beginning and closure. This arrangement fits in well with the prevalent biblical gender ideology, as has been established by feminist
critics in recent decades. Hence, rather than dwell further upon
issues of the relevance of the frame, let us now turn to particular images of femaleness and femininity in Samuel–Kings, and to
their implications for biblical gender ideology and reconstruc-
tions of pre-exilic sociology. En route we shall encounter chiefly
relational images—daughters, wives and mothers, unnamed as
well as named.

Part I: Women as Vehicles for Historiography: Liminality and Anonymity

Biblical ideology hardly distinguishes between the sex and gender roles allowed to women. Indeed, it encourages them to
seek social vocation and influence as well as biological fulfilment
almost exclusively in motherhood. Motherhood is portrayed as
historically meaningful not only for history but also for the
women-in-the-text. Through it they are supposed to acquire a
name for themselves. The first two essays in this collection
explore the dominant ideology from two perspectives: that of
daughters, and that of anonymous female characters.

In 'Living on the Edge: The Liminality of Daughters in
Genesis to 2 Samuel', Karla G. Shargent surveys the daughterly
status of biblical women. The survey leads up to the figure of
Michal, Saul's daughter and David's wife who was destined by
the main stream of biblical fiction not to become a mother.[1]

---

of the sexless entities they connote as women rather than, as many
commentators will have it, the other way round.

1. On Michal, see D.J.A. Clines and T.C. Eskenazi (eds.), *Telling Queen
Michal's Story: An Experiment in Comparative Interpretation* (JSOTSup, 119;

Shargent demonstrates that biblical daughters are depicted as doubly liminal, both temporally and spatially: they must move on from being nubile daughters into becoming wives and mothers, otherwise they are killed in (or by) the text; and no space, inside or outside, domestic or public, is safe for them. Among other things, this essay[1] illustrates how women, unless they do become mothers, are not accorded meaningful membership of the ongoing movement of biblical historiography.

Another way to mask, if not terminate, women's memory in history is to depict them as anonymous in relation to the named male characters around whom the action revolves. In 'Anonymous Women and the Collapse of the Monarchy: A Study in Narrative Technique', Adele Reinhartz explores the ways in which the namelessness of women serves the Davidic bias of the historiographers. She classifies anonymous female figures in Kings according to their textual linkage with male figures: Solomon (wives and the Queen of Sheba; harlot-mothers), Yoram (the cannibalistic mother) and prophets: Elijah and Elisha (mothers who enjoy miracles), Ahijah (Jeroboam's wife). The anonymous women mostly play conventional social roles, especially that of a mother. The main theme is the mother–son relationship. This theme connects with, and reflects on, a major theme in Kings as a whole: the collapse of the monarchy, which is tied up with the failure of kings and their royal mothers to emulate David. The anonymity serves to organize the stories, typify them, and deflect attention from female to male figures.

Part II: A Model Mother: Hannah

Hannah, the first maternal figure in Samuel–Kings, is portrayed as a paradigm wife-mother. The maternal ambition attributed to her figure is conventional enough in terms of the text's ideology; her story, however, is not. Hannah is unlike other biblical female figures who share her predicament. She is a

Sheffield: JSOT Press, 1991).

1.   On the topic of biblical daughters see also I. Rashkow, 'Daughters and Fathers in Genesis...Or, What is Wrong with This Picture?', in A. Brenner (ed.), *A Feminist Companion to Exodus–Deuteronomy* (The Feminist Companion to the Bible, 5; Sheffield: Sheffield Academic Press, 1994).

female subject who dares to make a bargain with God, and the bargain is accepted. Hannah's figure, and her affiliations with other figures in the story of 1 Samuel 1, are explored in three essays.

Yairah Amit, in '"Am I Not More Devoted To You Than Ten Sons?" (1 Samuel 1.8): Male and Female Interpretations', focuses on Elkanah's attempted consolation to his wife. She suggests that the interpretations of 1.8 by ancient and modern exegetes are mostly male-biased. They are offered from Elkanah's perspective and fail to take the female perspective of the textual Hannah into account. This, in Amit's opinion, is inappropriate, since Hannah holds the focal subject position in the narrative. Amit reads Elkanah's words as ultimately immature, inadequate and improper to the situation. Hannah's silence and departure to the temple are consequently read as an act of protest.

But Hannah has other textual relationships apart from the relationship with her husband. In 'Hannah: Marginalized Victim and Social Redeemer', Lillian Klein discusses Hannah's interaction with the other narrated characters—Peninnah, Eli and YHWH. Klein analyses the story from the perspectives of jealousy and mimetic desire (as defined by Girard), their disruptive sociocultural impact and the ensuing marginalization the victim may suffer; and the differences between female and male discourses. She reads Hannah as a marginalized victim of Peninnah's and Elkanah's displaced mimetic desire who, nonetheless, does not collaborate with the others' desire and behaviour. Although Eli too projects his shortcomings onto her, Hannah is heard, and her situation ameliorated, by YHWH. By not joining in the desire and its projection, Hannah neutralizes the damage wrought to the social unit, thus acting as a paradigmatic positive force of social redemption.

In 'Hannah and her Sacrifice: Reclaiming Female Agency', Carol Meyers focuses on another aspect of this literary figure: her cultic behaviour. Meyers establishes Hannah's prominence in the story, which is basically *her* story in which she is *named* and is a speaking agent. Although Hannah is often discussed in terms of her wifehood and motherhood, the implications of her vow and sacrifice usually receive much less attention in Bible scholarship, as does the participation of women in the cult throughout the Bible itself. Thus Meyers examines the text about Hannah for what can be gleaned from it about biblical women and worship.

Part III: The Women 'of' King David

The textual King David is depicted as a veritable lady-killer. Quite a few named women are linked to him as lovers or legitimized spouses. In King David's story, named women are usually reflections of his pronounced manly erotic nature. One, Tamar, is the daughter-signifier of his sweeping failure as a parent (2 Sam. 13.19). Other, unnamed women represent wisdom and prudence (chs. 14 and 20). In this volume we shall look at the first category, that of some female figures linked to David as sexual partners.

In 'The Pleasure of Her Text' Alice Bach rereads 1 Samuel 25 as Abigail's story, a self-contained narrative unit of which Abigail is the central figure. In so doing, Bach reverses the biblical custom of introducing a woman figure via her sexual connection with David. She sees Abigail as a 'good-sense wife', a sharp woman who uses verbal discourse to manipulate social and sexual codes wisely, in a manner that serves her own interests and, simultaneously, those of David and Nabal. Once married to David, Bach observes, Abigail loses her narrative power, political agency and verbal potency. Like other female figures whom David takes away from other men, Abigail is a subject and has an identity only up to the moment she is legally united with him. As his wife, the highly articulate Abigail becomes mute.

Shulamit Valler examines 'King David and "his" Women' in the 'Biblical Stories and Talmudic Discussions'. She reads the biblical David as a symbol of (biblical) masculine ideology. However, whereas the women linked to his name are secondary characters, they are nevertheless presented as not lacking actantial or verbal initiative. The talmudic David has undergone a transformation. From a worldly soldier, political leader and lover he has been developed into a spiritual believer, a self-sacrificing, unworldly person. This development, together with the Jewish sages' ideas about women and womanhood, motivates the talmudic readings and homilies of the women's stories. Valler cites discussions about David's marital relations in general and with named women, particularly with Michal, Abigail, Bath Sheba and Abishag. In order to present David as their scholarly and religious ideal, the Jewish sages sometimes change the narrative role of the female figures, and subdue the latter so that the textual women conform to their own ideology, which is even more stringent than the biblical gender ideology.

Carole Fontaine writes about 'The Bearing of Wisdom on the Shape of 2 Samuel 11–12 and 1 Kings 1–2'. Wisdom is viewed as a mediator, endowed by Yahweh for the ruler's private and public conduct and benefit. Solomon accepts the gift; David proves by his actions—especially those linked with the Bath Sheba affair—that he does not accept the divine gift. Thus, the reader is invited to view David in Solomon's light, to compare the father to the son whom he—wisely—chooses to be his successor.

'The Bearing of Wisdom' was published in 1986. In 'A Response to the Bearing of Wisdom', Carole Fontaine reflects on her previous essay and extends some of the points mentioned in it.

Part IV: Queen Mothers?

Ancient Israel and Judah did not have 'queens', in the sense that the biblical text does not acknowledge the legitimacy of female monarchs within pre-exilic Israelite or Judahite political organization. The concept of 'queen' as female monarch (the Queen of Sheba) or king's wife (Esther) is known, but relegated to foreign cultures. Athaliah's reign is denounced. There remain the issues of the formal or informal position of a king's mother, sometimes called 'queen mother' by analogy to later times and neighbouring cultures; and the meaning of the epithet נבירה, 'lady', which is at times assigned to royal females.

In 'The Status and Right of the *gᵉbirā*', Zafrira Ben-Barak reconsiders the notion that, in ancient Israel, the נבירה was a queen mother who enjoyed formal station and power analogous to those of her equivalents in other ancient Near Eastern monarchies. Ben-Barak analyses the cases of Bath Sheba, Maacah, Hamutal and Nehushta, mothers of young kings who succeeded in acquiring a following and position. She concludes that their status was granted to them personally by their royal sons. A chronological list of royal mothers from outside ancient Israel and Judah, from the thirteenth to the fifth–sixth centuries BCE, who managed to put their younger sons on the throne shows, according to Ben-Barak, that such royal women achieved power and status individually through ability, ambition and the royal son's favour. Therefore, she concludes that neither 'queen mother' nor נבירה had an official status.

But what about Maacah, or Athaliah, or Jezebel (whom Ben-Barak mentions but dismisses)? In 'Maacah—A Case Study: The Queen Mother in the Judaean Royal Court', Ktziah Spanier argues *for* an acknowledgment of the queen mother's official function within the Judaean court and realm. In Spanier's view, the גבירה, 'lady', assumed her official authority upon her son's accession to the throne and retained it for the duration of his rule (or her life). If Ben-Barak views the royal mother's influence as a consequence of her successful attempts to have her son enthroned, Spanier reads the paradigm differently: the son's accession is the consequence of his mother's being a favourite wife to his father. She examines Maacah's story for the sources of the queen mother's power, and concludes that those were ancestry, territories, court influence and imported cult.

And what about Jezebel, who certainly has power and influence? Rather than discuss the formal properties of her narrative, Tina Pippin has 'Jezebel Re-Vamped'. Pippin's concern is as much with colloquial cultural appropriations of 'jezebel' as with interpretations of the biblical character of Jezebel. Misogynist views of Jezebel, which women adopt, make for a 'bitch/witch', evil, sexual image; the complexity and royal spirit exhibited by her are interpreted as masculinity and otherness. Pippin traces the links between the biblical texts about Jezebel and intertexts in twentieth-century drama, poetry, film and art in order to 'deal with the cultural representations and the interactions of readers with the image of Jezebel'. The result is a plurality of Jezebel and jezebel images in the Bible, its interpretations, and contemporary texts. The images are 'colonized' (Pippin's term) and used against women and female sexuality; a line is drawn between Jezebel's life and death, and the jezebel metaphor.

Part V: Female, Femaleness/Prophets, Prophecy

Engagements between females and prophets or prophecy have already been discussed in the essays by Reinhartz and Pippin. In this section, the woman–prophet–prophecy cluster of themes is looked at from three different perspectives.

Jan Tarlin strives 'Toward a "Female" Reading of the Elijah Cycle'. He suggests that the Elijah cycle, ostensibly a patriarchal text about male bonding between the prophet and his God, can be read differently by appealing to a female readerly subjectivity. Traditional interpretations focus on 'male' figures-in-the-text: redactor, history, historical consciousness, inspiration and author. If the quest for these is put aside, the textual 'mirror' yields an impetuous, 'female' reflection rather than a 'male', ordered one. Then textual fragmentation, contradiction, circularity, ambiguity and open-endedness can be discerned. Tarlin finally suggests that his exercise in male 'feminized' reading points to the possibility of crossing the traditional boundaries of 'male' as against 'female' dualized subjectivity.

Fokkelien van Dijk-Hemmes, in 'The Great Woman of Shunem: A Dual Interpretation of 2 Kings 4.8-37', juxtaposes two options open to feminist critics: to wrestle with the biblical text for the presumably hidden liberating content, or to proclaim the irredeemably patriarchal, androcentric bent of Scripture and the powerful gender ideology deployed in it. Following Schweickart's proposal for a simultaneous dual (positive and negative) hermeneutic of male canonical texts, van Dijk-Hemmes proceeds to assess the story of the Shunammite twice. In the first (and resisted) reading, the text is seen as patriarchal propaganda for women's essential maternity *and* the superior life-giving properties of the male ('man of God'). In the second (liberating) reading, the sustained encounter between the woman and Elisha affirms that without her support and hospitality he would not have come to produce a miracle (which the textual ideology demands of him). Van Dijk-Hemmes concludes that the two interpretations are not mutually exclusive but, on the contrary, mutually supportive.

Since ancient times, male interpreters have been asking why King Josiah sends messengers to Huldah for an oracle (2 Kgs

22.14-20; 2 Chron. 34.22-28), whereas—according to the Bible's account of its own chronology—the prophet Jeremiah should have been available and consulted. Diana Edelman asks, 'Huldah the Prophet—of Yahweh or Asherah?'. Edelman tentatively suggests a composite history for a Huldah tradition: from a bare reference of consultation in 2 Kings 22, without knowledge of Huldah's original status as prophet of YHWH's consort Asherah, to a composition of an oracle; then the establishment of a link between the oracle story, and a story about the finding of the law scroll in the temple by a Deuteronomic editor. By the end of the process, it is tacitly assumed that YHWH was consulted rather than Asherah, and Huldah is presented as a female Jeremiah. Edelman hypothesizes that, when the final redaction was undertaken, Asherah's divine status was no longer acceptable. Whether this redaction suppressed the original (admittedly reconstructed) function of Huldah and Asherah consciously or otherwise remains a moot point.

Epilogue: Women's Status in Later
Historiography and History

Samuel–Kings is the historiography of pre-exilic 'Israel'. The weighty question of when this text unit finally achieved its MT form notwithstanding, the aim of the composition is clear: to account for the movement of history through certain lenses, in keeping with well-defined ideologies. Although decidedly indirect and a side issue for the writers, it seems, gender ideology is a constituent of the general ideological framework. The present collection has explored the compositional unit for women's lives, female voices, gendered types and women's presence in the written history.

By way of an epilogue, Tamara C. Eskenazi's essay outlines women's lives in the next biblical period, the so-called Persian period (sixth to fourth centuries BCE). 'Out from the Shadows: Biblical Women in the Post-Exilic Era' demonstrates how the biblical historiographical evidence (this time in Ezra and Nehemiah) concerning women's lives has been misinterpreted but, also, that it needs to be supplemented by external (archaeological and inscriptional) material. In Eskenazi's words, the 'recovery of women's stories and traditions' is an important task of feminist bible scholarship.

Part I
WOMEN AS VEHICLES FOR HISTORIOGRAPHY: LIMINALITY AND ANONYMITY

LIVING ON THE EDGE:
THE LIMINALITY OF DAUGHTERS IN GENESIS TO 2 SAMUEL

Karla G. Shargent

Two and a half years have passed since I set off on a journey to study what the Hebrew Bible has to say about daughters.[1] When I look back now on the first stages of my travels, it seems as if I were moving through a wilderness devoid of resources. That is, it did not take me long to realize that biblical commentaries, for instance, rarely give separate consideration to the category of daughters—even when daughters figure largely in the biblical texts being analyzed.[2] And works stylized as anthropologies of the Bible also make little room for the subject of daughters. They are either considered under the rubric of children, where they quickly become buried under an avalanche of

---

1.   I am greatly indebted to Carol L. Meyers for first suggesting such a journey, as well as for the many ways in which she has subsequently furthered my thinking about biblical daughters. I want to thank, too, several of my colleagues at Duke University for their personal and professional support as I struggled with the ideas for this paper: F. Volker Greifenhagen, Ann Burlein and Sandie Gravett. An earlier version of this paper was read at the 1992 AAR/SBL Annual Meeting in San Francisco, CA.

2.   As an illustration of this general pattern, one needs only examine the standard analyses of Gen. 19.30-38 (Lot and his daughters in the cave of Zoar). Most often this narrative is read as an aetiology of the Moabites and Ammonites; cf. W. Brueggemann, *Genesis: A Bible Commentary for Teaching and Preaching* (Interpretation; Atlanta: John Knox, 1982), pp. 176-77; C. Westermann, *Genesis 12–36: A Commentary* (trans. J.J. Scullion SJ; Minneapolis: Augsburg, 1985), pp. 310-15. Alternatively, it is read as a story that further ridicules Lot; cf. G.W. Coats, *Genesis: With an Introduction to Narrative Literature* (FOTL, 1; Grand Rapids: Eerdmans, 1983), pp. 146-48. Either way, scant notice is given to the initiative and intelligence displayed by the two daughters.

information about sons,[1] or they are used, in a rather fragmentary way, to illuminate certain social practices (for instance marriage customs, adoption issues, rights of inheritance). The latter tendency, in particular, is characterized by an intense focus on a few isolated texts among the legal materials, the rich narrative portrayals of daughters being either ignored or used only sparingly to illustrate the legal imperatives.[2] And although biblical scholarship informed by feminist perspectives has been a beacon of hope—insofar as it spotlights many of the previously neglected biblical narratives that involve women—it, too, still tends to ignore the category of daughter as daughter.[3]

If it had not been for my reading of Mieke Bal's *Death and*

1. In his chapter on children, Roland de Vaux spends two full pages discussing the issue of children's education. Only at the end does he notify us that 'The preceding paragraphs concern only the education of boys. Girls remained under the control of their mothers, who taught them what they needed to know for their duty as wives and housekeepers' (R. de Vaux, *Ancient Israel: Its Life and Institutions* [trans. J. McHugh; New York: McGraw-Hill, 1961), p. 50.

2. De Vaux is probably the most attentive to the narrative portions of the Hebrew Bible. But even he still determines the issues to be considered by relying to a great extent on the legal texts; see de Vaux, *Ancient Israel*, esp. pp. 19-61. Johannes Pedersen, too, structures his view of the social order of ancient Israel by using the law codes. And unlike de Vaux, he spares almost no attention for the narratives; see J. Pedersen, *Israel: Its Life and Culture* (London: Oxford University Press, 1926), I, II. Hans Walter Wolff, in a rather surprising shift, constructs his anthropology in a way that leans heavily on the Psalms and wisdom books; see *Anthropology of the Old Testament* (trans. M. Kohl; Philadelphia: Fortress Press, 1974).

3. Survey articles on women in the Bible are very illuminating in this regard. Phyllis Bird mentions daughters only once, in passing, in the context of her discussion of inheritance laws; see 'Images of Women in the Old Testament', in R. Radford Ruether (ed.), *Religion and Sexism* (New York: Simon & Schuster, 1974), p. 53. And the more recent article by Susan Niditch also fails to consider daughters as a separate category: 'Portrayals of Women in the Hebrew Bible', in J.R. Baskin (ed.), *Jewish Women in Historical Perspective* (Detroit: Wayne State University Press, 1991), pp. 25-42. Even books purporting to survey women in the Hebrew Bible ignore the role of daughters; cf. J.G. Williams, *Women Recounted: Narrative Thinking and the God of Israel* (Sheffield: Almond Press, 1982), and A. Brenner, *The Israelite Woman: Social Role and Literary Type in Biblical Narrative* (The Biblical Seminar, 2; Sheffield: JSOT Press, 1985).

Dissymetry and Phyllis Trible's *Texts of Terror* I might have reneged on my journey entirely, considering it a fool's quest that had led me only up a blind alley. But in these two books I found intimated the possibility of constructing a study in which the explicit focus was the portrayal of daughters across a whole spectrum of biblical narratives. Mieke Bal's work was important to me as an example of a full-length study that foregrounds, for several biblical women, their role as daughters (including Jephthah's daughter, the Judges 19 concubine and the Timnite wife of Samson). Consequently, our understanding of these women is both revitalized and complicated. Of course, the identification of these women as daughters is not, for Bal, of the first order of importance. Her principal interest is in the ways in which their stories can be read as a working out of a conflict between virilocal and patrilocal marriage in ancient Israel.[1] Furthermore, although Bal does occasionally extend her readings to include the stories of daughters in other parts of the Hebrew Bible, the primary focus of her study is just the one book of Judges.

Phyllis Trible does not limit herself to one biblical book. Her work, *Texts of Terror*, bridges the distance across several different biblical books as it retells the stories of Hagar (Genesis), Tamar (2 Samuel), an unnamed concubine (Judges) and the daughter of Jephthah (Judges). Yet even though three of the aforementioned women have in common the fact that their being identified as daughters is integral to the unfolding narratives in which they play a role, Trible nowhere makes explicit mention of that fact! For her what these stories have in common is that they are all 'sad stories' with 'women as victims'.[2]

Suffice it to say that although these two books gave me the courage to press on with my journey, neither of them provided me with a sure framework for conceptualizing a study of biblical daughters. With no secure positioning, I fell prey to intense feelings of insecurity. At just this juncture, though, a new path was opened up for me by the feminist theorizing of Linda Alcoff. She asserts that 'the position that women find themselves in can be actively utilized...as a location for the construction of

---

1. See D. Jobling, 'Mieke Bal on Biblical Narrative', *RSR* 17 (1991), p. 5.
2. P. Trible, *Texts of Terror* (Philadelphia: Fortress Press, 1984), p. 1.

meaning'.[1] And so by a process best characterized as an inside-out revisioning I transformed my lack of a standpoint into a standpoint: the insecurity under which I was operating became the position from which I began to recognize the insecurity of the narrative daughters of the Hebrew Bible. However, whereas my insecurity partly proceeds out of a world of biblical scholarship which still has difficulty even recognizing the presence of daughters in biblical narratives, the insecurity of biblical daughters can be said to operate at least partly because their textual world is one that positions them on the boundaries.

When Victor Turner speaks of boundary states he uses the term 'liminality'. For him it is a way to refer to that which is neither here nor there, and to recognize persons who are defined as 'betwixt and between assigned societal positions'.[2] As Turner goes about further specifying this concept, he reviews a number of traditional societies in which societal members partake in ceremonial rites of passage; it thus becomes clear that for him liminality is something that happens along the temporal dimension of human existence. Yet the Bible's construction of daughters positions them liminally along the axes of both time and space. That is, a synchronic reading of narratives involving daughters in Genesis through 2 Samuel[3] betrays a temporal liminality of daughters wherein the text's conceptualization of the daughter role is confined to the narrow span of time that marks

1. L. Alcoff, 'Cultural Feminism versus Post-Structuralism: The Identity Crisis in Feminist Theory', in E. Minnich, J. O'Barr and R. Rosenfeld (eds.), *Reconstructing the Academy: Women's Education and Women's Studies* (Chicago: University of Chicago Press, 1988), p. 286.

2. V. Turner, *The Ritual Process* (Chicago: Aldine, 1969), p. 95.

3. The decision to focus on the narratives of Genesis through 2 Samuel was somewhat arbitrary, yet also shaped by several constraints. My main concern was to move towards redressing the general neglect of biblical scholarship towards those daughters portrayed in biblical narratives. But since narrative depictions of daughters in the Bible are concentrated in the two books of Genesis and Judges, it behooved me to shape a study that took advantage of that fact. At the same time there are no sustained narratives involving daughters in either Kings or Chronicles, which explains why I stop with 2 Samuel. And including a consideration of daughters or daughter imagery from the Latter Prophets or Writings would have greatly overburdened this paper.

the move from childhood to adulthood. Meanwhile, these same narratives also engage in a spatial liminalization of daughters so that they have no secure place of their own. Although daughters portrayed in the narratives of the Hebrew Bible are free to move about almost everywhere, nowhere is safe for them.

The resulting double jeopardy effects a positioning for biblical daughters that is particularly precarious. And although all the narrative daughters in Genesis through 2 Samuel partake, to some degree, in this liminalization, it is in the figure of Michal—and more precisely as she is narratively introduced in 1 Samuel 19—that we find perhaps the most vivid and concise embodiment of a biblical daughter in a liminal state.

The Temporal Liminality of Biblical Daughters

Our commonplace understandings of the daughter role accept it as one that can possibly extend over the entire lifespan of a woman. Of course, the particular contents of the role are apt to change: a middle-aged woman responsible for the care of her elderly parents has a configuration of rights and responsibilities quite at odds with those of a five-year-old girl heavily dependent on others for her wellbeing. Still, we scarcely hesitate in our recognition of both of them as daughters.

Biblical discourse works otherwise. By and large, the Bible limits its understanding of daughters to just those women who have come to sexual maturity. (Although all women are daughters, for biblical writers all daughters are only young women!) It is not that the text explicitly conveys the ages of the daughters depicted in its narratives. Rather, the contexts within which they are introduced allow us to infer at what point in their life cycle they become narratively visible.

For the most part, biblical daughters appear on the scene in response to a need by male characters for wives. Rebekah, for instance, is introduced into the biblical text so as to appear providentially before the servant of Abraham; the latter has undertaken a journey under the specific directives of his master in order to find a wife for Isaac (cf. Gen. 24.1-15).[1] Rachel,

---

1. Versification and English translations of the biblical text rely on the New Revised Standard Version, unless otherwise noted.

Rebekah's daughter-in-law, is also ushered into the text when a patriarch is required to marry. In her case, of course, Jacob's journey to Nahor is motivated primarily by his need to flee from Esau's anger; but he has also been directed by his father, Isaac, to find a wife (cf. Gen. 27.41–29.12). (Jacob ends up with not one but two wives, for his meeting with Rachel results in his marriage to both her and her sister Leah!) The Midianite daughters of Reuel are brought into the story of Moses at the point at which he is seeking refuge from the anger of Pharaoh. But a mere five verses after their introduction, Zipporah, the eldest daughter, becomes Moses' wife—even though Moses ostensibly was not looking to get married (cf. Exod. 2.15-21). The daughters of Shiloh are inserted into the text consequent to the need of a certain number of Benjaminites for wives; only by their marriages is the continued existence of the tribe of Benjamin assured (cf. Judg. 21.15-24). And, finally, Michal comes to the notice of her father, Saul, only when it is learned that she loves David (1 Sam. 18.20). Their subsequent marriage at least temporarily suggests a hope for the reconciliation of the Saulide and Davidic parties.

Not all biblical daughters become wives. Yet even for those who do not, it is still their maturing sexuality that is the focal point of their identification. Indeed, for these daughters the biblical narratives tend to move with breathtaking speed from introducing them into the text to embroiling them in a sexually loaded activity. So Tamar, daughter of David, is introduced in v. 1 of 2 Samuel 13; by v. 14 we learn of Amnon's rape of her. With Dinah, Jacob and Leah's daughter, the move happens even more quickly: Genesis 34 opens (v. 1) with an introduction to her; immediately (v. 2) the text relates her abduction by Shechem (leaving aside for the moment the notice of her birth back in Gen. 30.21). And the very introduction of Lot's daughters coincides with information about their sexual maturity— although in this latter case their actual sexual activity is diverted to the later episode with their father (Gen. 19.8, 30-38).

The rule of the Bible whereby daughters are seen only when they become sexually mature young women has one possible exception: Jephthah's daughter. One might plausibly argue that she is still a prepubescent girl when she comes out to dance and sing before her father. But even her story includes intimations of her sexuality. After all, her final words are a request that she be allowed to go to the mountains with her companions and bewail her virginity (cf. Judg. 11.37).

If biblical daughters are first introduced into the text only when they have come of age, under what circumstances do they exit from the text? That is, at what point do their stories end? If 'endings, however conventional, overdetermine narrative logic, and in this sense [they] might be thought of as a taxonomy of *telos*',[1] then the conclusions to biblical narratives involving daughters ought to speak to the text's ultimate intended goal for them. From this standpoint, the textual imperative for daughters is of an extremely limited nature: they must become mothers. Ideally this occurs within the confines of marriage, and preferably to a man identified as an Israelite. But it is just possible to be a mother without the benefit of marriage. However, failing to become a mother (and/or wife) condemns a daughter to death.

It should, then, occasion little surprise to note that in many of the narrative depictions of daughters endings reinforce beginnings. That is, a daughter who comes into the narrative because a male character needs a wife finds herself reconfigured as a wife (and mother) in the concluding episode of that very same narrative. Rebekah exemplifies this pattern most convincingly. She is introduced near the beginning of Genesis 24, and the last words of this same chapter inform us that she became the wife of the patriarch Isaac (cf. v. 67). Moreover, her future role as mother is also adumbrated in the concluding portion of Genesis 24, for immediately before she departs on her journey to Isaac, her family blesses her with the words 'May you, our sister, become thousands of myriads; may your offspring gain possession of the gates of their foes' (v. 60). With regard to Zipporah, the eldest Midianite daughter of Reuel, the narrative fragment that introduces her and her sisters concludes with the notice that she has become, first, Moses' wife, and, secondly, Gershom's mother (cf. Exod. 2.16-22). And in the case of the daughters of Shiloh, the last we hear of them is that they have

1. N. Miller, *The Heroine's Text: Readings in the French and English Novel, 1722–1782* (New York: Columbia University Press, 1980), p. xi.

become wives to the remaining unmarried Benjaminites (cf. Judg. 21.23). Although no explicit notice is given about their becoming mothers, their move into this role is absolutely necessitated by the narrative context. After all, the whole point of their forced marriages is to repopulate the tribe of Benjamin; the disaster which precipitated the marital unions will be overcome only when the daughters become mothers to a new generation of Benjaminites (cf. Judg. 20–21).

The narrative construction of several other daughter stories is rather more complicated, yet it scarcely matters insofar as these daughters, too, end up as mothers. So, for instance, the daughters of Zelophehad are featured in two different, yet related, texts (Num. 27.1-11; 36.1-12), and in neither one are they introduced under the pretext of men looking for wives. Nonetheless, the concluding verses of Numbers 36—which also close the whole book—contain the notice that these daughters have married kin relations of their father ('sons of their father's brothers' [v. 11]). As with the Shilonite daughters, the text does not explicitly report their becoming mothers. But the very reason they married was to guarantee the retention of their inheritance within the clan. If they do not have children, transfer of the inheritance to an outside clan is again a risk.[1] A somewhat reversed situation presents itself in the conclusion of the story of Lot's daughters. That is, their story comes to an end once it is reported that they have borne children. But the prior information about their becoming wives is missing because, of course, no men are available to them to marry (cf. Gen. 19.31). Their sons result from sexual relations with their father (Gen. 19.36). And finally, in the story of Rachel situations are

---

1.   The story of the daughters of Zelophehad is complicated in yet another way. Besides the two narratives in Num. 27 and 36 that feature them, the Bible refers to them three other times. Num. 26.33 lists their names in the context of a tribal census; the verse thus serves as a sort of proleptic introduction to the ch. 27 narrative. Josh. 17.3-6 again mentions their names, while also reviewing how they came to have an inheritance 'among the kinsmen of their father' (Josh. 17.5). And 1 Chron. 7.15 refers, in passing, to the fact that Zelophehad had daughters. In none of these texts is their wifehood or motherhood clearly articulated, although both roles are implied in their inclusion in the Chronicles genealogy.

presented that are both like and unlike that of her mother-in-law Rebekah. Thus, both women become wives to patriarchs, and both are mothers to two sons of the line of Abraham (Rebekah is mother to Esau and Jacob; Rachel to Joseph and Benjamin). Yet Rachel's attainment of these two roles is fraught with more uncertainty than was the case with Rebekah. First, she is married to Jacob only after he has already married her sister Leah. Secondly, she becomes a mother only after Leah, Bilhah and Zilpah all have children. Moreover, when she gives birth to her second son, she dies (Gen. 35.16-19). Her life, unlike the lives of the other matriarchs, is cut short. Is this punishment for her earlier deception of her father Laban, when she hid the *tᵉrāpîm* from him?[1] Yet Jacob does set up a pillar over her grave as a memorial, so she is commemorated by later generations of Israelites (Gen. 35.20).

Even given the narrative byways into which some of the above daughter stories have wandered, they have all still ended in approximately the same way: with daughters becoming mothers (and/or wives). But what of those daughters who fail to negotiate the passage leading to motherhood (and wifehood)? They die. The text is unable (or unwilling) to envision any other livable alternative for them.

This message is conveyed most explicitly by the book of Judges. The daughter of Jephthah who, we are told, 'had never slept with a man' (11.39), affirms her father's vow and so dies by his hand. The Timnite daughter, whose marriage to Samson was annulled by her father and who had no children, goes up in flames along with her father, the two of them dying at the hands of their Philistine compatriots (cf. Judg. 14.20–15.6). And the concubine in ch. 19 who rejects her husband and returns to her father's house also dies; the chapter closes with the notice that her husband dismembered her and distributed her body

---

1.   Esther Fuchs also suggests this as a possible interpretation, although she characterizes it as problematic both because of the unusual severity of such a punishment (given the crime) and its textual disjunction from the scene describing the crime (i.e., the 'crime' is narrated in Gen. 31; the 'punishment' is not reported until Gen. 35); cf. E. Fuchs, '"For I Have the Way of Women": Deception, Gender, and Ideology in Biblical Narrative', *Semeia* 42 (1988), p. 81.

parts 'throughout all the territory of Israel' (v. 29).

The death of three other biblical daughters are of a different sort; they are much less brutal than the deaths of the Judges daughters, though no less tragic. In the book of Genesis, for example, Dinah is killed not *in* the text, but *by* the text.[1] Ostensibly ch. 34 is her story, since it opens with news about her visit to the women of the land (v. 1). But, as it turns out, she functions in the narrative only as the pretext for the struggle between the Shechemites and the sons of Israel.[2] The text never conveys to us the ultimate fate of this daughter; the last words about her tell us that her brothers took her out of Shechem's house, and so went away (v. 26). What happens to Dinah after that? The Bible never says.

In 2 Samuel, daughters are killed off in yet another way: they experience a 'death-in-life'. The reader takes leave of Michal at the end of ch. 6 with the news that she 'had no child to the day of her death' (v. 23). Whether she was childless because it was understood that YHWH had made her barren or because David no longer visited her, the consequences for her are the same: isolation and abandonment.[3] A similar fate befalls Tamar. After she is raped by Amnon, her brother Absalom takes her into his house, and so she remains, 'a desolate woman' (13.20). Though cared for by her brother behind the walls of his house, her father evinces no concern for her, nor does she ever seem to have become a wife or mother.

Motherhood or death. For biblical daughters the 'choice' is

1. I am borrowing language here from J. Cheryl Exum. In referring to the story of Michal, Saul's daughter, she speaks of a murder that 'does not take place in the story, but rather by means of the story'; J.C. Exum, 'Murder they Wrote: Ideology and the Manipulation of Female Presence in Biblical Narrative', *USQR* 43 (1989), p. 19.

2. Cf. N. Aschkenasy, *Eve's Journey: Feminine Images in Hebraic Literary Tradition* (Philadelphia: University of Pennsylvania Press, 1986), p. 125; T. Frymer-Kensky, 'Law and Philosophy: The Case of Sex in the Bible', *Semeia* 45 (1989), p. 95; S.L. Gravett, 'Subject in Genesis 34: A Literary Analysis' (unpublished paper, Duke University, 1990), pp. 15-16.

3. These two reasons for Michal's barrenness have long been recognized by readers of the Bible. Exum suggests, additionally, a third interpretation: Michal deliberately refused to have sexual relations with David (out of spite?). See Exum, 'Murder they Wrote', p. 26.

stark and uncompromising, and it all seems to turn on their maturing sexuality. That is, it is precisely their coming of age as sexual beings that gets them noticed by the biblical text in the first place. At the same time, this recognition places them at a terrible risk, for unless their sexuality is appropriately channelled (given the patriarchal context) so that they mother a new generation (preferably of Israelites), they lose that notice—and their life! Does not Rachel speak truly of the plight of all daughters—and express something of the precariousness of their temporal existence—when she pleads, 'Give me children, or I shall die!' (Gen. 30.1)?

The Spatial Liminality of Biblical Daughters

The dominant paradigm by which we think about social space splits the world into just two main spheres: the public and the private (or domestic). And this dichotomous view of the social world also marks quite strongly certain aspects of the construction of gender. That is, the private or domestic realm, which includes all those activities and institutions that are centered around the home and family, is associated especially with female identity: women 'belong' in the home. Meanwhile, the public domain, which is identified with all those activities and institutions outside the home and family, is linked with male identity: men govern the world beyond the house.[1] Yet when we read biblical narratives involving daughters, this commonplace understanding of gendered space(s) is everywhere subverted.

In the first place, the biblical text actually locates many of the most significant and positive words and activities of daughters

---

1. My definitions of public and private are derived most immediately from C.L. Meyers, *Discovering Eve* (New York: Oxford University Press, 1988), p. 32. The work on the public/private dichotomy is, of course, voluminous. From the standpoint of feminist anthropology, see the articles by Michelle Zimbalist Rosaldo, Sherry B. Ortner, Louise Lamphere and Peggy Sanday in M. Zimbalist Rosaldo and L. Lamphere (eds.), *Woman, Culture, and Society* (Stanford: Stanford University Press, 1974). Also of significant importance is the 'revision' of the understanding of this dichotomy in M. Zimbalist Rosaldo, 'The Use and Abuse of Anthropology: Reflections on Feminism and Cross-Cultural Understanding', *SIGNS* 5 (1980), pp. 389-417.

out in the public sphere. We witness this occurrence particularly in the story of Zelophehad's daughters. When they come forward to present their case before not only the leaders of the people, but all the congregation, they take up their position 'at the entrance of the tent of meeting' (Num. 27.2). If we read this place analogously to the city gate of Israel's later settled existence, the implication is that these daughters make their legal claim at the place recognized as the most appropriate for settling important social, economic or judicial matters—one which is, furthermore, the most visible and accessible site to the entire community of Israelites.[1]

The affirmative linkage of biblical daughters to public places is also evident in the work we see them perform. Instead of portraying daughters laboring within the domestic compound at such tasks as grinding grain or spinning and weaving cloth,[2] the Bible determinedly positions them out in the open, drawing water and herding sheep. This is how we are introduced to Rebekah; she is one of the daughters of the townspeople who come out of the city at evening to draw water from the well (Gen. 24.13-15). And Rachel is introduced in a similar fashion. She is a shepherd. Her job of caring for her father's sheep includes the task of watering them at the communal well. And it is at this site, where all the shepherds of the area congregate, that she first meets Jacob (Gen. 29.2-12). Moreover, this type-scene reappears almost exactly in the story of the daughters of Midian, for it is when they come to water their father's sheep at the well that they first encounter Moses (Exod. 2.15-17).

If biblical daughters are remarkably visible and active in public arenas, what happens to them in private settings? As it turns out, expectations built on traditional readings of a public/private split are further thwarted when considering this question, for

---

1. That the city gate functions in this manner is well attested in the Hebrew Bible. See the brief discussions by C.C. McCown; 'City', *IDB*, I, pp. 634-35; 'Gate', *IDB*, II, p. 355.

2. These are among the tasks Carol Meyers identifies as probably being the particular responsibilities of women in ancient Israel; see Meyers, *Discovering Eve*, pp. 145-48. Her analysis depends not only on the biblical testimony but also on archaeology and comparative ethnography.

the insides of houses take on the meanings of invisibility or negativity for biblical daughters.

The invisibility of a daughter inside the house is supremely exemplified in the Rebekah story of Genesis 24. In the first scene involving this daughter we see her in conversation with Abraham's servant out at the city well. Immediately afterwards, she runs to her mother's household to report what has happened (cf. v. 28). Laban, upon seeing the gifts of jewelry received by his sister, not only rushes out to meet the servant, he is extremely effusive in his greeting. 'Come in,' he says, 'O blessed of the Lord. Why do you stand outside when I have prepared the house...?' (v. 31). While the subsequent scene is thus fixed inside of the house, all the activities and conversation revolve around these two men; Rebekah virtually disappears. Not until the end of this scene does she reappear—and then only as the passive recipient of more jewelry and clothes (cf. v. 53).

Another instance of a disappearing daughter transports us to the book of Judges. In the opening verses of ch. 19 we are introduced to a nameless concubine who has returned to her father's house consequent to some sort of discord with her Levite husband. Four months later the Levite comes after her, and according to the Hebrew of v. 3, the concubine brings him to her father's house, presupposing that she came out of the house to greet him and facilitate an introduction to her father. What happens next? Her father convinces the Levite to stay and lodge in the house. The ensuing five days are a dizzying round of dinner parties at which 'the two men sat and ate and drank together' (v. 6; cf. also v. 8). But where is the daughter? Like Rebekah, she has been entirely effaced from the house.

The two previous examples cannot be taken to mean, though, that biblical daughters are never portrayed in the privacy of the home. However, when the narratives do locate them there, the site holds mainly negative meanings for them, expressed primarily in terms of deception and violence. Deception colors especially the relationship between daughters and their fathers.[1] Thus,

1.   For this insight I am indebted to Esther Fuchs. See E. Fuchs, 'Who is Hiding the Truth? Deceptive Women and Biblical Androcentrism', in A. Yarbro Collins (ed.), *Feminist Perspectives on Biblical Scholarship* (SBL

when Laban comes into Rachel's tent, looking for his missing *t͏̄erāpîm*, his daughter—by claiming that 'the way of women is upon me' (Gen. 31.35)—successfully foils his recovery of them. And when Saul comes into the house looking for David, he discovers that Michal, his daughter, has used a *t͏̄erāpîm* to fool both him and his messengers (cf. 1 Sam. 19.13-16). His words to Michal at this point, 'Why have you deceived me...?' (1 Sam. 19.17), aptly summarize the way that this scene, played out in a domestic setting, characterizes the father–daughter relationship in the Bible.

If the dynamics of the father–daughter relationship in the space of the house bespeak deception, then the relationship of sister to brother is marked by sexual violence. David's daughter, Tamar, is violated by her half-brother Amnon. This occurs in a supremely private place: the bedroom (i.e. the inner chamber) of Amnon's house (2 Sam. 13.10). Afterwards she is summarily ejected from this house (cf. 2 Sam. 13.15-19).

If biblical daughters cannot necessarily expect homes to be safe havens, the space outside the house offers no secure alternative. Indeed, stepping outside of the house can constitute a real risk.[1] Thus, when Dinah, daughter of Leah and Jacob, goes out to visit the women of the land, she is abducted and raped by Shechem (Gen. 34.1-2). And when Jephthah's daughter comes out to greet her father and celebrate his victory over the Ammonites, she meets a sentence of death, caught up in a vow not of her own making (Judg. 11.34-40). The concubine of Judges 19 is brought out of a house, abandoned by both her husband and her host to the vicious acts of the men of Gibeah (Judg. 19.22-26). Even being part of a group does not guarantee safety, for it is when the daughters of Shiloh go out to dance that they are abducted by the Benjaminites (Judg. 21.20-23).

We have travelled a full circle. If we earlier discovered that public places could hold meanings of activity, community recognition and positive self-worth for daughters, we end here

Centennial Publications; Atlanta: Scholars Press, 1985), pp. 139-40.

1. Exum also recognizes the dangers of stepping outside for daughters. But she does so with the assumption that staying inside the house would guarantee their safety. We have already seen that this is not necessarily true; cf. Exum, 'Murder they Wrote', pp. 29-30.

with the notice that to go outside also means for daughters the potential risk of danger and death. And sandwiched between these contradictory messages about 'the outside' for daughters is the message that the space inside the house carries meanings of invisibility and negativity for them.

So where, then, do daughters belong? Contrary to the gender assumptions of the public/private dichotomy, which would confine daughters to the private sphere, the narrative daughters of the Hebrew Bible are remarkably mobile and can be found in the most disparate locations: at the city well, before the entrance of the Tent of Meeting, out in the fields herding sheep. As concerns belonging, though, in the sense of having a secure refuge that is at all times safe for them, daughters are unable to claim any space as inherently their own. They thus exist spatially in a liminal zone, a place that is securely rooted neither here nor there.

The Incarnation of Liminality in the Figure of Michal

The preceding two sections could not be, and were not meant to be, exhaustively comprehensive treatments of the daughters in Genesis–2 Samuel (I have in mind, minimally, this article's complete neglect of the Gen. 38 Tamar and Achsah, daughter of Caleb). Indeed, we can be grateful for the fact that one paper cannot encompass all the daughter stories that appear in Genesis–2 Samuel (much less elsewhere in the Hebrew Bible). However, enough specific examples were elucidated to be suggestive of a pattern expressive of the liminality of biblical daughters. And although feminist biblical scholarship is accustomed to thinking about the 'otherness' of the female given the patriarchal text and context of the Bible, one of the aims of this article was to demonstrate how this 'otherness' works on biblical daughters in quite specific ways. Temporally, biblical daughters are marginalized, insofar as the narrative attention of the text is weighted towards that narrow in-between time when daughters are neither young, dependent children nor fully mature adults. Spatially, biblical daughters are fragmented, because the text positions them in quite diverse locations while at the same time refusing to privilege any one site as the place of their belonging and security.

This twofold liminality of biblical daughters finds its most concentrated realization, perhaps, in 1 Sam. 19.11-17, one of the earlier episodes involving Michal. Her temporal marginalization can be most clearly identified by following the vocabulary used to name her both here and in some of the verses preceding and following this episode. Prior to the 1 Samuel 19 episode mention is made of Michal in only three verses (1 Sam. 14.49; 18.20; 18.27), and in all three of these places she is identified as Saul's daughter. However, the latter two of these verses conjoin this identification with information that directs her towards David, her eventual husband (1 Sam. 18.20: 'Now Saul's daughter Michal loved David'; 18.27: 'Saul gave him his daughter Michal as a wife'). The two verses in ch. 18 thus adumbrate her role as David's wife, and in her very next textual appearance—which also opens the episode with which we are primarily concerned—this is how she is identified (1 Sam. 19.11; 'But Michal, David's wife, told him...'). Seemingly, then, by ch. 19 Michal has securely achieved the transition from child to adult, from daughter to wife. The narrative here seems to bear this out, for her activity as reported in this episode has as its goal saving David from the murderous intentions of Saul: that is, she acts *for* her husband and *against* her father.

Peculiarly, though, her actions have precisely the opposite effect. David's escape into the night works to separate Michal from her husband; they will not meet again for at least seven years.[1] Meanwhile, Michal finds herself re-engaged in a relationship with her father: the subsequent dialogue in v. 17 is the only reported conversation between them in the biblical text. Her uneasy positioning at this point in the narrative—as both wife and daughter, and yet neither—is signalled partially by the text's refusal to identify her as either one. In all of the references to her in this episode (except the first, where she is

1. That is, their reunion takes place sometime after David's seven-year rule in Hebron has come to an end (1 Kgs 2.11). See D.J.A. Clines, 'Michal Observed: An Introduction to Reading her Story', in D.J.A. Clines and T.C. Eskenazi (eds.), *Telling Queen Michal's Story: An Experiment in Comparative Interpretation* (JSOTSup, 119; Sheffield: JSOT Press, 1991), p. 45.

identified as David's wife) she is designated simply as 'Michal' (cf. 1 Sam. 19.12, 13, 17 [twice]). Furthermore, when we pick up her story later in 1 Sam. 25.44 the text continues its ambivalence: here she is both daughter and wife ('Saul had given his daughter Michal, David's wife, to Palti son of Laish...').

If Michal, in this episode, is positioned temporally as if on a threshold, her spatial location works to reinforce this same positioning. The text identifies the locale as David's house (v. 11). A further plausible inference is that the scene is set specifically in the upstairs bedroom of the newly-married couple. A place intended to encourage the most intense intimacy between the two, it becomes a matter of some comedy that David, almost immediately in the episode, flees from it. The tragedy for Michal is that she assists (even plans?) her husband's escape—ostensibly from Saul, but also from herself. And once she has let David down through the window (one of the markers between inside and outside), we can imagine her eyes continuing to follow him as he disappears into the night. Standing within the house, yet looking outside, she comes to be the very embodiment of liminality.

But then she turns away from the window, and makes preparations for the confrontation with her father and his messengers. As her bedroom privacy is overrun by men on a menacing political mission, the meaning of the place becomes twisted. If Saul ends up accusing and condemning her, she, in turn, lies to him. And so it is that biblical daughters—torn by competing loyalties and demands, and unsure of their positions—struggle to survive.

Anonymous Women and the Collapse of the Monarchy: A Study in Narrative Technique

Adele Reinhartz

Introduction

The narrator of the books of Kings was no objective reporter. Rather, in giving his[1] account of the succession of Solomon to the monarchy, and its aftermath, he attempted to explain two colossal tragedies in the history of ancient Israel: the division of the kingdom into Israel and Judah, and the destruction of these two at the hands of foreign powers. In keeping with the historiographical perspective of biblical narrative as a whole, the narrator interpreted these events in the context of the covenantal relationship between God and the people Israel. The monarchy collapsed because Israel 'did not obey the Lord their God; they transgressed His covenant—all that Moses the servant of the Lord had commanded. They did not obey and they did not fulfil it' (2 Kgs 18.12).[2] Specifically, the narrator attributed the division of the monarchy to God's anger with Solomon, who 'did what was displeasing to the Lord and did not remain loyal to the Lord like his father David' (1 Kgs 11.6). Similarly, the destruction of Israel and Judah was largely the fault of their kings, who were not 'wholehearted with the Lord...like [their] father David' (1 Kgs 15.4; cf. 1 Kgs 14.8), and 'did what was

---

1. The use of the masculine pronoun is deliberate. Because the narrator does not appear as a character in the narrative, it is not possible to say with certainty whether the narrator is male or female. Nevertheless, the relative lack of focus on female characters implies, at least in my opinion, a male narrator.

2. All biblical quotations are from the *Tanakh: A New Translation of the Holy Scriptures* (New York: Jewish Publication Society, 1985).

displeasing to the Lord' (cf. 1 Kgs 15.26; 2 Kgs 24.20).[1]

These comments illustrate a predominant element of the narrator's technique, namely, his penchant for comparing and contrasting his characters. David, who disappears from the narrative some chapters before Solomon angers God, provides the narrator with a basis of comparison for judging subsequent rulers: 'For David had done what was pleasing to the Lord and never turned throughout his life from all that He had commanded him, except in the matter of Uriah the Hittite' (1 Kgs 15.5). As the monarchy continued to disintegrate, a second point of comparison is seen in the prophets such as Elijah and Elisha, who were 'moved by zeal for the Lord, the God of Hosts' and stood up to challenge the Israelites and their kings 'who have forsaken Your covenant, torn down Your altars, and have put Your prophets to the sword' (1 Kgs 19.14).[2]

In these passages, the narrator compares characters in an explicit, even heavy-handed, manner, in order to pass a negative judgment on those he considers responsible for the collapse of the monarchy. Elsewhere, however, he uses this method with somewhat more subtlety. By the narrative motifs he recounts, by the way he describes his characters, by what he conveys, what he suppresses and what he transforms, he invites us to make similar comparisons. In doing so, he encourages us to see things his way, thereby supporting his basic premises regarding the downward slide of Israel into disobedience and destruction.

In this essay, I shall accept the narrator's invitation by exam-

1.   See G. Savran, '1 and 2 Kings', in R. Alter and F. Kermode (eds.), *The Literary Guide to the Bible* (Cambridge, MA: Harvard University Press, 1987), p. 147; and D.J. McCarthy, 'Compact and Kingship: Stimuli for Hebrew Covenant Thinking', in T. Ishida (ed.), *Studies in the Period of David and Solomon and Other Essays* (Tokyo: Yamakawa-Shuppansha, 1982), pp. 75-92.

2.   But cf. C. Fontaine, 'The Bearing of Wisdom on the Shape of 2 Samuel 11–12 and 1 Kings 3', *JSOT* 34 (1986), pp. 61-77 (reprinted in this volume), who suggests that 1 Kgs 3 implies a comparison with 2 Sam. 11–12, according to which Solomonic wisdom is contrasted with Davidic folly. See also C. Meyers, 'The Israelite Empire: In Defense of King Solomon', *Michigan Quarterly Review* 22 (1983), pp. 412-28, who suggests that the aggrandizement of David as compared with the Solomonic era, which is characteristic of both ancient and modern sources, is not completely faithful to the history of the Solomonic empire.

ining a group of stories featuring characters whose contribution to the narrator's overall agenda is often overlooked.[1] As anonymous female characters, they are the narrative antonyms of the major players—named male kings and prophets[2]—in this, the concluding portion of the Deuteronomistic history.[3] Just as the narrator compares David with Solomon, and the kings of Judah and Israel with their prophets, so we can compare these unnamed women, and the stories in which they appear, with one another, and with other figures and stories as occasion arises. These comparisons can then be used as a lens through which to reconsider the narrator's own activity in the narrative as a whole.

The first act of comparison has in fact already been made. With the decision to focus on unnamed female characters, we in effect unite them as a group by gender and anonymity, and separate them from the named male characters in Kings. The second act is to further divide the stories in which they appear into three categories. One category portrays the consorts of King Solomon; a second pictures women pressing a king for judgment of a dispute over their sons; the third features women who petition a prophet on behalf of a son threatened by illness or starvation. I shall examine each group separately before reuniting them in my conclusions.

1.   Anonymous female characters in Kings have often been discussed individually, or contrasted with one or two others, as references in these notes and the bibliography will show. To my knowledge, however, no published study to date has studied them as a group in the context of the narrative as a whole.

2.   It must be noted, however, that not all female characters in Kings are anonymous, nor are all kings and prophets named. See, for example, the prophetess Huldah (2 Kgs 22.14), Queen Jezebel (1 Kgs 16.31–2 Kgs 9.37), the men of God and sons of prophets (1 Kgs 13, 2 Kgs 6.1, 9.1), and the king of Edom (1 Kgs 3.9).

3.   It was Martin Noth (*The Deuteronomistic History* [JSOTSup, 15; Sheffield: JSOT Press, 1981 (1943)]) who first labelled the narrative line in Joshua, Judges, Samuel and Kings, introduced by Deuteronomy, the Deuteronomistic history. For critique of Noth's hypothesis see R. Nelson, *The Double Redaction of the Deuteronomistic History* (JSOTSup, 18; Sheffield: JSOT Press, 1981).

King and Consorts

Royal Wives

1 Kgs 11.3 tells us that Solomon 'had seven hundred royal wives and three hundred concubines'. Of these, only one is named, and then only in passing. As the mother of Rehoboam, the Solomonic scion who rules Judah after the division of the monarchy, Naamah the Ammonite is named in the formula with which the narrative normally introduces the kings of Judah.[1] She receives no further characterization in the narrative.

Aside from this formulaic and indirect reference, the king's consorts are concentrated in 1 Kings 3–11.[2] All we know about most of them is that they were not Israelite, but rather 'Moabite, Ammonite, Edomite, Phoenician, and Hittite women, from the nations of which the Lord had said to the Israelites, "none of you shall join them and none of them shall join you, lest they turn your heart away to follow their gods"' (1 Kgs 11.1-2; cf. Deut. 7.3-4; 23.4, 8-9).

Of the one thousand members of this group, only one is characterized beyond this brief reference. She is the daughter of Pharaoh, King of Egypt. About her we are told several things. First, her marriage to Solomon was politically motivated, in order to forge an alliance between Solomon and her father (1 Kgs 3.1). Secondly, she lived temporarily in the City of David, until Solomon had finished constructing a palace for her elsewhere (3.1, 7.8, 9.24).[3] Thirdly, her father Pharaoh gave the city of Gezer to Solomon as dowry after capturing and destroying

1. For other examples, see 1 Kgs 15.2, 22.42 and 2 Kgs 8.26; 14.2; 15.2; 18.2; 22.1; 23.31, 36; 24.8, 18; not all Judahite kings have their mothers mentioned in the text, however. Cf. 2 Kgs 16.2.

2. 1 Kgs 3–11 is considered by many scholars to be a distinct unit in 1 Kings, coming from various sources possibly including a Solomon saga. See J. Gray, *I and II Kings: A Commentary* (OTL; London: SCM Press, 2nd edn, 1970), p. 114; and Meyers, 'The Israelite Empire', p. 423, for discussion.

3. For detailed discussion of the portrayal of Pharaoh's daughter in Kings and Chronicles, see S.J.D. Cohen, 'Solomon and the Daughter of Pharaoh: Intermarriage, Conversion, and the Impurity of Women', in *Ancient Studies in Memory of Elias Bickerman (JANESCU* 16–17 [1984–85]), pp. 23-37.

the city and killing its Canaanite residents (9.16).

Although she receives more mention than any other royal consort, Pharaoh's daughter is characterized only minimally; she does not speak, and, as far as we are told, she acts only in accordance with what the important men in her life—her father Pharaoh and her husband Solomon—decide. Her presence at the beginning of the list of Solomon's wives in 11.1, however, accords her a role as the exemplar of Solomon's harem as a whole. The omission of her name and other markers of personal identity that might have differentiated her from her peers is consistent with the narrator's thesis that it is these foreign women, as a group, that led to Solomon's downfall.

What is true of one is, therefore, by implication, true of all, and vice versa. Hence we may assume that Solomon's motivations in acquiring these woman as wives and concubines were at least in part diplomatic and political. Once acquired, however, he 'clung to and loved' them (11.2), and they turned his heart away from the Lord and towards other gods, such as 'Ashtoreth the goddess of the Phoenicians, and Milcom the abomination of the Ammonites' (11.4). This is proof, suggests the narrator, that 'he was not as wholeheartedly devoted to the Lord his God as his father David had been' (11.3).

The negative judgment of the narrator upon Solomon for loving foreign women, expressed explicitly in 1 Kgs 11.1-3, is also conveyed by silence regarding the offspring of these unions. Yet that there were offspring is indicated in the formulaic reference to Naamah the mother of Rehoboam and the naming of several Solomonic daughters who married his prefects (1 Kgs 14.11-15). This is surprising in the context of biblical narrative, in which the main purpose of marriage, and particularly the marriage of kings, was the production of male heirs.[1]

This silence is even more striking, however, in light of the content and structure of 1 Kings 11 itself. After recounting the Lord's anger with Solomon in 1 Kgs 11.1-8 and his promise to tear most of the kingdom away from his house in the generation of his son (11.9-13), the narrator describes the adversary that

1. The importance of this is assumed, for example, in God's promises to David in 2 Sam. 7.12-16. Cf. also 2 Sam. 12.24, regarding the birth of Solomon.

the Lord raised up against him: Hadad the Edomite (11.14). In some respects, Hadad is the mirror image of Solomon. Like Solomon, he married a close relative of Pharaoh, and an anonymous one at that (11.19). But unlike Solomon, Hadad is portrayed as the father of a son, Genubath, born of Pharaoh's sister-in-law and raised in Pharaoh's palace (11.20). Although nothing more is heard of this son, it may be suggested that the adversary of Solomon is accorded the kind of conventional treatment by the narrator that Solomon himself is denied.

As the Lord's words in 9.12-13 suggest, however, the principal comparison in 1 Kings 1–11 is not between Solomon and Hadad, but between Solomon and his father David. Solomon's spiritual inferiority to David is also implied by a comparison of the narrative treatment of their wives and children. While it is certainly the case that David's relationships with Michal, Bathsheba and Abigail are not portrayed in an unambiguously positive way, it is significant that they are recounted in detail.[1] Furthermore, the issue of royal heirs is faced directly, in the case of Michal by explaining why she did not produce any offspring (2 Sam. 6.23), and in the case of Bathsheba, by describing how it came to pass that Solomon was born and destined for kingship (2 Sam. 12.24).

The anonymous, and narratively barren,[2] royal consorts are therefore made to bear a heavy load as the rationale for the downhill process which results in division of the kingdom and the eventual destruction of both Israel and Judah. The narrative absence of their names and offspring—prime markers of identity—implies the narrator's wish that these women themselves had been absent from Solomon's life.

1. See the portrayal of Michal in 1 Sam. 18 and 19, of Abigail in 1 Sam. 25 and Bathsheba in 2 Sam. 11 and 1 Kgs 1–2. For studies of these royal women, see D.J.A. Clines and T.C. Eskenazi (eds.), *Telling Queen Michal's Story: An Experiment in Comparative Interpretation* (JSOTSup, 119; Sheffield: JSOT Press, 1991); M. Sternberg, *The Poetics of Biblical Narrative: Ideological Literature and the Drama of Reading* (Bloomington: Indiana University Press, 1985), pp. 186-222; and A. Berlin, *Poetics and Interpretation of Biblical Narrative* (Bible and Literature Series, 9; Sheffield: Almond Press, 1983), pp. 23-32.

2. They are narratively barren in the sense that their childbearing activities are not recounted in the narrative, though clearly Naamah gave birth to Rehoboam and others gave birth to the daughters named in 1 Kgs 14.

The Queen of Sheba

Between the description of the Lord's conditions to Solomon for the continuation of his dynasty in 1 Kgs 9.3-9 and the Lord's confirmation of Solomon's failure to fulfil them in 1 Kgs 11.9-13 stands the story of another anonymous,[1] foreign queen about whose offspring the narrator is silent. Yet in other elements of her characterization, the Queen of Sheba has little in common with the other foreign queens in 1 Kings 3–11. Where they are minimally portrayed, she is the 'star' of a narrative of her own, 1 Kgs 10.1-13, in which she claims narrative equality with Solomon along with parity in status, wealth and wisdom.[2] Where they are characterized as a group of a thousand, she is unique. Where they are silent, she is loquacious; where they are passive, she is active, initiating a state visit accompanied by great pomp and ceremony. Perhaps most important, whereas they are linked to Solomon by marriage or concubinage, she is autonomous; she arrives with her entourage as a visiting foreign dignitary, and departs, with her attendants, as the same.[3]

The Queen of Sheba therefore stands out boldly from the group of anonymous consorts in 1 Kings 3–11. In fact, the character in this narrative block whom she most resembles is not someone with whom she would be linked on the basis of anonymity and gender, but rather a named male character, namely King Hiram of Tyre. Such comparison is invited by the direct reference to Hiram in the midst of the Sheba narrative (10.11).

There are differences, to be sure, in their narrative portrayal, beyond the issues of names and gender. For example, Hiram does not initially visit Solomon himself but communicates with

1. In this book, most kings and queens of foreign nations are given proper names in addition to their titles, such as Hiram, king of Tyre (1 Kgs 5.15) and Queen Tahpanes (1 Kgs 11.19); or have titles which function as names, such as Pharaoh, king of Egypt (1 Kgs 11.18).

2. Solomon is wealthier, however. According to 1 Kgs 10.23 he 'excelled all the kings on earth in wealth and in wisdom'.

3. J.B. Pritchard (*idem* [ed.], *Solomon and Sheba* [London: Phaidon, 1974], p. 9) sees hints of a sexual liaison between Solomon and Sheba in the use of the verb בוא, 'come'. Of all the women with whom Solomon was associated, it is the Queen of Sheba who most captured the imagination of Jews, Christians and Muslims alike. For discussion, see the essays in Pritchard (ed.), *Solomon and Sheba*.

him by means of envoys or messengers (5.15, 20). Furthermore, the Hiram–Solomon relationship is an ongoing one, with Hiram providing materials and labour for the construction of Solomon's temple (5.20-25), whereas our narrator presents only one encounter between Solomon and the Queen of Sheba.

Beyond these differences, however, these two figures have much in common. Each is impressed with Solomon's wisdom and his wealth. Secondly, each is in a formal relationship of parity and equality with Solomon, despite the fact that, at least according to the narrator, Solomon surpassed them both, and all kings, in wealth and wisdom (cf. 10.23). This parity is important for the narrative; only a king who was rich and wise himself could recognize Solomon's wisdom and give him the help he needed for building the temple; only a wise and rich queen could think up riddles to test Solomon's wisdom and bring gifts that he would appreciate and value.

Both Hiram and the Queen of Sheba function narratively to illustrate the keen interest in, and the recognition of, Solomon's divinely-given wisdom, a trait that the narrator of 1 Kgs 5.14 attributes to the rulers of the world. In the case of Hiram, the king's judgment of Solomon's wisdom seems to be based on the latter's decision to build the temple, and to use Sidonian labour and wood (5.17-21). The judgment of the Queen of Sheba is based on Solomon's ability to answer her riddles in a way that apparently exceeded her expectations, and that, along with his wealth, literally left her breathless (10.5).

Yet in contrast to 1 Kgs 3.16-28, in which the readers 'observe' the process by which Solomon wisely decides in whose custody to place a harlot's son, 10.1-3 provides us with no opportunity to judge Solomon's wisdom for ourselves. The riddles are not recounted, only the comment of the narrator, apparently in accord with the judgment of the queen herself, that 'Solomon had answers for all her questions; there was nothing that the king did not know, [nothing] to which he could not give her an answer' (10.3). This omission would be less obvious were it not for the fact that her speech in praise of his wealth and wisdom is reported at length (10.6-9).

This pattern of omission and provision attests to the strong hand of the narrator: he withholds information but asks that we

Similarly, in his critique of Solomon's idolatry, the narrator makes an explicit comparison between the two kings, criticizing Solomon for not remaining 'loyal to the Lord like his father David' (1 Kgs 11.6). The Lord's angry act of tearing the kingdom away from Solomon and giving it to an underling (1 Kgs 11.11) is somewhat softened for the sake of David: this event will not occur in Solomon's lifetime, and one tribe will remain for Solomon's son (11.12-13).

As we have seen, the portrayal of anonymous women indirectly contributes to this latter contrast between Solomon and David. This is apparent in the ways in which the portrayal of Solomon's wives differs in detail and in length from that of David's wives. Most suggestive here is the silence concerning the names and personalities of his wives, and procreative results of these marital or quasi-marital relationships. This silence implies that neither they nor their offspring will be needed in the ensuing narrative just as they were not needed in the history of the kingdom, since the dynasty was to be removed from Solomon.

Mothers and Kings

Harlot Mothers

There are two stories in which a woman turns to the king for judgment of a dispute concerning the life of a son. The first story in the narrative sequence describes the famous Solomonic judgment of the two harlots (1 Kgs 3.16-28). The case is presented in great detail by one of the harlots (3.17-21). She argues that her housemate accidentally killed her own newborn, and then switched the babies to make it appear that it was the speaker's child who had died. This presentation is followed by the back and forth accusations of the two women, until Solomon interrupts by summarizing the case: 'One says, "This is my son, the live one, and the dead one is yours"; and the other says, "No, the dead boy is yours, mine is the live one"...' (3.23). Solomon's risky suggestion to cut the living child in half by the sword reveals the true mother, who would rather give up her child to the other than have him die (3.26-27). The narrator views this case as a prime example of the king's wisdom (3.28).

trust and accept his judgment. This is similar to the strate;
employed in describing the king's wives. In the case of tl
Queen of Sheba, we are asked to believe the narrator regardir
Solomon's wisdom; the attitude to Solomon is positive, yet w
as readers are not given the opportunity to judge. Similarly, w
are not told how and why Solomon came to worship the idol
of his foreign wives, yet we are asked to believe the narrator'
negative judgment that Solomon was idolatrous and henc(
deserving of the punishment set out by the Lord in 9.6-9.

Conclusion

The portrayal of the anonymous queens in Solomon's life, and,
in particular, the contrast between his consorts and the autonomous Queen of Sheba, is consistent with the ambivalent characterization of Solomon in 1 Kings 3–11. On the one hand, his
reported weakness for foreign women and his alleged inability
to refrain from worshipping their gods prove to be his undoing.
On the other hand, Solomon is wise and wealthy. These praise-
worthy characteristics are indicative of divine favour (1 Kgs
3.10-14) and, somewhat ironically, are displayed in his encounter
with the foreign queen with whom the themes of marriage and
idolatry are not played out.[1] In the final analysis, it is the latter
portrait that dominates, accounting for his removal from divine
favour.

In both sides of this portrayal, however, the narrator invokes
King David, inviting comparison between Solomon and his
father. While the Lord grants Solomon wisdom as a unique gift
(1 Kgs 3.12), he also promises him 'long life, if you will walk in
My ways and observe My laws and commandments, as did
your father David' (1 Kgs 5.21). On the positive side of his
portrayal, therefore, the narrator presents Solomon as the
worthy successor to his father David.

1. It is worth noting that the only relationship of equality portrayed
between Solomon and a woman is one which does not end in marriage; she
is the queen whom he does not marry. Indeed, to have married her would
have been to destroy the parity of their relationship. To demote her from
her unique position, turning her into merely another foreign woman ir
Solomon's massive harem, is a transformation which would have rur
completely counter to her characterization in 1 Kgs 10.

This story may therefore be placed alongside the Queen of Sheba narrative as an expression of the narrator's positive assessment of King Solomon's wisdom. Another narrative similarity between the two stories may be found in the riddle motif, although, as I have already noted briefly, this is here played out in a different manner. In contrast to the Queen of Sheba story, in which the content of the riddles that demonstrate Solomon's wisdom is not conveyed to the reader, the story of the harlots portrays at length and in detail the dilemma before the king. This allows the reader to marvel, along with 'all Israel' (3.28), at the wisdom of his solution. This wisdom consisted not only in devising a trick which would expose the 'real' mother, but also, as some commentators note, in being able to see beyond the stereotype of the harlot to the women's identities as mothers.[1]

Yet in the course of describing the dilemma, the narrator in fact creates a second riddle, to which no solution is provided.[2] Which speaker is the woman to whom the king presented the child? Most commentators have assumed that the speaker in 3.17-21 is the woman referred to as the mother in 3.26. But this identification is not made at all clear in 3.26-27, which connects the identity of the real mother with her response to Solomon's offer to divide the child in two. In this case, the reader, while privy to the words of the two women, is not given access to the visual and other identifying details which would have been available to the king in distinguishing the speakers from one another.

What emerges is a lack of differentiation between the two women. Not only are they harlots and mothers of newborn sons, living in the same house and engaged in the same activity, namely sleeping in the same bed with their children, but they are both anonymous. The refusal of the narrator to differentiate

1. See P. Bird, 'The Harlot as Heroine: Narrative Art and Social Presupposition in Three Old Testament Texts', in M. Amihai, G.W. Coats and A.M. Solomon (eds.), *Narrative Research on the Hebrew Bible* (*Semeia* 46; Atlanta: Society of Biblical Literature, 1989), pp. 119-39; and W.A.M. Beuken, 'No Wise King without a Wise Woman (I Kings III 16–28)', in A.S. van der Woude (ed.), *New Avenues in the Study of the Old Testament* (Leiden: Brill, 1989), pp. 6-7.

2. See S. Lasine, 'The Riddle of Solomon's Judgment and the Riddle of Human Nature in the Hebrew Bible', *JSOT* 45 (1989), pp. 61-86.

between them nominatively results in confusion as to which of the two initial speakers was 'the woman whose son was the live one' (1 Kgs 3.26).[1]

The riddle that is therefore asked of the reader is: which is the mother of the living son? This in turn raises another, more abstract question: by what criteria does one label her as the 'real' mother? Most commentators assume the 'real' mother to be the biological mother.[2] This is not the only possibility allowed by the story, however. It is also possible to read this story not only as a deconstruction of the notion of harlotry—a harlot can be a good mother—but also as a deconstruction of the notion of biological motherhood. Solomon awards the child to the woman who displays greater veneration for the life of the child. One may imagine that she would also be the one better able to raise the child. This would appear to be an endorsement of the concept of motherhood as a social rather than primarily a biological institution, and perhaps it is indeed in this that his wisdom lies. Furthermore, while there is no biological father in the picture, Solomon acts as father since he is the one who quite literally provides one of them with a living child to raise. Therefore, in symbolic fashion at least, he not only creates a mother but also rehabilitates her from her harlotry by providing symbolic paternity for her child.[3]

Cannibal Mothers

In sharp contrast is the second story in this category, 2 Kgs 6.26-30.[4] This story too focuses on a dispute between two

---

1. As Beuken ('No Wise King without a Wise Woman', p. 6) notes, the two women are differentiated only at the point of their response to Solomon's proposal to divide the child. See also K.A. Deurloo, 'The King's Wisdom in Judgment: Narration as Example (I Kings iii)', in van der Woude (ed.); *New Avenues*, p. 18.

2. See B.O. Long, *1 Kings—With an Introduction to Historical Literature* (FOTL, 9; Grand Rapids: Eerdmans, 1984), p. 68.

3. This point is hinted at by Fontaine in 'The Bearing of Wisdom'; she comments that the child is in effect born twice, the second birth being his new lease of life as a result of Solomon's judgment.

4. See S. Lasine, 'Jehoram and the Cannibal Mothers (2 Kings 6.24-33): Solomon's Judgment in an Inverted World', *JSOT* 50 (1991), pp. 27-53; and B.O. Long, *2 Kings* (FOTL, 10; Grand Rapids: Eerdmans, 1991), pp. 92-99.

women over the life of a child, a dispute which one of the women brings to the attention of the king. Here the king is not named within the pericope but from the context is presumed to be King Joram of Israel (2 Kgs 3.1, 8.16). Unlike the story in 1 Kings 3, however, this story is directly tied to a historical situation, namely the famine in Samaria resulting from the siege of King Ben-hadad of Aram (2 Kgs 6.24). The woman calling for help from the king of Israel is not anxious to preserve the life of a child, but, on the contrary, is complaining of breach of contract: a second woman has failed to fulfil a prior agreement by refusing to give up her child for food, as the speaker had done with her own.

Like 1 Kgs 3.16-28, this story overturns the assumptions and expectations of the reader. In this case, however, the result is negative, even shocking. In the content of her complaint, the woman is admitting to cannibalism of the worst possible sort, and displays an attitude towards human life that the king, and with him probably most readers, find unacceptable. It is no wonder that the king has no wisdom and can only react in grief at the depths to which his besieged subjects have sunk. Indeed, it is difficult to image what the Solomonic solution to this dilemma would have been.

Like the story in 1 Kgs 3.16-28, this story illustrates a broader theme. But whereas the theme in the earlier story is wisdom, here it is despair and destruction. The story illustrates the fact that the consequences of disobedience as set out in Deut. 28.56-57, the worst of which is maternal cannibalism, have indeed come to pass. In this way, the story describes the divine judgment against the people Israel.

Conclusion
Solomon's wise judgment and the veneration of human life displayed by his act as well as by the mother in 1 Kings 3 stand in contrast to the despair of King Joram and the disturbing inhumanity of the mother in 2 Kings 6. The sequence and specific narrative contexts of these stories in themselves illustrate the narrator's views concerning the progressive deterioration of the monarchy and of the material and moral situation of the people.

Mothers and Prophets

The Miracles of Elijah and Elisha

Like those in the previous category, the stories in this group also feature mothers and endangered sons;[1] nevertheless, the structure of these stories and their characterization of the mothers are quite different from those in 1 Kings 3 and 2 Kings 6.

In 1 Kgs 17.8-24, the widow appointed by God to take care of Elijah is in danger of starving, as is her son (17.13). Although she does not directly ask Elijah for help, he prevents their death by means of a multiplication miracle: 'The jar of flour did not give out, nor did the jug of oil fail, just as the Lord had spoken through Elijah' (2 Kgs 17.16).

This is only a temporary reprieve, however, since some time later the son falls mortally ill.[2] At this point the widow, who was somewhat passive in the first part of the story, becomes active, accusing Elijah of causing his death. Again, she does not ask him directly for a miracle, although her accusatory tone may be read as implying such a demand. Elijah responds by petitioning God on her behalf, and his own. The miracle is performed out of sight of the mother, but upon seeing her child alive, she acknowledges Elijah as a man of God, who has the word of the Lord in his mouth (17.24).

Similar stories are told with respect to Elijah's successor, the prophet Elisha. In 2 Kgs 4.1-7, the widowed wife of a son of the prophets calls out to Elisha for help: her children are to be taken as slaves in repayment of debts. Like his mentor, Elisha responds with a multiplication miracle, providing her and her children with enough oil to repay their debts and support themselves thereafter. Unlike her counterpart in 1 Kings 17, this woman is not portrayed as praising Elisha; the narrative is sufficiently unambiguous to allow the readers to draw their own conclusions regarding the prophet's miraculous abilities.

The very next pericope tells of another woman whom Elisha

1.   This motif is also present in 2 Kgs 11.1-3, in which the saving woman is not the child's anonymous mother but his named aunt.

2.   Gray (*I and II Kings*, p. 382) argues that the child did not in fact die. Whether he did or did not reach the point of death, the emphasis is clearly on the prophet's ability to bring him back to life.

helped. The Shunammite woman, though still anonymous,[1] is characterized much more lavishly than the unnamed women in 1 Kings 17 and 2 Kings 4.1-7.[2] The first section of her story provides a variation on the annunciation type-scene.[3] In thanks for providing him with food and shelter, Elisha promises her a son, despite her barrenness and age. Not having asked for such reward, she is sceptical, but in fact does conceive and bear a son within the year (2 Kgs 4.17).[4] Some time later, this son dies. She puts him on Elisha's bed, and goes out in search of the prophet. When she finds him, she clasps his feet, an act which brings home to Elisha her great distress, and the disconcerting fact that the Lord had not made this event known to him (4.27).

Like the widow in 1 Kings 17, the Shunammite woman links the prophet with the death of her son: 'Did I ask my lord for a son: Didn't I say: "Don't mislead me"?' (2 Kgs 4.2). Like Elijah, Elisha performs the miracle by resurrecting the son, upon which his power is recognized by the woman, who again, this time in praise, 'fell at this feet and bowed low to the ground' (2 Kgs 4.37). Like the earlier story, this one conveys a double message. While it glorifies prophetic prowess, it also, through the voice of the woman, implies the limitations of that prowess, at least from her point of view. In each case, the woman becomes trans-

1. See B.O. Long, 'A Figure at the Gate: Readers, Reading, and Biblical Theologians', in G.M. Tucker, D.L. Peterson and R.R. Wilson (eds.), *Canon, Theology, and Old Testament Interpretation: Essays in Honor of Brevard S. Childs* (Philadelphia: Fortress Press, 1988), p. 168, for a brief discussion of her anonymity.

2. See A. Rofé, 'The Classification of the Prophetical Stories', *JBL* 89 (1970), p. 433; A. Dim, 'Ha-Isha ha-gedolah mishunem (2 Kings 4)' (Hebrew; 'The Great Woman of Shunem'), in *Proceedings of the Eighth World Congress of Jewish Studies A: The Period of the Bible* (Jerusalem: World Union of Jewish Studies, 1982), p. 21; Long, *2 Kings*, pp. 55-62.

3. On literary conventions and type-scenes see R. Alter, *The Art of Biblical Narrative* (New York: Basic Books, 1981), pp. 47-53; on the annunciation type-scene, and the ways in which the story about the Shunammite woman differs from the norm, see R. Alter, 'How Convention Helps us Read: The Case of the Bible's Annunciation Type-Scene', *Prooftexts* 3 (1983), pp. 125-26.

4. On the effect on the reader of the fact that the conception and birth of this son was not at the woman's request, see Long, 'A Figure at the Gate', p. 171; and Sternberg, *The Poetics of Biblical Narrative*, p. 310.

formed by the threat to the life of her son into an assertive, angry woman accusing the prophet in her life, to whom she is indebted for earlier favours, of nevertheless contributing to the death of her son. While the prophet in each case responds appropriately, thereby reinstating himself in her confidence, the reader is left with a hint of narrative ambivalence.[1]

The similarities among these stories suggest that they are all working with common motifs.[2] In all cases there is an anonymous woman who directly or indirectly petitions a prophet for the life of her unnamed son;[3] the father is either absent altogether or, in the case of the Shunammite woman, a minor figure. The prophet responds affirmatively, saving the son by miraculous means. None of these stories is tied directly into the history of the monarchy, which is the main plot line of the narrative, and all ultimately glorify the power of the prophet.

The Prophecy of Ahijah

The fourth example in this group employs the same motifs but turns them upside down. 1 Kgs 14.1-18 tells of the anonymous wife of King Jeroboam of Israel, who is sent by her husband to inquire of the prophet Ahijah concerning the fate of their ill child, Abijah. Although in disguise, in compliance with the demand of her husband, she is recognized by the prophet, who gives her a message to take back to Jeroboam: the king has acted wickedly and his dynasty will be destroyed. As soon as she returns to her city, Ahijah pronounces, the son will die, yet this will be a fate preferable to that which awaits the rest of Jeroboam's family: the son, at least, will be buried. 1 Kgs 14.17-18 records the fulfilment of this prophecy regarding the death and burial of the son.

This passage clearly explores the same central theme as the other three in its portrayal of a mother in contact with a

1.   See Rofé, 'The Classification of the Prophetical Stories', pp. 433-34; and Long, 'A Figure at the Gate', p. 174.

2.   These stories, and other similar ones including 2 Kgs 11.1-3, may be said to constitute a type-scene in the sense spoken of by Alter ('How Convention Helps us Read', pp. 47-53).

3.   Although 2 Kgs 4.1-7 speaks of the widow and her children, it is her son who is emphasized, as indicated by his speaking role in 4.6.

prophet over the life of her son. In the characterization of both woman and prophet, however, as well as in the outcome of her visit, the story provides a contrast with the others. Where the other sons are anonymous like their mothers, hers is named. Yet they survive, while hers does not. Whereas the women in the other stories act autonomously, this woman acts as an agent of her husband. Where they are active in petitioning the prophet, she is completely silent and passive, with no clues provided concerning her feelings. She does not even petition the prophet for her son's life, but is sent merely to discover his fate.[1]

The woman's passivity is most poignant in the description of her return to the city, which according to the prophecy is the moment of her child's death. A different woman might have vowed never to return to Tirzah again. Unlike the other anonymous mothers, she accepts the absolute authority of the prophet as she does that of her husband, and will not rise up to challenge their words. Her complete self-effacement is symbolized by the fact that not only is she anonymous, but she goes in disguise to a blind man who nevertheless knows her identity by virtue of divinely-given knowledge.[2]

Another difference between this passage and the other three can be seen with respect to the narrative context. Whereas the other three stories are disconnected from the political framework of the narrative plot as a whole, this story is tied into the main plot of the narrative of Kings by the content of Ahijah's prophecy and the fate of the son. This narrative context provides the key to the purpose of the story. Whereas the other stories focus rather directly on the power of the prophets and their interactions with the various women, in this story the main focus is on the judgment of the prophet against Jeroboam, the husband of the woman and the father of the sick child. That the prophet has divinely-given powers which presumably could have saved the child is indicated by his recognition of the woman despite his blindness.

The death of Jeroboam's son Abijah suggests a comparison with the death of another king's son, namely, the first child of

---

1. Cf. R.L. Cohn, 'Convention and Creativity in the Book of Kings: The Case of the Dying Monarch', *CBQ* 47 (1985), pp. 606-608.

2. See R. Coggins, 'On Kings and Disguises', *JSOT* 50 (1991), pp. 59-60.

David and Bathsheba (2 Sam. 12). This death too is foretold by a prophet, Nathan, as a punishment for the father, David (2 Sam. 12.14). The differences between the two stories, however, are as instructive as the similarities. Whereas David implores God directly for the life of his child (2 Sam. 12.16), Jeroboam sends his wife in disguise only to ask the prophet Ahijah about his son's fate. The death of David's child atones for David's sin; his next child with Bathsheba, Solomon, is favoured by God and inherits his kingdom (2 Sam. 12.24). The death and burial of Jeroboam's son function ironically as a mark of Solomon's own favour, and a sign of Jeroboam's disfavour; the death of this child marks the end of Jeroboam's dynasty.

Conclusion

The story of Jeroboam's wife therefore illustrates the contrast between king and prophet, according to which the prophet, as mouthpiece of the Lord, pronounces negative judgment upon the king. This contributes to the characterization of the post-Solomonic kings as displeasing to both Lord and narrator, in contrast to the prophets who honour the Lord and are therefore honoured by the narrator as well. The glorification of the prophet is clearly at work in the other three examples in this group of stories, which illustrate the power of the prophet, a power that is dependent on divine co-operation (1 Kgs 17.14, 21; 2 Kgs 4.33). Secondly, in its echoing of the themes of 2 Samuel 12, this story is consistent with the narrator's ongoing effort to portray the Israelite kings negatively in contrast to David. It is useful to the narrator in justifying the eventual fate of the kingdom, now divided. This contrast is in fact made explicit in the words of the Lord conveyed by Ahijah to Jeroboam's wife, in 1 Kgs 14.8-9:

> I tore away the kingdom from the House of David and gave it to you. But you have not been like My servant David, who kept My commandments and followed Me with all his heart, doing only what was right in My sight.[1] You have acted worse than all those who preceded you; you gone and made for yourself other gods and molten images to vex me...

1.   In 1 Kgs 15.5, however, the Lord does not overlook David's chequered past, as narrated in 2 Sam. 11–12.

Female Anonymity and Narrative Technique

Our comparisons of the stories within each group reveal the narrative use of similar motifs. Yet the contrasting ways in which these are played out reveal the narrator's agenda in each case, illustrating the contributions of these stories to his overall programme. The Queen of Sheba stands out in comparison with the anonymous queens and concubines of Solomon; they in turn are striking in their minimal characterizations when compared to the consorts of Solomon's father David as described in 1 and 2 Samuel. The king's ability or inability to provide wise judgment in a dispute between two women about the fate of a child expresses the narrator's evaluation of the king in question, and ultimately comments on the collapse of a divided monarchy, a major preoccupation of the narrator. Finally, the success or failure of a mother's explicit or implicit petition to the prophet for the life of her son becomes a vehicle for expressing the divinely sanctioned power of the prophet, which contrasts with the divine and narrative displeasure at the behaviour and religiosity of the kings of Israel and Judah.

In most cases, the anonymous women play out the conventional roles often assigned to women in biblical narrative: they are consorts of the king, mothers, widows and harlots, roles that only women can play. Within each group of stories, however, there is at least one in which the anonymous female character behaves in a counter-stereotypical way. The Queen of Sheba comes to Solomon as head of state, like her royal male counterparts. The besieged mother eats her child and complains of another mother's unwillingness to kill and share hers.[1] The silent wife of Jeroboam passively accepts divine judgment and contributes through her passivity to her child's death.

Yet one motif which binds all of these stories to one another, and ties them into the narrative as a whole, is that of the mother–son relationship. This theme is prominent in the stories featuring disputes between two women as well as those in which a mother approaches a prophet about the life of her son. It is

---

1. For a discussion of the sharing motif, see Lasine, 'Jehoram and the Cannibal Mothers', p. 31.

conspicuous by its absence from the stories about the king's consorts, where, on the basis of biblical stories about other leaders and their spouses, we might expect to find it.

By looking briefly at other stories in the books of Kings which focus on mother–child relationships, it becomes clear that the narrator employs this theme rather liberally in order to contrast Solomon with David and to document the progressive collapse of the monarchy. For example, the succession of Solomon to the Davidic throne in 1 Kings 1–2 would not have come to pass were it not for the petition of Bathsheba, Solomon's mother, to her dying husband David: 'the eyes of all Israel are upon you, O lord king, to tell them who shall succeed my lord the king on the throne. Otherwise, when my lord the king lies down with his fathers, my son Solomon and I will be regarded as traitors'.[1]

This theme continues in 1 Kgs 2.19-22. Solomon's first recorded interview on becoming king is with his mother, who, in an ironic twist on the mother–son theme, petitions Solomon on behalf of Adonijah, his half-brother, for the hand of Abishag the Shunammite. This time, however, Bathsheba is unsuccessful; not only does Solomon turn down this request but he also arranges for the death of Adonijah himself.

Whereas Bathsheba—like the Shunammite and other anonymous women—attempted to save and promote her son, Queen Athaliah, mother of Ahaziah, reacted to the news of his death by killing all who were of royal stock (2 Kgs 11.1). Only Ahaziah's son Joash survived, thanks to the resourcefulness of his aunt Jehosheba who, taking on the protective role of mother, 'secretly took Ahaziah's son Joash away from among the princes who were being slain, and [put] him and his nurse in a bedroom' (11.2) where they hid for six years during Athaliah's reign.

Finally, the fate of children throughout Kings is considered to be symptomatic of the evil of the kings of Israel and Judah as

1.   Much has been written on Solomon's succession to the throne. See R.N. Whybray, *The Succession Narrative: A Study of 2 Sam. 9–20 and 1 Kings 1 and 2* (SBT, 2.9; London: SCM Press, 1968); D.A. Knight, 'Moral Values and Literary Traditions: The Case of the Succession Narrative (2 Samuel 9–20; 1 Kings 1–2)', in P.J. Haas (ed.), *Biblical Hermeneutics in Jewish Moral Discourse* (*Semeia* 34; Atlanta: Scholars Press, 1985), pp. 7-23, and the essays in Ishida (ed.), *Studies in the Period of David and Solomon.*

well as indicative of their fate. King Ahaz, King of Judah, is condemned for following the 'ways of the kings of Israel', which included consigning his son to the fire 'in the abhorrent fashion of the nation' (2 Kgs 16.2). Like King Jeroboam, King Hezekiah of Judah is given a prophecy concerning his progeny: some of his sons 'will be taken to serve as eunuchs in the palace of the king of Babylon' (2 Kgs 20.18).

The stories featuring anonymous women are therefore closely tied to the narrative line of Kings, its major themes and the interpretation of Israelite history that it presents. What separates them from stories about other women is the anonymity shared by their female characters. This observation raises the question of the narrative significance of anonymity.

It may certainly be the case that these female characters remained unnamed in 1 and 2 Kings because the narrator did not know their names, did not care to report them if he did know, or to make them up if he did not know. While it is impossible to know the intention of the narrator, or the author who created the narrator, in not naming these characters, our discussion does allow us some observations on the effect of their anonymity on the reader, or at least on this particular reader.

First, the characters' anonymity can be used as an organizing principle to group them and their stories together in search of narrative coherence.[1] This is of course one way in which it has been used in this essay. By doing so, I have constructed a reading of the narrative which imports narrative significance to the perceived similarities and differences among these stories, and between this group of stories and others in the books of Kings.

Secondly, the anonymity of these characters deflects attention away from them as individuals to their roles in the narrative, and towards seeing them in typified fashion as harlots, queens or mothers.[2] The expectation that anonymous characters act in

---

1. According to reader-reception critic Wolfgang Iser (*The Implied Reader* [Baltimore: Johns Hopkins University Press, 1974], pp. 283-84), the building of a coherent reading of the text is the primary enterprise of the reader.

2. On the relationship between typification and anonymity, see M. Natanson, *Anonymity: A Study in the Philosophy of Alfred Schutz*

typified fashion also causes us to pay attention when they do not. In his portrayal of these women, the narrator exploits typification by both conforming to and departing from the stereotypical roles often assigned to women in biblical narrative.

Thirdly, the anonymity of these female characters directs the reader's attention to the named male characters with whom they interact. Hence, the stories featuring anonymous women urge us to reflect upon the wisdom and folly of Solomon, the evil of Jeroboam, the helplessness of Joram and the prophetic prowess of Elijah and Elisha. The minimally-characterized anonymous female figures aid in the characterization of named male characters around whom the narrative as a whole is structured.

These characters and the stories in which they appear therefore contribute to the narrator's attempt to account for the collapse of the monarchy. They focus our attention on the various comparisons and contrasts so important in his theory, by helping in the characterization of the various kings and prophets who loom large in the narrative. In doing so, the stories also contribute to the characterization of the narrator himself. Although anonymous, like the women we have studied, and not present in the narrative as a character himself,[1] his strong presence can nevertheless be felt throughout.[2] This is a result of both his direct comments and his mode of narration. Not only does he make frequent comparisons between, direct comments about and value judgments on the characters, their acts and their fates, but he also manipulates the flow of information and asks us to trust him. We must take his word that Solomon answered the Queen of Sheba wisely, since we do not hear her riddles or his answers. We must believe that Solomon was led into idolatry by his wives—we do not see him worshipping Milcom and Ashtoreth.

By refraining from portraying these events, the narrator

(Bloomington: Indiana University Press, 1986), p. 25; *idem, Phenomenology, Role and Reason* (Springfield, IL: Charles C. Thomas, 1974), pp. 163, 164, 170; and A. Reinhartz, 'Anonymity and Character in the Books of Samuel', *Semeia* (forthcoming).

1. This would be the case, for example, with a first-person narrator.
2. On the notion of narrative voice, see Berlin, *Poetics and Interpretation*, pp. 57-59.

avoids ambiguity and forestalls the possibility of multiple interpretations. Such restrictiveness may be unwelcome after the
subtlety of the narrator in Samuel, who engages the reader by
presenting complex and ambiguous characters such as Saul,
David and Jonathan, and their very human relationships. But the
heavy-handedness of our Kings narrator may be understood
on the grounds that it was his way of explaining grand tragedy.
In the face of the conquest of Israel and Judah at the hands of
the Assyrians and Babylonians, and its enormous implications
for the notions of the covenantal relationship between God and
Israel, ambiguity is a risky proposition: the reader must hear
and, hearing, must understand. Only by understanding, and
repenting, can the evil decree be reversed, and the people be
worthy of the redemption and return to the land. In this, the
narrator of Kings is in accord with divine prophecy as declared
by his canonical successor, the prophet Isaiah:[1]

> Return, O Children of Israel, to Him to whom they have been so
> shamefully false; for in that day everyone will reject his idols of
> silver and idols of gold, which your hands have made for your
> guilt (Isa. 31.6-7).

> And the ransomed of the Lord shall return,
> And come with shouting to Zion,
> Crowned with joy everlasting.
> They shall attain joy and gladness,
> While sorrow and sighing flee (Isa. 35.10).

---

1. This assumes that the narrator's historical location is after the
destruction of Judah and before the return from exile under Ezra and
Nehemiah. This in fact corresponds to the conclusions of source critics
concerning the historical situation of the redactor. See Gray, *I and II Kings*,
p. 6, who suggests that Kings had a pre-exilic compilation and exilic
redaction.

Part II
A MODEL MOTHER: HANNAH

'AM I NOT MORE DEVOTED TO YOU THAN TEN SONS?' (1 SAMUEL 1.8): MALE AND FEMALE INTERPRETATIONS

Yairah Amit

Until recently the tradition of biblical exegesis has been a male domain: the voices of women have been absent from the attempt to understand the text and from work of textual interpretation. This lack is particularly conspicuous in the case of those biblical passages which describe interaction between men and women, where the latter's attitudes and behaviour are interpreted only by men. It is reasonable to assume that attention to the exegetic voice of women could contribute to a richer and more discriminating understanding of the text. The following notes on 1 Sam. 1.8 suggest that a woman's point of view may shed fresh light on the verse and on the situation it depicts.

The story of the birth of Samuel and his consecration to the temple (1 Sam. 1.1–2.11)[1] begins with an exposition, in which the characters are introduced and the customary practice of Elkanah and his family is described (vv. 1-7a).[2] Every year

---

1. For a detailed discussion of the story's outline see U. Simon, 'The Story of Samuel's Birth: Structure, Genre, and Meaning', in *idem* (ed.), *Studies in the Bible and Exegesis* (Hebrew; Ramat Gan: Bar Ilan University Press, 1986), II, pp. 57-60. Simon does not include 2.11b in the story but adds 2.18-21 to it.

2. Hannah's acts of crying and her avoidance of food do not belong to the exposition of customary conduct; they are characterized as unique to this specific visit, when the situation has reached a critical stage; see, for example, H.W. Hertzberg, *I & II Samuel* (OTL; repr.; London: SCM Press, 1964 [1960]), p. 24; Simon, 'Samuel's Birth', p. 68. R.W. Klein (*1 Samuel* [WBC, 10; Waco, TX: Word Books, 1983], p. 7) notes that the description of that specific day is broken by the long parenthetical clause of vv. 4b-7a.

Elkanah would take his wives with him to kneel at the altar of the Lord of hosts at the temple of Shiloh, over which Eli and his sons presided (vv. 1-3). The uniqueness of this exposition resides in the fact that it singles out and emphasizes the specific details of the day of the occurrence and presents them as part of the general description of customary events (vv. 4-7a). The opening 'One such a day' (v. 4) and the closing 'This happened year after year: Every time she went up to the House of the Lord, the other would taunt her' (v. 7a),[1] explain that what occurred yearly also occurred on that day. The reader thus learns that the disproportion in the distribution of sacrificial portions and the anger that Peninnah caused Hannah were not isolated incidents, but, rather, regularly recurring phenomena. So the question arises: what was different this time, and why did the customary distribution of the portions of the family sacrifice to the women and the sons now provide an opportunity for exceptional behaviour on the part of Hannah, which resulted in the birth of Samuel and his consecration to the temple? From what is related we find that, as usual, Peninnah received many portions by virtue of her sons and daughters, whereas Hannah received one portion only.[2]

Lest the reader interpret the paucity of portions as an

However, some interpreters also see in v. 8 a description of this family's daily life; for instance, M. Abernik, *The Book of Samuel A, B* (Hebrew; Presburg, 1872), pp. 7-8: '*Whenever* he saw her crying he said "Am I not more devoted to you..."' (emphasis mine). See also R. Alter, *The Art of Biblical Narrative* (New York: Basic Books, 1981), pp. 82-83. Nevertheless, interpreting Elkanah's words as repetitive diminishes their effectiveness. It is more likely that v. 8 represents the first scene of the story itself.

1. In the Peshiṭta we find, 'Thus *she* did', and in the Vulgate 'Every time *they* went up'. In 42 Hebrew MSS the word בבית ('in the house') is written בית ('house'; a case of dittography?). These and other differences show that the verse is corrupt. The version to be preferred is, therefore, 'and thus she [Peninnah] did, year after year, every time they went up to the House of the Lord, so she provoked her [Hannah]...'.

2. This interpretation is grounded in the LXX[b] for v. 5, and many commentaries explain מנה אחת אפים as 'a larger portion'. P.K. McCarter (*I Samuel* [AB; Garden City, NY: Doubleday, 1980], pp. 51-52, 60) notes that the meaning is 'a single portion equal to theirs (= to the portions of Peninnah and her children)'.

indication of less love, the narrator adds that, contrary to what would be expected, it was childless Hannah who was the beloved wife: 'but to Hannah he would give one portion only—though Hannah was his favourite—for the Lord had closed her womb' (v. 5). Elkanah's greater love for Hannah was a cause of pain to Peninnah, and Peninnah gave expression to her jealousy: 'Moreover, her rival, to make her miserable, would taunt her that the Lord had closed her womb' (v. 6).

The first scene of the narrative therefore opens with a description of Hannah weeping and refraining from eating (v. 7b). The break in the customary situation presented in the exposition is the result of the behaviour of Hannah, who has reached a crisis point. According to U. Simon,

> Hannah's expectations for the annual pilgrimage have again come to nothing, and her rival has again poured salt upon her wounds when Hannah receives her single sacrificial portion. The cumulative effects of her continuing disappointment by God and the recurring vexation at the hands of her rival brought on a crisis this time—'so that she wept and would not eat'.[1]

This behaviour of Hannah caused Elkanah to attempt to speak words of comfort to his wife, but, far from being consoled, she reacted with increased resistance by leaving the chamber in the direction of the Lord's temple.[2]

Hannah's unexpected reaction to Elkanah's words of comfort obliges us to search out the exact meaning of his words. Such an examination reveals two possible interpretations. According to that adopted by most exegetes, Elkanah makes use of a rhetorical question to proclaim that his love for Hannah is better for her than ten sons. According to the other interpretation, Elkanah is telling Hannah that he loves her more than the ten sons borne to him by Peninnah.

It is doubtful whether this second interpretation, which is characterized by a specific reference to Peninnah's ten sons and

---

1. Simon, 'Samuel's Birth', p. 70.
2. On the interpretation of the term לשכה ('chamber') as a room in the temple, where sacrificial meals were eaten, see the LXX for v. 18 and the proposed emendations for v. 9; cf. *BHK* and Simon, 'Samuel's Birth', p. 71 n. 21.

proposed by Rashi, Ralbag and recently Eslinger,[1] among others, fits the meaning of the verse, given the use of the same idiomatic expression in Ruth 4.15: 'for he is born of your daughter-in-law, who loves you and is better for you than seven sons'. In both texts the number of sons is typological, seven and ten, and is invoked rhetorically, for exaggeration, rather than literally. Similarly, in 1 Sam. 2.5, 'While the barren woman bears seven, the mother of many is forlorn'. In the present case, the preference for the hyperbolic number of sons, ten rather than seven, underscores the extent of Elkanah's love for Hannah.[2] This interpretation reflects great sensitivity for Hannah's pain and portrays Elkanah as one who declares that Hannah's position and importance mean more to him than all ten of Peninnah's sons who are, as we know, his own flesh and blood.

This interpretation, which has failed to acquire many adherents, is problematized by Hannah's subsequent behaviour. For, after the sensitive revelation of love which it presumes, a revelation that would simultaneously have constituted a painful blow for Peninnah and her children, Hannah makes no attempt to please her husband by at least eating.[3] By this reading, her

1. L.M. Eslinger, *Kingship of God in Crisis: A Close Reading of 1 Samuel 1–12* (Bible and Literature Series, 10; Sheffield: Almond Press, 1985), pp. 75-76. Radak mentions this interpretation as a second option. He prefers the one found in the Jonathan translation; and see below.

2. On the use of typological numbers see Radak and, recently, Y. Zakovitch, *Ruth* (Hebrew; Miqra LeYisra'el; Tel Aviv: Am Oved; Jerusalem: Magnes, 1990), p. 114. Zakovitch contends that 'the numbers "seven" and "ten" are interchangeable: the tradition of "ten" plagues (Exod. 7–12) as opposed to the tradition of "seven" plagues (Ps. 78; 105), the "seven" Canaanite nations (Deut. 7.1, for example) as opposed to the "ten" Canaanite nations (Gen. 15.19-21), and the use of the number "seven" represent: many...'. A. Brenner (*Ruth and Naomi: Literary, Stylistic and Linguistic Studies in the Book of Ruth* [Hebrew; Tel Aviv: Afik, Sifriyat Po'alim and HaKibbutz HaMe'uchad, 1988], p. 114) suggests that in Ruth 4.15 the author has preferred the typological number 'seven' because of the association with Hannah's story and the number's occurrence in the psalm ascribed to Hannah (1 Sam. 2.5b) and presented as her thanksgiving upon the birth of Samuel. J.G. Baldwin (*1 & 2 Samuel* [TOTC; Downers Grove, IL: Inter-Varsity Press, 1988], pp. 51-52) understands the expression 'am I not better to you than X sons' as a common idiom.

3. That Hannah did not eat is made clear by what follows. Only after

departure would have to be perceived as indifference to her husband's words, even as an expression of protest. Whoever accepts this interpretation can ask: is there no limit to Hannah's demands? It should be noted here that most exegetes describe the character of Hannah as remarkably sensitive and long-suffering, and there are even those who single her out in contrast to Rachel: 'When Rachel saw that she had borne Jacob no children, she became envious of her sister; and Rachel said to Jacob, "Give me children, or I shall die". Jacob was incensed at Rachel, and said, "Can I take the place of God, who has denied you fruit of the womb?"' (Gen. 30.1-2).[1]

Most exegetes follow Jonathan, who translated: 'my friendship is better to you than ten sons'. According to Radak's interpretation, this means: 'my desire and love for you are better for you than ten sons'. This interpretation views Elkanah's rhetorical question as implying that he knows better what is good for Hannah than she does herself. Hannah is depicted as a woman who does not appreciate her own good fortune. To put it more bluntly, seen in this perspective, she is an ingrate. In Abrabanel's words: '"better to you than ten sons" is to say that I am better and of more benefit to you than ten sons whom you bore would be'.[2] It is not surprising that Abrabanel also concludes his interpretation of Elkanah's words by representing Hannah's silence as the only possible reaction by such an ungrateful woman: 'and the text does not record Hannah's response for she had nothing to say'. Smith too believes that Elkanah deserved a positive answer from Hannah, but he moderates his criticism by adding that, since she wanted

speaking to the priest and receiving his blessing was she able to relax and eat: 'So the woman left, and she ate…' (v. 18). Cf. Ralbag, 'and she did not eat and did not drink as it is written, "so that she wept and would not eat" and as she said, "I have drunk no wine or another strong drink"'. However, Eslinger (*Kingship of God*, pp. 75-76) thinks that 'Hannah appears to humour Elkanah by eating'.

1.   See Z. Adar, *The Biblical Narrative* (Hebrew; Jerusalem: Education Department of the World Jewish Agency, 2nd edn, 1963), pp. 15-22, especially pp. 18-19.

2.   See Abrabanel, in *A Commentary on the Former Prophets* (Hebrew; Jerusalem: Torah VeDa'at Publishing House, 1955), p. 172.

children for his sake, his attempt to comfort her was the cause of renewed anguish.[1]

Adar's interpretation is of interest,[2] as he notes that 'Elkanah does not tell Hannah that she is dearer to him than ten sons but rather that he is better for her than ten sons'. Moreover, he applauds Elkanah's words, since 'he does not make demands of Hannah, and all he desires is only to be good to her because he loves her'. Adar believes that Elkanah's statement 'surmounts to some extent the biological perspective which was typical of ancient patriarchal societies, and contains some perception of the value of a woman as an independent personality, and a new, more human sense of love'. He even defines this and similar narratives as a 'kind of experiment in examining the nature and depth of the husband's love: will he continue to love his dear one even when he discovers she is barren?'. Apparently, Adar senses that in praising Elkanah as a lover he may be slighting Hannah; therefore he adds: 'Indeed these words of Elkanah reveal to the reader the charm of Hannah's character, thus adding to the meaning of the entire chapter'. The utmost in enthusiasm concerning Elkanah's words and character as a loving husband is to be found in the exegesis of Simon:

> Hannah weeps *out of frustration and shame* and refuses to eat her portion. Elkanah, her husband, comes to her aid, and in appealing to her heart, he tries to convince her that there is no point in crying, in not eating, and in a sorrowful heart, because his love for her is better for her than ten sons. These words of comfort also relate indirectly to Peninnah's taunts: while her rival enjoyed the good fortune as having borne children, Hannah had the advantage as Elkanah's beloved wife, and even if Peninnah were to bear ten sons, they would carry less weight than Elkanah's love as a husband.[3]

According to Simon, these words of Elkanah testify to true love, and he regards their utterance as Elkanah's finest hour.

Simon is not the only one to heap praise upon Elkanah's phrases. Segal found in them 'the tender love of a husband for

1.   H.P. Smith, *The Books of Samuel* (ICC; Edinburgh: T. & T. Clark, 1899), pp. 7-8.

2.   Adar, *Biblical Narrative*, pp. 17-18.

3.   Simon, 'Samuel's Birth', p. 70.

his wife'.[1] According to Adar, they represent Elkanah as one who 'tries to pamper and compensate for her barrenness with his love'.[2] In his view, 'Hannah's silent anguish arouses Elkanah to express his tender assurance of love', and Hannah of the sorrowful heart appears as a delicate image of beautiful character. Alter finds Elkanah's words a 'touching effort to console his beloved wife, [which] though also a periodically repeated action, is given the emphasis of direct quotation as a climactic conclusion of the exposition—perhaps as a way of fully dramatizing Elkanah's tender devotion to Hannah...'.[3]

Thus far we have heard from the men, and not one woman is to be found to speak in the name of Hannah, to analyse her reaction and to illuminate Elkanah's words differently. Perhaps the possibility which Adar dismisses out of hand and which has been proposed by only two exegetes—Rashi and Ralbag—represents not what was said but what Hannah would have liked to hear: that she was worthy, and that she mattered to Elkanah.

If these expectations are realistic, and that is what Hannah would have liked to hear, her reaction may be understood differently. Apparently, the soothing words uttered by her husband did not afford her comfort or consolation.[4] On the contrary, they were even more annoying and disheartening than Peninnah's remarks. In other words, Hannah's silence, her persistent refusal to eat and, finally, her departure were intended to express her pain at what her husband said.

It would seem to me that, in interpreting the passage, consideration should be given to the use of the first-person subject

1.   M.Z. Segal, *The Books of Samuel* (Hebrew; Jerusalem: Kiryat Sefer, 1956), pp. 1, 7.

2.   Adar, *Biblical Narrative*, pp. 17, 19. The significance of Elkanah's endeavour is similarly expressed in Klein, *1 Samuel*, p. 7.

3.   Alter, *Art of Biblical Narrative*, p. 83.

4.   According to K.L. Chafin, *1, 2 Samuel* (The Communicator's Commentary; Dallas: Word Books, 1989), p. 29, Elkanah's last question reflects 'a certain insensitivity. Her answer was to go to the temple in "bitterness of soul", where she prayed and "wept in anguish"'. Cf. Eslinger's different point of view in *Kingship of God*, pp. 75-76, and nn. 1 and 3 on p. 71, above.

אנכי ('I') in conjunction with the second-person objective case לך ('to you'). Elkanah wonders why she cries and does not eat when he is, so he believes, better for her than ten sons. Elkanah's words reveal him to possess the egocentricity of a child who perceives himself as the centre of his world and is disappointed when his behaviour fails to receive the attention he expects. Elkanah is revealed as one who cannot accept the fact that Hannah wants to be mother to her children and not mother to her husband. According to this interpretation, Elkanah's flow of questions is the complaint of a man who never matured, who perhaps enjoys moving back and forth between two women when one is the mother of his children and the other continues to fulfil the oedipal role of his own mother. Elkanah is thus indifferent to Hannah's pain, and he finds it easy to decide for her that his closeness to her is more important for her than her own children would be. It would seem that his self-esteem knows no bounds. He determines that his presence is equivalent to the satisfaction of having ten children, and it is no wonder that he chooses the large typological number in order to make his point. Furthermore, the vulnerable economic circumstances of a woman who has no sons should probably also be taken into consideration, especially if the husband dies and the woman is left with no children. Elkanah is therefore guilty not only of insensitivity to his wife's feelings but also of disregard for her future.

Naturally, Hannah, who thus understood her husband's words, was not encouraged, did not eat or drink, and only looked for a suitable opportunity to get away from the feast and pour out her troubles before her Creator. Hannah's remarkable sensitivity and capacity for suffering are expressed in the fact that she did not leave the table immediately but, rather, continued to respect the occasion of the family sacrificial feast and only afterwards dared to stand up and leave. It should also be recalled that in ancient society, where a woman's status was determined by her fertility, Hannah did not have much of a choice. Therefore, this distancing from her husband and from the family ceremony should be regarded as the resistance and protest of a woman isolated within her own family, a woman deprived of being understood even by her husband. If it is possible to speak of Hannah's delicacy and virtue, they are found in the noble and silent way in which she expresses her protest.

HANNAH: MARGINALIZED VICTIM AND SOCIAL REDEEMER

Lillian R. Klein

Ethnographic materials indicate that varying degrees of marginalization are an effective means of social control. In the relatively closed society of biblical literature described in 1 Samuel extreme marginalization, physical isolation, was stipulated for individuals who demonstrated an 'abnormal' physical condition or social behavior, for instance menstruation, disease or anti-covenantal conduct. However, not all marginalization is physical. Most individuals at some time or another have experienced, at least briefly, the emotional marginalization of being an 'outsider', an 'Other' in specific situations.

This emotional marginalization is a significant component of the narrative of Hannah (1 Sam. 1). Each of the three individuals with whom Hannah interacts—her rival wife, Peninnah, her husband, Elkanah, and the priest, Eli—contributes to her emotional marginalization in a different way. The motives for and methods of marginalization used by each of the characters comment upon the social milieu even as they delineate interpersonal relationships and character.

Hannah is the loved but barren wife of a man who has two wives—a familiar motif in the Hebrew Bible. Sarah is barren when Hagar conceives, and even when he has fathered a son by Hagar, Abraham puts Hagar at Sarah's disposition, confirming which wife he loves.[1] Rachel, the beloved of Jacob, is

---

1. Sarah gave Hagar to her husband as a wife for purposes of conception (Gen. 16.3). In a feminist reading of Hagar, Savina J. Teubal (*Hagar the Egyptian: The Lost Traditions of the Matriarchs* [San Francisco: HarperCollins, 1990], pp. 75-81) finds that the close relationship between Hagar and Sarah is undermined by Abraham; and that, instead of conflict between two women in one household, the issue at hand is the custom of acquiring an

also barren while Leah bears him many sons. In traditional readings, all three fruitful wives provoke the barren but loved ones—Sarah, Rachel and Hannah—thus increasing their suffering.

In the Hebrew Bible women are usually portrayed as jealous of each other. Indeed, jealousy and seductiveness are the chief transgressions projected upon women.[1] In narrative depictions of men the chief male transgressions are theft, intrigue, rape and murder. Nevertheless, it is not clear that such masculine behavior is necessarily recognized as transgressions; see for instance the aftermath of the rape of Dinah (Gen. 34). The text may just suggest that 'men are like that'. We may regard analogously the persistent narrative stance on feminine jealousy, which has the text imply that 'women are like that'.

A convenient tool for exploring jealousy in the context of biblical Hebrew narrative is offered by Renea Girard's concept of 'mimetic desire'. Girard coined this term for the complex of attitudes and actions arising from imitation of another generated by desire of what the other has. This acquisitive mimetic desire thus subsumes jealousy, rivalry and all the actions taken to gain the object of desire.[2] Such conflictual and destructive mimesis is a disruptive force and must be subjected to social constraints; there must be a '"normal" mechanism to interrupt and reverse'

---

heir, male or female, through a woman's handmaid. I find her suggestion that the feminine bond is broken by masculine intervention an interesting parallel to the argument of this paper.

1.   One exception is the lack of envy among the women in the Song of Songs. The 'daughters of Jerusalem' demonstrate no jealousy of the Shulammite maiden they themselves call the 'fairest among women' (1.7; 5.9; 6.1), although Michael V. Fox suggests that they may tease her (*The Song of Songs and Ancient Egyptian Love Songs* [Madison: University of Wisconsin Press, 1985], p. 158); 'Suspicion of that sort [jealousy] is not suggested anywhere in the Song, not even when the Shulammite mentions the love that other girls must feel for her beloved' (Fox, *Song of Songs*, p. 170).

2.   'When any gesture of appropriation is imitated, it simply means that two hands will reach for the same object simultaneously: conflict cannot fail to result' (R. Girard, *To Double Business Bound* [Baltimore: Johns Hopkins University Press, 1978], p. 201).

its disordering effects.[1] Without social control of rivalry, it can escalate into reciprocal forms and gather sufficient strength to destroy the social unit's functional entity. Although the term 'mimetic desire' usually refers to this acquisitive form, desire may also be expressed in 'non-acquisitive forms—those that are good to imitate'.[2] Although mimetic desire is part of human nature, we are not necessarily at its mercy; the acquisitive form can be deliberately bridled and not allowed to generate social conflict.

In its acquisitive form, mimetic desire is directed toward an object that the subject desires *'because the rival desires it'*[3] (author's emphasis). To imitate the desires of someone else is to turn this someone else into a rival as well as a model. Of the three entities—subject (the one desiring an object), rival (the one who is in possession) and the object of desire—Girard accords the rival the dominant role because the rival's desiring an object 'alerts the subject to the desirability of the object'.[4] It follows that two desires converging on the same object are bound to clash;[5] therefore, uncontrolled mimesis coupled with desire necessarily involves conflict. Furthermore, once the possessor–rival realizes that what he or she has is desirable, it becomes more valuable, and he or she becomes zealous to retain it. Should the desiring subject attain the coveted object, the positions are reversed: the former rival in turn assumes the position of desiring subject in order to regain the object. With reciprocal exchange, mimetic desire and its attendant violence spreads, potentially to engulf the social order.

The prevalent cultural accommodation to mimetic desire, the focus of Girard's work, occurs in cultures which channel mimetic

1. Sacrificial scapegoats, Girard postulates, were 'mimetic free-for-alls' that could terminate a disruptive mimetic crisis and reunite 'the entire community against a single, powerless antagonist' (Girard, *Double Business*, p. xii).

2. R. Girard, *Things Hidden since the Foundation of the World* (Stanford: Stanford University Press, 1987), pp. 288-90.

3. R. Girard, *Violence and the Sacred* (Baltimore: Johns Hopkins University Press, 1977), p. 145.

4. Girard, *Double Business*, p. 140.

5. Girard, *Violence and the Sacred*, p. 146.

desire as sacrifice, a safe outlet within the society which thereby protects the society from dissolution. The sacrificial victim is an individual who has, by some means or another, demonstrated difference but who is innocent of the charges, thereby first an Other, then a victim. By projecting the social ills of both sides (subject and rival) onto the innocent but different individual, and by sacrificing this Other, the society maintains social cohesion, at least for the moment.

Literary and sociological evidence suggests, however, that the social groups reflected in biblical literature were directed to govern the basic human impulse of acquisitive mimetic desire by *exposing* it as such within the social group, lest it disrupt the culture; and, if necessary, by *displacing* it outside the social group, with foreign social groups it regards as 'evil' or danger-ous.[1] Marshall Sahlins describes

> the tribal plan...as a series of more and more inclusive kinship-residential sectors...The close kinsmen who render assistance are particularly near kinsmen in a spatial sense: it is in regard to people of the household, the camp, hamlet, or village that compassion in required, inasmuch as interaction is intense and *peaceable solidarity essential.*[2]

Under the circumstances described by Sahlins, striving toward social solidarity, which implies rejection of mimetic desire within the intimate social group, is characteristic of primitive social organizations. Such communities typically take pains to maintain cohesive and harmonic social unity, beginning with the family. Within the household, pooling of goods and services makes necessities available to all, eliminating differentiation of members 'in favor of the coherence of the whole'; it is 'the *constituting activity* of a group'[3]. Kinship is a social aspect of mutual aid, and generosity, not competitive pricing, effects material exchanges.[4]

---

1.   Non-acquisitive mimetic desire is considered a positive social value.
2.   M. Sahlins, *Stone Age Economics* (Chicago: Aldine–Atherton, 1972), p. 198.
3.   Sahlins, *Stone Age Economics*, p. 93.
4.   M. Sahlins, 'Exchange Value and the Diplomacy of Primitive Trade', in J. Helm, P. Bohannan and M.D. Sahlins (eds.), *Essays in Economic Anthropology Dedicated to the Memory of Karl Polanyi* (Proceedings of the 1965 Annual Spring Meeting of the American Ethnological Society; Seattle:

This is obvious even in contemporary households: parents do not charge their children, other relatives, or guests for food.

The Hebrew Bible, although it recognizes sacrifice and the sacrificial crisis, does not accept them as necessary. Unlike the literature of sacrificial societies, the Bible does not seek to hide the workings of mimetic desire. It does the opposite: it directs attention to the negative aspects of mimetic desire (jealousy and violence), often by displacement of the sacrificial victim, exposing the misunderstood 'necessity' of sacrifice in order to thwart human sacrifice. There is no denial that sacrifice, often displaced as animal sacrifice, played an important role in the evolving biblical community, but biblical literature discloses that this group sought to reject *human* sacrifice within the community as an unavoidable consequence of mimetic desire. But mimetic desire is, according to Girard, part of human nature. It may be displaced, but it is not nullified. Even though individuals may not be sacrificed, they may still be victimized through the effects of mimetic desire.

The Hebrew Bible consistently exposes individuals who are controlled by mimetic desire, that is, imitating another by desiring what the other has.[1] Indeed, the Ten Commandments are specific stipulations against various forms of mimetic desire, so that acquisitive mimetic desire is essentially anti-covenantal.[2] But two women married to one man are repeatedly depicted in a reciprocal exchange of mimetic desire: they both wish to be fertile and (most) loved. Each woman makes the Other a model and rival; each is jealous (desires what the Other has) and zealous (desires to retain what the Self has) at the same time. In

University of Washington Press, 1965), pp. 103-107.

1.   For example: the serpent desires YHWH's power, the first woman desires the serpent's promised wisdom, Cain desires the divine approval Abel receives, Jacob desires Esau's birthright, Joseph's brothers desire his most-loved status.

2.   The commandments which most clearly repudiate mimetic desire are: 'You shall not kill' (Exod. 20.7); 'You shall not commit adultery' (20.8); 'You shall not steal' (20.9); 'You shall not bear false witness against your neighbor' (20.16); 'You shall not covet your neighbor's house; you shall not covet your neighbor's wife, or his manservant, or his maidservant, or his ox, or his ass, or anything that is your neighbor's' (20.17), and cf. the equivalent commandments in Deut. 5.

fact, the word most used for 'second wife', צרה, means a female
'rival' or 'foe' or 'opponent', the feminine form of the masculine
צר, 'enemy' (with all the implications retained in the feminine
form). Thus the language conveys (and thereby shapes) the
expected behavior of two women who share a husband even
though that behavior is disparaged by the social norms.
Masculine mimetic desire is displaced onto the female.

With such displacement, it is understandable that female
rejection of mimetic desire occurs only once in the Hebrew Bible.
This is unexpected in a social structure where kinship status is
demonstrated by forms of etiquette, where reciprocity and co-
operation determine the economic aspects of domestic decisions,
all aimed at 'maintaining domestic contentment'.[1] In such a social
organization it is singular that the women, at the center of
household life, are not shown in any acts of reciprocal generosity.

Hannah, who is the rival wife to Peninnah, refuses to enter
into the subject–rival competition and is victimized. The rival
wife's actions draw attention to Hannah as an Other—a barren
woman in a society that valorizes fertility—which Hannah
experiences as a 'torment'. If Peninnah is jealous because
Elkanah loves Hannah, if she is using Hannah's lack of fertility
to attract Elkanah's love for herself, then Peninnah's mimetic
desire is the basis of Hannah's being emotionally marginalized in
this quarter, despite the narrator's observation that YHWH had
closed Hannah's womb. In other words, Peninnah is exploiting
YHWH's action (his closing of Hannah's womb) by responding
to mimetic desire—contrary to YHWH's commandments and the
social code[2]. With masculine mimetic desire ostensibly displaced
onto the females, Elkanah initially appears as a non-mimetic
'norm' for his rival wives.

In the social structure described in the Hebrew Bible several
women might stand in a variety of relationships to a man. The
primary relationship is usually with an אשה, 'wife'; and some men
have several wives without any further distinction between
them. A woman may also be a שפחה, 'handmaid', usually to a
wife; a פלגש (or even more indelicately, לחנה), 'concubine' to the

---

1.   Sahlins, *Stone Age Economics*, p. 77.
2.   But in accord with the language.

husband; or a female slave. Peninnah is defined as none of these. She is a second wife, a צרה. Peninnah is an opponent–foe–rival wife because this word has been selected to describe her; this does not mean that she is any of these for Hannah. Notably, Hannah never shows any envy of Peninnah. Hannah wants a child, but she does not project her desire onto Peninnah. Nothing in the text suggests that Hannah wants a child because Peninnah has children or because Peninnah taunts her. Hannah's desire arises from within and is maintained as a personal, as yet unfulfilled wish.

Under the circumstances of the 1 Samuel 1 narrative, Hannah's need to bear children according to the precepts of this culture suggests that she does not take the cultural prescriptions lightly. Accordingly, she must be thoroughly familiar with the cultural disdain of mimetic desire. Although Hannah suffers Peninnah's torments, there is no suggestion that she seeks to gain revenge, that is, to generate reciprocal mimetic desire. In this tale of feminine jealousy, Hannah shows no jealousy; by keeping her desire to herself, she does not express it mimetically, acquisitively. Desire remains introspective for this woman; it is a *good* mimetic desire. Hannah desires to have what women have, a child; she does not desire to have a child because Peninnah has children. She does not perpetrate masculine displacement of mimetic desire on the female, and she proves herself an Israelite observant of the covenantal strictures. There is, however, no feminine bonding depicted; Peninnah's mimetic desire obviates that possibility. Hannah is marginalized as a childless Other in a culture where a woman's purpose in life is depicted as reproduction and associated tasks.

Elkanah, as a devout Israelite, may be assumed to be familiar with the narratives of Israelite history, including explicit as well as implied statements of masculine rejection of mimetic desire. He must also know about Sarah and Hagar, about Leah and Rachel; in fact, Elkanah may think his experience of female jealousy is buttressed by those biblical narratives. After all, the language reinforces jealousy among second wives: they are 'enemy–rival–wives'.

Perhaps that is the reason Elkanah seeks to advance Hannah's personal desire for a child as mimetic desire (her wanting what Peninnah has) and thereby elicit jealousy between his wives. He gives portions of sacrifice to each member of his family and thus differentiates between the two women in terms of their fruitfulness. That Peninnah's tormenting Hannah is associated with Elkanah's portion-giving is implied by the sequence of the narrative. Even though Peninnah and Hannah are introduced and contrasted in terms of fruitfulness in 1.2, Peninnah's tormenting Hannah is not mentioned until immediately *after* Elkanah's giving of the portions; and the association of motherhood and torment is supported by the following line: 'And her rival wife really provoked her, to irritate her because YHWH had closed her womb' (1.6). Elkanah reinforces Peninnah's advantageous status at the sacrifice, and Peninnah 'rubs it in'.

The action is summarized as an annual event: 'And so *he* [Elkanah] *did* year by year, as often as *she* [Hannah] went up to the house of YHWH *she* [Peninnah] provoked *her* [Hannah]' (1.7). Elkanah assigns portions; when Hannah goes to the house of YHWH, Peninnah provokes her. There is no suggestion of Peninnah's hostility during the rest of the year or at least no suggestion that it is intense; the antagonism seems exacerbated by the visit to the temple at Shiloh and Elkanah's portion-giving that is associated with that visit.

Elkanah's sense of justice apparently demands that he give equal portions to each member of his family: nevertheless, he gives one—a generous one—to Hannah,[1] one to Peninnah, his second wife, and one to each of the latter's sons and daughters (1.4). This public display of difference—and it is *difference* that marks the victim—is augmented by provocations from Peninnah, Hannah's rival wife, year after year. Elkanah's actions exacerbate disharmony in his family even though biblical literature suggests other, less divisive ways of being just. Elkanah could have learned from Joseph, who gave each of his brothers by Leah a portion of food, of clothing and of gold; but Benjamin, a brother of his own mother, Rachel, he gave five times as much, so that each group of mothers' sons received an equal portion

---

1. מנה אחת אפים, 'a portion more'. This is frequently rendered as 'a double portion'; but cf. the articles in this volume by Amit (p. 69) and Meyers (p. 94).

(Gen. 43.34). In so doing, Joseph honored the mothers equally, whether or not that was his primary intention.

Now Hannah has no children, but to honor his wives equally Elkanah could give his wives equal portions; that is, one to each of the children and their mother, and an equivalent number of portions to Hannah, so that the women would be equal in their shares. Elkanah gives Hannah only one portion, but one *generous* portion (1.6); his inconsistency draws attention to his restricting of Hannah's portion and enlarging it at the same time, neither of which is a comfort to Hannah. This annually repeated disparity in his portion-giving and its equally repeated consequence in Peninnah's provocations of Hannah suggest that his experience of the women as jealous of one another—over him—is not altogether discomfiting to him. The one woman (Peninnah) wants his love, the other (Hannah) his children. Elkanah seems to aid and abet strife between the women.

One must question Elkanah's motives in his interactions with his wives. It seems that the generation of mimetic desire in this narrative does not arise from the two women but from Elkanah. Insofar as they identify themselves with their reproductive functions, Hannah and Peninnah are types of the women Esther Fuchs says are created 'in the image of patriarchal desire'.[1] By fostering mimetic desire between the women Elkanah may be displacing his own discontent, his desire for a son from the woman he loves. As a result, the women in strife become a foil for Elkanah's apparent 'purity'.

According to Jung, such a projection cannot occur without a 'hook'; in other words, it must be feasible in the situation described. It is certainly possible that a barren woman be jealous of a fertile one, but equally likely that she *not* be jealous, especially in a society that valorizes repudiation of envy and emphasizes generosity and cohesiveness within the family unit. The women could comfort and console each other, even closing rank as women against the male Other. Displacing his frustrated desire for a child by Hannah, Elkanah projects mimetic desire between the two women and thereby initiates a 'divide and conquer' tactic with the women in his household.

1.   E. Fuchs, 'The Literary Characterization of Mothers and Sexual Politics', *Semeia* 46 (1989), p. 151.

Hannah does not rise to the bait. The unfulfilled desire that Elkanah projects outward on others, Hannah keeps for herself and turns inward. She refuses mimetic desire and concentrates on her own desire: she internalizes her pain by weeping and not eating, and by speaking her heart out to one whom she believes will listen. Between Peninnah and Elkanah, both of whom project their mimetic desires on her, Hannah is an example of what James G. Williams calls a 'marginal' female, 'different to the point of being *too* different'.[1]

Hannah is addressed by two men: her husband Elkanah, and the priest Eli. Both these men are presented as admirable. Elkanah appears with full genealogy as an Ephraimite who lives in the Ephraimite territory (1.1) and practices religious devotion: he goes to sacrifice at the altar at Shiloh annually (v. 3). All of these attributes endorse the virtuousness of the individual. Eli the priest may be inferred to be righteous as an attribute of his position. But, as often happens in the Hebrew Bible, these initial impressions give way to ambiguity as the narrative develops. In fact, both of these men are so involved with their own perceptions that they fail to comprehend a suffering woman, a woman who is wife to the first and a devotee of the temple of YHWH to the second.

Elkanah is described as loving Hannah (1.8). That his love is current and not in the past is attested to by the Hebrew syntax.[2] However, such a rare, bald statement of love from a presumably reliable narrator is confounded by Elkanah's 'conversation' with Hannah. In his speech to her, Elkanah notes that Hannah weeps and does not eat. His response is to cajole her: 'Hannah, why do you weep? And why do you not eat? And why is your heart morose? Am I not more to you than ten sons?' (1.8). Elkanah's 'consoling' of Hannah does not allow her

1. J.G. Williams, 'Between Reader and Text: A General Response', *Semeia* 46 (1989), p. 174. Even though Williams is referring to a 'harlot' as a marginal female, the concept applies equally to Hannah, a woman at the other extreme of female marginality.

2. The simple past (without *waw*) of 'for he loved Hannah' is followed by a reversal of the normal verb–noun sequence, which signals a temporal change (to past perfect) so that the following phrase reads 'and YHWH had shut up her womb' (1.5).

time to answer his initial questions, which would effect communication between husband and wife, but would also draw him into involvement. That his questions are rhetorical and thus not intended to probe Hannah's situation is evident from their quick succession. While they do not allow Hannah to convey her thoughts or feelings, Elkanah's questions do relinquish some tacit information about him. His questions are typical of what psycholinguist Virginia Satir classifies as the 'Blamer Mode'. Such speakers 'don't bother about an answer; that is unimportant. The blamer is much more interested in throwing weight around than really finding out anything'.[1] Elkanah is depicted as imposing himself without regard for the Other, who happens to be his suffering wife.

Furthermore, these questions also reveal that Elkanah, as typical of a 'blamer', 'longs to be connected'.[2] His last question, 'Am I not more to you than ten sons?', expresses this desire in a formulation which precludes an answer, thereby making overtures toward connection even as he closes off the possibility. Only with this question does Elkanah allow time for Hannah's answer, which she wisely forfeits.

Significantly, Elkanah's third question uses a form of the word רע, which means 'morose' or 'unsatisfied' when it refers to countenance or heart, as it does here, but primarily means 'evil' or 'destructive'. The stronger implications are usually ignored in translations, which ameliorates Elkanah's judgment of his wife and thus alters the relationship to Hannah depicted by the narrative.[3] In the Hebrew one hears 'evil' even as one understands 'morose', 'unsatisfied'.

Notably, Elkanah's consoling judgment of Hannah is followed by *his* claim for love, which I paraphrase as 'is not your love for me greater than your desire for even ten sons?'. Elkanah does not comfort his wife with his love *for her*. As a male, Elkanah does not have his entire existence connected to procreation as the female Hannah is supposed to do in the patriarchal culture.

---

1. V. Satir, *The New Peoplemaking* (Mountain View, CA: Science and Behavior Books, 1988), p. 87.
2. V. Satir, *Conjoint Family Therapy* (Palo Alto, CA: Science and Behavior Books, 3rd edn, 1983), p. 258.
3. RSV: 'Why is your heart sad?'.

He has already fathered sons and daughters; his responsibility for generation has been fulfilled. Although his frustration suggests that he wants children by the woman he loves, he apparently 'loves' Hannah without regard for the need she has, as a woman in this culture, to bear children. His suggestion that he is more than 'ten sons' makes light of her deprivation as it attempts to equate conjugal love with parental love.

Furthermore, all of Elkanah's questions to Hannah fall under the psycholinguistic category of verbal attacks. The first three are in the 'Blamer Mode' under the disguise of affectionate concern, and the fourth hides the attack under a presupposition—that Elkanah's love is 'worth more than' the love of ten sons.[1] The skilled attacker may bury verbal abuse under surface signals of tenderness and affection, claiming tender loving care for which the recipient should be grateful, but in fact the recipient will more likely be burdened with a second layer of hurt, which leads to confused misery and confusing guilt. Elkanah ostensibly tries to diminish Hannah's suffering by attempting to show that it is unjustified, claiming that her love for him is more valuable than 'ten sons'; in fact, he increases it. When Hannah is not granted the dignity of her suffering, she suffers even more. Elkanah's use of these modes of verbal attack discloses a man who is threatening, angry and punishing beneath the surface. He typically directs his anger at the weakest target, in this case Hannah.

Elkanah's use of verbal attack supports the claim that he is frustrated because the woman he loves is barren. It is psychologically understandable that he unloads his anger on the object of his frustration, especially since she is the weakest target available. In an interesting twist, Elkanah does not suffer from mimetic desire; there is no 'object' he wishes to take from someone else. However, his actions instigate mimetic desire between his two wives. A foil for Hannah's non-mimetic handling of her own inner desire, Elkanah is betrayed by his mode of speech as well as his deeds. Hannah, even though she is rival to Peninnah and object to Elkanah, is an innocent victim.

It is clear that Elkanah assumes dominance in his 'conversation'

---

1. Satir, *Peoplemaking*, p. 87.

with Hannah by taking the first 'turn'[1] and by establishing the topic—and this is all well and good. But Elkanah abuses his dominance by asking questions without allowing an answer three times, and by concluding with a question which cannot be answered. He thus maintains the first and last word, destroying any possibility of verbal exchange and effectively maintaining dominance. As long as Hannah is wife but not mother, Elkanah marginalizes her through verbal attack and renders her speechless.

Later (1.21-23), when Hannah is no longer in a socially weak position, Elkanah's manner of speech to her is entirely different. Hannah initiates the conversation and establishes the topic. She, unlike Elkanah, does not verbally attack; and she allows her husband ample opportunity to answer. Hannah's conflict-avoiding behavior is, according to linguist Deborah Tannen, typically female: 'To most women, conflict is a threat to connection', and women struggle 'to keep the ties strong...and accommodate to others' needs while making what efforts they can at damage control with respect to their own needs and preferences'[2]. Male focus on status, hierarchy and rank allows Elkanah to attack Hannah under the guise of protection (domination); with female focus on interdependence, Hannah *expects* her actions to be influenced by others.[3] She has no need to suppress Elkanah's response. On the other hand, Elkanah's verbal aggression in 1.8 is typical of the male: 'male behavior typically entails contest...Furthermore, oral performance in self-display is part of a larger framework in which many men approach life as a contest'.[4]

After the birth of her son, Hannah does not go up to make the annual offer at the house of the Lord. She wishes to remain at home until her son is weaned, at which time she brings him to abide at the temple, as she promised (vv. 24-28). She sends her husband off with her 'rival' (vv. 21-22a), clearly demonstrating

1. 'Turns', a linguistic concept, refers to the sequence of conversational speeches. Elkanah simply speaks first, thus has the first 'turn'.
2. D. Tannen, *You Just Don't Understand: Women and Men in Conversation* (New York: Ballantine Books, 1990), pp. 150-52.
3. Cf. Tannen, *You Just Don't Understand*, p. 152.
4. Tannen, *You Just Don't Understand*, p. 150, citing Walter Ong.

that she harbors no jealousy. Hannah's remaining at home also interrupts the pattern of provocation established by her husband's portion-giving. In contrast to Hannah's sure knowledge of what she will do is Elkanah's response, which closes with the weak 'only, may the Lord establish his word' (v. 23). And when she does bring Samuel to Shiloh, Hannah brings her own provisions: 'a three-year-old bull, an ephah of flour, and a skin of wine' (v. 24). Hannah has extricated herself from Elkanah's disruptive and isolating conduct.

Hannah's experience with Eli is hardly better. Like Elkanah, Eli judges Hannah—this time explicitly—before she can say a word: Eli's questions are in the simple 'Blamer Mode', without any overlaid and contradicting emotional element; they are neither rhetorical nor a trap for self-incrimination. Hannah does respond, and her words constitute the climax of this part of the narrative. In the structure of her response, Hannah almost literally centers her words on the most significant aspect of her visit to the temple: 'I have been pouring out my soul before YHWH' (1.15c).[1] The phrase she uses, 'pouring out', is suggestive of the male part in a sexual encounter; despite her deprived existence, Hannah appears the stronger, the 'male', and 'pours out' her heart to God. Her conception shortly thereafter attests to the success of her plea. Eli's response is so non-specific and impersonal that it cannot be considered significant in her change from barrenness to fertility (v. 17). Like Elkanah, Eli speaks from a verbal protective barrier and maintains distance.

It is curious that Eli immediately presumes that Hannah is drunk (vv. 13-14). Other conditions could as easily explain her behaviour: she could be a habitual lip-mover, one who 'mouths' ideas unconsciously; she could 'mouth' her prayers consciously, the better to communicate; she could be in grief, as indeed she is. Mere 'mouthing' seems insufficient evidence for the unquestioned judgment Eli makes. When his presumption proves utterly false, Eli fails to accept responsibility for his misjudgment; instead, he utters easy platitudes that could apply to any person, any prayer. Hannah is judged abnormal (drunken) and thereby marginalized, and this by a man to whom she has not

1. Cf. the English translations for 1.15c.

turned, a man who unjustly criticizes her with the authority of his position.

Hannah's independent resolution of her inner turmoil, so that she eats (there is no mention of drink) and 'her countenance was no longer' (v. 18)[1] is followed by Elkanah's 'knowing' Hannah and her conception.

Elkanah and Eli attend to superficial 'ritual' aspects of belief without perceiving deeper significances which lie in human relationships to one another and to YHWH. Hannah, although she receives the brunt of Peninnah's mimetic desire, is never shown in active reciprocity. Hannah clearly wishes to have children as Peninnah does but, despite provocation, the text does not demonstrate any projecting, acting out or other demonstrations of envy on her part. It is Hannah who evolves as the social ideal, despite projection of mimetic desire on her by Elkanah and Peninnah and judgment of her by both Elkanah and Eli.

According to James G. Williams, 'In those tales where the woman acts only for the sake of the hero or the man's world, she is a persona on the boundary, a mediator who may quickly become a victim'.[2] Not interacting in any roles in the subject–rival–object triangle of mimetic desire, Hannah becomes its victim. However, because Hannah does *not* respond to mimetic desire, she is able to curtail mimetic interaction in the entire family and lead it to a more socially acceptable interaction. Hannah is a woman in a boundary situation, a situation 'where the woman, by virtue of her very tenuous, sometimes marginal status, can lead the male...over the threshold into a safer or better zone for his survival and success'.[3] She is a social redeemer.

Finally, Hannah only speaks her heart to, and is only heard by, YHWH. Her marginalization in the world of men, of human power, is emphasized by Elkanah's failure to let her speak and Eli's failure to respond meaningfully to her emotional appeal. She is also marginalized in the world of women by Peninnah's uncontrolled jealousy, repeatedly precipitated by Elkanah's

1. In the Hebrew, ten words precede the five-word central phrase, and fourteen words follow.
2. Williams, 'Reader and Text', p. 177.
3. Williams, 'Reader and Text', p. 175.

actions. YHWH's hearing of Hannah attests to the fact that YHWH listens to the heart, and that of female as well as male. Hannah's meaningful relationship with YHWH overrides all human marginalization, which happens to be consistently related to anti-covenantal, acquisitive mimetic desire. This narrative shows that a woman can reach YHWH by opening her heart when males, even powerful men like Elkanah and priests like Eli, may project their own weaknesses on the 'weaker' women or be absorbed in empty ritual. And although Elkanah and Eli project Hannah as diminished (by Elkanah as morose, with implications of evil; by Eli as drunk), her strength of character and integrity of belief finally render *her* the noble core of the narrative, and both Elkanah and Eli as ambiguous by comparison. The narrative describes victimization of an innocent, and victim-reversal; so that Hannah evolves from an Other into a paradigm, a model of woman, and redeems her family from mimetic desire.

And the rival wife? Her jealousy and mimetic desire (she is zealous for the motherhood Hannah is expected to be jealous of) serve as a foil for Hannah's refusal of mimetic desire. In this respect Hannah seems to resist 'biblical sexual politics'.[1] The implicit traditional interpretation of women as jealous of each other in opposition to the explicit cultural and religious mores suggests, perhaps, the magnitude of the threat of female bonding to the patriarchal system. But even Hannah desires a *son* (not a *child*, or a *daughter*), and the narrative depicts her as relinquishing the joys of parenthood, thus limiting her function to reproduction and nursing, the biologically programmed aspects of being a female. Hannah refuses the mimetic desire and envy despised in the patriarchal culture but displaced upon women; at the same time, the desires she achieves are those ascribed to women in the patriarchal system. Victim and redeemer, Hannah reinforces the patriarchal image of women.

---

1.   Fuchs, 'Characterization of Mothers', p. 162.

HANNAH AND HER SACRIFICE:
RECLAIMING FEMALE AGENCY*

Carol Meyers

The road from Samuel's birth to his emergence as one of the great national leaders of ancient Israel is marked by several complex narratives. All of these serve to prepare the reader or audience for the role Samuel will ultimately play in the critical and momentous transition of Israel from its tribal existence to its monarchic political structure. As is often the case for such pivotal figures, the prefiguring of Samuel's national prominence involves a birth and childhood narrative. Thus, willy-nilly, a woman—the mother of the man destined for greatness—enters the biblical story.

Hannah is introduced in the second verse of 1 Samuel 1 and appears throughout the narrative of that chapter. Her role in the Samuel story culminates in the poem, attributed to her in its superscription, of 1 Sam. 2.1-10.[1] Finally, a postscript to her role in the story of her son's birth and dedication to Yahweh comes in 2.21, which records the birth of Samuel's five siblings—three more boys and two girls.

According to the biblical tale, Hannah was one of two wives of a prominent Ephraimite named Elkanah. Unlike her co-wife

* This paper appears as 'The Hannah Narrative in Feminist Perspective' in J. Colesin and V. Matthews (eds.), *Go to the Land I Will Show You: Studies in Honor of Dwight W. Young* (Winona Lake, IN: Eisenbrauns, 1994).

1. This poem is usually called the Song of Hannah for reasons summarized by P.K. McCarter, *I Samuel* (AB, 8; Garden City, NY: Doubleday, 1980), p. 74. Most exegetes suggest that the song has been inserted into the narrative. A tenth-century date has been proposed by D.N. Freedman, 'The Song of Hannah and Psalm 113', *EI* 14 (1978), pp. 56-69.

Peninnah, Hannah had no children. Although her inability to conceive apparently did not dampen her husband's love for her, she suffered from the taunting of Peninnah. Her distress was particularly acute during the family's annual trek to Shiloh, where Elkanah's differential allotment of the sacrificial portions—only one portion to Hannah, for she was only one individual—caused her to weep and left her unable to partake in the sacrificial feast (1 Sam. 1.8).

In the context of one of these trips to Shiloh, Hannah was overcome with distress, offered an ardent prayer to Yahweh, and then made a vow. If God would answer the prayers and provide a son to her, that child would be dedicated to Yahweh. Eli, the priest at Shiloh, encouraged her and sent her home with her family, whereupon she conceived and gave birth to Samuel. Hannah's next trip to Shiloh involved handing over her child to the care of Eli and giving voice to her eloquent prayer of thanksgiving and praise.

Embedded in this narrative is a verse—1 Sam. 1.24—describing a sacrifice brought to the sanctuary at Shiloh at the time that Samuel was entrusted to the priests at the 'house of Yahweh at Shiloh'. This verse provides two pieces of information about the ritual act it records: it lists the commodities brought to the sanctuary,[1] and it gives Hannah an integral role in the presentation of these materials, along with her son, to the sanctuary.

Neither Hannah's actions in this verse nor her position in the narrative have ever figured very prominently in the traditional historical-critical, form-critical, or even more recent literary-critical treatments of the books of Samuel or of the Samuel story. The commentaries do not subject Hannah's role to special exposition. Indeed, by the very titles they assign to 1 Samuel 1 (or 1 Sam. 1–3),[2] they obscure the prominent position of Hannah

---

1.   These are examined in C. Meyers, 'An Ethnoarchaeological Analysis of Hannah's Sacrifice', in D.P. Wright, D.N. Freedman and A. Hurwitz (eds.), *Pomegranates and Golden Bells: Studies in Biblical, Jewish, and Near Eastern Ritual, Laws and Literature in Honor of Jacob Milgrom* (Winona Lake, IN: Eisenbrauns, forthcoming).

2.   Some examples of the way commentaries label this narrative are: 'The Legitimacy of Samuel' (1 Sam. 1–3), in W. Brueggemann, *First and Second Samuel* (Interpretation; Louisville, KY: John Knox, 1990), pp. 10-28;

in the opening section of the books of Samuel. Yet this narrative in general and 1 Sam. 1.24 in particular contain valuable information when considered from the analytical perspectives of feminist biblical analysis.

Traditional modes of biblical scholarship do not entirely ignore the fact that Hannah was a woman. However, feminist inquiry involves posing questions that diverge from those that have long prevailed in biblical studies as the result of the long dominant sociology of the discipline. That is, biblical studies have been traditionally pursued more in seminaries than in universities and more by men than by women.[1] Androcentric orientation and bias have thus tended to preclude attention to the Bible as the product of a living community of women as well as men. And theological agendas have interfered, albeit perhaps subconsciously, with recognition of a woman's initiative and deed in the ritual sphere. Hannah's role has been marginalized, trivialized or ignored. Furthermore, all too often her actions in bringing a sacrificial offering to a major national shrine have been viewed as atypical; or, worse, the text has been reviewed as corrupt.

Consideration of the place of Hannah as a woman in the poignant narrative of 1 Samuel 1 will thus be a central focus rather than a side issue of this inquiry. Her position as one of the small company of prominent biblical females will serve as an

---

'Birth and Dedication of Samuel' (1 Sam. 1), in G.B. Caird, *The First and Second Books of Samuel (IB, II; Nashville: Abingdon Press, 1953), pp. 876-82; 'Samuel et Eli' (1 Sam. 1–3), in L.P. Dhorme, *Les Livres de Samuel* (Paris: Gabalda, 1910), pp. 16-45; 'Samuel's Birth Narrative' (1 Sam. 1), in R.P. Gordon, *1 & 2 Samuel* (OTG; Sheffield: JSOT Press, 1984), pp. 23-24; and 'The Child Asked of God' (1 Sam. 1.1-20) and 'Samuel Comes to Eli' (1 Sam 1.21–2.11), in N.H.W. Hertzberg, *I & II Samuel* (trans. J.S. Bowden; OTL; London: SCM Press, 1964), pp. 10-28. But cf. 'Hannah's Trial and Trust' (1 Sam. 1.1-18) and 'Hannah's Faith Rewarded' (1 Sam. 1.19-28), in W.G. Blaikie, *The First Book of Samuel* (Expositor's Bible; New York: Armstrong & Son, n.d.), pp. 1-24.

1. See C. Meyers, *Discovering Eve: Ancient Israelite Women in Context* (New York: Oxford University Press, 1988), pp. 6-23, for a discussion of contemporary biblical scholarship with respect to the social sciences and to gender. See also D.C. Bass, 'Women's Studies and Biblical Studies: An Historic Perspective', *JSOT* 22 (1982), pp. 6-12.

introduction. Then, rather than examine the quest for maternity that serves as the theme for the narrative and that has been treated as an annunciation type-scene in recent literary and feminist analyses,[1] I will take a close look at 'Hannah's Sacrifice', a designation used here to describe Hannah's trip to Shiloh with ritual offerings as well as with her young son. That episode within the well-known biblical tale provides a rare opportunity to recognize and evaluate a woman's ritual act. Since the primary actor in the sacrificial passage of 1 Sam. 1.24 is a woman,[2] in contrast with the overwhelming predominance of males in cultic contexts in the Hebrew Bible, a feminist perspective is de rigueur in considering Hannah's sacrifice.

1 Samuel 1: A Woman's Story

That the first chapter in the books of Samuel is a woman's story can be established first by examining the personnel involved. The cast of characters in 1 Samuel 1 includes five individuals: the Ephraimite Elkanah, his two wives, Hannah and Peninnah, the priest Eli and the infant Samuel. Eli and Samuel become prominent in the succeeding chapters. Elkanah is introduced in v. 1, ostensibly as the focus of the ensuing narrative. Of the two women, Peninnah plays only a minor role. But Hannah plays a major part in the tale, so much so that the narrative of Samuel's birth could as well be called the Hannah Narrative.

Hannah's prominence is evident in several ways. For one thing, her name is mentioned fourteen times between 1 Sam. 1.1 and 2.21. Samuel, whose acclaimed birth is apparently the motivation for the narrative, is named only three times. Peninnah also appears three times, and their husband is named eight times. Interestingly enough, given the association formed here between Samuel and his eventual priestly role, Eli is mentioned

---

1. See R. Alter, *The Art of Biblical Narrative* (New York: Basic Books, 1981), pp. 82-87, and A. Brenner, *The Israelite Woman: Social Role and Literary Type in Biblical Narrative* (The Biblical Seminar, 2; Sheffield: JSOT Press, 1985), pp. 92-98.

2. Textual variants make the identity of the person offering the sacrifice somewhat ambiguous, but the case for that person being Hannah is a strong one. See discussion below.

ten times. Still, Hannah's name appears more frequently than does Eli's and as often as those of all other members of her family combined.

Hannah's name is also prominent in comparison to the appearance of the names of other major female figures in the Hebrew Bible. Not surprisingly, given the focus on pre-national family 'history' in the Genesis narratives, the matriarchs are the women whose names are most frequently mentioned in the Hebrew Bible. The name Sarah/Sarai, for example, appears some 55 times, Rebekah 30 times, Rachel 46 times and Leah 34 times. Women appearing in all other contexts, no matter how important they may have been, are named far less frequently—if they are named at all.[1] For example, Miriam's name appears only fifteen times, Deborah's nine times, Jael's six times, Bathsheba's ten times, Michal's sixteen times, Huldah's twice. With fourteen mentions, Hannah features prominently among the major female figures of the Hebrew Bible.

The matriarchs, the first group of women, figure extensively because of their maternal roles. For the second group, the focus is on some other aspect of their 'lives'; this is true even for Bathsheba, though of course her role as Solomon's mother cannot be ignored. Hannah fits into the latter group (all prominent biblical women other than the matriarchs of Genesis) with respect to frequency of mention. That is, she is hardly mentioned as often as are the female ancestors of the Genesis narrative. Furthermore, although her maternal function is certainly the focus of the narrative, she belongs to the second group thematically speaking, too: a dimension of female behavior other than maternity is a significant part of the Hannah story.

Hannah's prominence as a named individual is also noteworthy in light of the overall pattern of female names—or lack thereof—in the Hebrew Bible. The names of Israelite women represent only a small percentage, 8 percent, of attested

---

1.   Esther, as the central figure of a biblical book ten chapters in length, is not included in this statement. But note that Ruth, also the main figure in a biblical book, is mentioned only 12 times (although Naomi, perhaps the true heroine of that book, is named 22 times).

Israelite personal names.[1] Many females who figure in narratives are not named at all. In the epic traditions of Joshua through Samuel, the story of Samson's birth bears some similarity to that of Samuel: in both, a barren women conceives a child who is dedicated to Yahweh; and sacrifices and prayers are part of the sequence of events in both tales. Yet the mother of Samson is denied the visibility of a named individual; she remains the wife of Manoah throughout the narrative. Similarly, the tragic story of Jephthah's daughter (Judg. 11) involves remembering the event but not the name of the virgin who was sacrificed as a burnt offering in fulfillment of her father's vow. With biblical texts so restrained in giving women personal names,[2] Hannah's named visibility allows her a modicum of individuality despite her role as wife to Elkanah and mother of Samuel.

Another dimension of naming likewise offers exceptional status to Hannah, in that she is one of a series of biblical women who name their offspring. The accounts of women naming their children are found in narratives dealing with the premonarchic period of Israelite history.[3] The role of women in giving names is apparently indicative of an authoritative social role, at least within the family setting, since the child receiving the name thereby comes under the influence of the namegiver.[4] Certainly

1. I. Ljung, *Silence or Suppression: Attitudes toward Women in the Old Testament* (Acta Universitatis Upsaliensis; Uppsala Women's Studies, Women in Religion, 2; Stockholm: Almqvist & Wiksell, 1989), p. 27. Ljung bases her calculations on the material in M. Noth, *Die israelitischen Personennamen im Rahmen der gemeinsemitischen Namengebung* (BWANT, 3.10; Stuttgart: Kohlhammer, 1928), which lists 1426 personal names, of which 1315 are those of men, giving a figure of 9 percent for female names. However, Noth includes extrabiblical materials, such as the Elephantine letters, which have proportionally more female names. Ljung apparently excludes extrabiblical names in considering the figures for the Hebrew Bible.

2. Cf. Reinhartz's essay in this volume.

3. Ljung, *Silence or Suppression*, pp. 17, 18-27. Ljung also notes the general absence of women as name-givers in P narratives and as part of the generational chains in P's genealogies.

4. See J. Pedersen, *Israel: Its Life and Culture* (2 vols.; London: Oxford University Press, 1926), pp. 245-49. Ljung (*Silence or Suppression*, p. 103 n. 14) refers to H. Ringgren's observation (in *Israelite Religion* [Philadelphia: Fortress Press, 1966]) that knowing someone's name affords some sort of control; she also suggests that the patriarchal impulse to name wells,

the details of the Hannah–Samuel story depict a mother making decisions about the future of her child; Hannah participates in the social authority implicit in the giving of a name.

This discussion of names and naming practices with respect to women in the Hebrew Bible reveals a distinctive role for Hannah. Likewise, several literary features of the 1 Samuel 1 narrative present her as an active person rather than as a passive, dependent female. In looking at all the verbs associated with the noun 'woman' in the primary history (Genesis through 2 Kgs), Ljung found that 'woman' was the subject of verbs exactly the same number of times (51) as it was the object of verbal forms.[1] In the 1 Samuel narrative Hannah is the subject of the verb over three times more often than she is the object. The narration of her story makes Hannah a social actor and imbues her with a dynamic quality not typical of texts dealing with women.

The frequent use of dialogue and direct speech in the construction of the Hannah story also affords her the measure of visibility and individuality that is more a concomitant of reported speech than of descriptive narration. In his perceptive discussion of dialogue in the Hebrew Bible, R. Alter emphasizes that direct speech functions to reveal nuances of character and relationships and that spoken language, in transferring the nonverbal thought into words, is an effective mechanism for revealing the essence of the speaker.[2] In light of this, it is worth noting that there are ten instances of recorded speech in the 28 verses of 1 Samuel 1. Hannah is the only character in that chapter to be part of each of these dialogic episodes: six times she is the speaker (to God, Eli, Samuel and Elkanah) and four times she is addressed by another (twice by Elkanah and twice by Eli). In contrast, Elkanah speaks only twice and is spoken to but once; Eli also speaks only twice and is addressed twice; and Samuel is spoken about just once (to God? to the household?) when he is named in 1.19. Hannah's character is thus revealed

springs and places represents not only etiological expression but also the establishment of rights of control.

1.   Ljung, *Silence or Suppression*, p. 113.
2.   Alter, *The Art of Biblical Narrative*, pp. 66-70.

far more fully than that of any of the other participants in her story.

In addition, Hannah's dialogic centrality culminates in the ten verses of poetry attributed to her. None of the other persons featured in 1 Samuel are credited with poetic utterance except for Samuel, for whom only one poetic passage, two verses in length (1 Sam. 15.22-23), is recorded. The latter, along with Hannah's song, are the only poetic passages in all of 1 Samuel. Hannah is thereby distinguished, as are relatively few other biblical personages, by association with poetic speech.

Hannah's Sacrifice

This discussion of Hannah's prominence in 1 Samuel 1 serves as a background to a consideration of her role in bringing sacrificial materials to the shrine at Shiloh. The MT of 1 Sam. 1.24 portrays her as weaning her son and then taking him, along with the bull, flour and wine, to the house of Yahweh. However, the LXX and probably also 4QSam[a] have a much fuller text, which presumes that Elkanah also went up to Shiloh, that *he* brought the sacrifices, and that the two of them together offered the sacrifice.[1]

The reasons that some prefer the LXX/4QSam[a] over the MT can be related to certain ambiguities in identifying the agent of the vow and its fulfillment. In 1 Sam. 1.11 Hannah makes a vow; 1 Sam. 1.21 has Elkanah fulfilling a vow—one that is not previously mentioned; and in 1 Sam. 1.27 Hannah refers to the terms of *her* vow. The role of Elkanah in this votive language is difficult. Is he participating in Hannah's vow or fulfilling one of his own, which is otherwise not mentioned? These questions are not easily resolved. But removing the agency of the sacrificial act from Hannah, with LXX and 4QSam[a], does not resolve the issue either; and in the process, it deprives Hannah of a cultic role that legitimately belongs to her. It is easier to consider the circumscribed cultic activities for women at the time of the LXX

---

1.   So McCarter, *I Samuel*, pp. 56-57, following a suggestion (personal communication) by F.M. Cross. Cf. Cross's hypothesis, in 'A New Qumran Biblical Fragment Related to the Original Hebrew Underlying the Septuagint', *BASOR* 132 (1953), pp. 15-26, about 4QSam[a] as *Vorlage* of the LXX. McCarter accepts the LXX as the original in his translation.

and 4QSam[a] as a basis for their texts than to forego the MT with Hannah's premier role in the sacrifice of 1.24.

Hannah's sacrificial agency, as expressed by the MT, is congruent with the prominence she holds in the narrative of 1 Samuel 1 as described above. It is also consistent with what can be inferred about female participation in cultic events as suggested in recent feminist biblical scholarship.

Hannah's activity in making a vow and bringing sacrificial goods to Shiloh is probably best understood in the context of family religion. Indeed, the spectrum of cultic behavior revealed in 1 Samuel 1 reveals the private, personal piety of Elkanah and his family and should not be considered an early version of the pilgrimage festivals prescribed in Pentateuchal legal texts. Indeed, such visits for prayer and for making and keeping vows, precisely because they represent family ritual rather than public or institutional cultic activity, are not mentioned at all in the Pentateuch.[1]

Hannah's sacrifice thus stands as an example of women's religion as it existed at some point early in the history of Israel. The dominant and official roles in the Israelite cultus were reserved for males, but public cultic office and official ritual events were not the sum total of religious practice in ancient Israel or in any society for that matter. That the pre-eminent male role in Israelite ceremonial life was not so comprehensive as to deny other family members direct activity in the cultic sphere has long been noted.[2] Indeed, there has been a tendency to view male and female roles as being virtually the same except for the matter of priestly eligibility, despite gender differentials in certain texts prescribing specific cultic activities.[3]

The older studies granting some importance to women's religious behavior have now been enhanced and given a firm theoretical base by an approach which examines such behavior in

1. So M. Haran, *Temple and Sacrifice in Ancient Israel* (Oxford: Clarendon Press, 1978), pp. 304-307. Haran's view is similar to that of Pedersen, *Israel*, pp. 376-82, 385.

2. As by C.J. Vos, *Women in Old Testament Worship* (Delft: Judels & Brinkman, 1968), p. 49.

3. One of the first examples of this perspective is I. Peritz, 'Women in the Ancient Hebrew Cult', *JBL* 17 (1898), pp. 111-48.

light of anthropological data dealing with gender and religion.[1] Perhaps the most important methodological lesson to emerge from the quest to reconstruct the role of Israelite women in cultic activity is that biblical materials are insufficient, since they are mostly centered on the male-dominated public life of Israel, and they may even distort a social reality quite different from the formal canonical stance. It is becoming increasingly clear that women everywhere have critical roles to play in religious life, even if those roles are ignored or minimized in the public record.[2]

The validity and autonomy of Hannah's actions, as an example of family religion, should not be questioned. Her sacrifice comes as the result of the vow that she made during a family pilgrimage to Shiloh. Although a legal text in Numbers (30.6-8) would appear to make a woman's vow subject to the veto of her husband, there is no indication that Elkanah acted in this way in 1 Samuel. That law may be later than the activities recorded,[3] and the very existence of such a law is probably a good indication that women in early Israel were indeed accustomed to making and carrying out their own vows. Furthermore, Hannah's autonomy in making a vow at Shiloh is authenticated by the fact that pilgrimages and concomitant votive acts are two of the most characteristic religious acts of

1. Two articles by P. Bird are programmatic in bringing the analytical perspective of anthropological gender studies to bear upon the consideration of the religious roles and activities of both men and women in ancient Israel: 'The Place of Women in the Israelite Cultus', in P.D. Miller, Jr, P.D. Hanson and S.D. McBride (eds.), *Ancient Israelite Religion* (Philadelphia: Fortress Press, 1987), pp. 397-420; and 'Women's Religion in Ancient Israel', in B.S. Lesko (ed.), *Women's Earliest Records from Ancient Egypt and Western Asia* (BJS, 166; Atlanta: Scholars Press, 1989), pp. 283-98.

2. For a striking example from the contemporary world, see S.S. Sered, 'Conflict, Complement, and Control: Family and Religion Among Middle-Eastern Jewish Women in Jerusalem', *Gender and Society* 5 (1991), pp. 10-29.

3. So J.T. Willis, 'Cultic Elements in the Story of Samuel's Birth and Dedication', *ST* 26 (1972), p. 59. Willis also points out that even if the MT of 1 Sam. 1.21 is correct in attributing a vow to Elkanah (although many text critics would delete 'his vow'), his vow could not have been the same as his wife's.

women as observed in ethnographic research.[1]

In vowing that her son will be dedicated to Yahweh and in bringing a sacrifice along with her son in fulfillment of that vow, Hannah's religious actions bridge the realms of private and public religious life. Her motivation is individual, personal and wrenchingly private. Acts prompted by similar profound feelings must surely have been carried out by countless Israelite women; yet those of Hannah are uniquely visible. Biblical tradition has preserved her tale because it enters the public realm—partly because she interacts with the leading priestly figure of the day at the major shrine of the premonarchic era, and partly because her behavior adumbrates the national prominence of Samuel. Although some feminist biblical critics would emphasize the barren woman type-scene of the Hannah story as an indication of female behavior in the service of patrilineal if not patriarchal interests,[2] it seems that the national purview of this tale transposes it beyond the sexual politics of domestic life and into the realm of national service. The private *is* the public in this instance; were it not so, Hannah would be as invisible as her sisters.[3]

Furthermore, Hannah's visibility comes at a time of political dysfunction in Israelite history. It is precisely in biblical texts dealing with the premonarchic period that most of the examples of women in significant public roles are clustered. In such decentralized eras, marked by social upheavals, and with no dominant national power structure, women frequently emerge as significant social actors. At the very least, their status is usually higher than in more stable periods; for it is just at such unsettled times that all persons with marginal access to power find themselves

1.   See the sources cited in Bird, 'Women's Religion', p. 297 n. 37.

2.   E. Fuchs ('The Literary Characterization of Mothers and Sexual Politics in the Hebrew Bible', in A. Yarbro Collins [ed.], *Feminist Perspectives on Biblical Scholarship* [SBL Centennial Publications, 10; Chico, CA: Scholars Press, 1985], pp. 118-19) asserts that these type-scenes all promulgate a patriarchal ideology with male and female in a power-structured relationship that subordinates women.

3.   For another instance of female religious activity in the public domain in biblical Israel, see C. Meyers, 'Of Drums and Damsels—Women's Performance in Ancient Israel', *BA* 54 (1991), pp. 16-27.

able to transcend the normal criteria that might otherwise limit their actions.[1]

A woman's visibility and centrality in the Hannah Narrative of 1 Samuel 1 and her agency in a ritual act thus reveal an otherwise hidden aspect of women's cultic life. In addition, Hannah's sacrifice signifies an instance of female activity—albeit related to maternal functions—with national implications. By the very individuality of her characterization and behavior, she is represented as contributing to the corporate welfare of ancient Israel. Although the Hebrew Bible as the story of Israel may be primarily the story of men, occasionally women such as Hannah can be discerned. Such women may be the exceptions in terms of the canonical record; but they should hardly be considered unique within the dynamics of daily life, at least in the rural context of ancient Israel.[2]

1.   See the discussion of these dynamics, and works cited, in J.A. Hackett, 'Women's Studies and the Hebrew Bible', in R.E. Friedman and H.G.M. Williamson (eds.), *The Future of Biblical Studies: The Hebrew Scriptures* (SBL Semeia Studies; Atlanta: Scholars Press, 1987) 141-64. Cf. the discussion of the private–public dichotomy in C. Meyers, *Discovering Eve*, pp. 173-76.

2.   The changing pattern of gender relationships, over time and in different socioeconomic settings, is examined in C. Meyers, 'The Creation of Patriarchy in the West: A Consideration of Judeo-Christian Tradition', in A. Zagarell (ed.), *The Foundations of Gender Inequality* (Kalamazoo: New Issues Press, forthcoming).

Part III
WOMEN AND MONARCHS

THE PLEASURE OF HER TEXT*

Alice Bach

That which you are, that only can you read.

Harold Bloom, *Kabbalah and Criticism*

No sooner has a word been said, somewhere, about the pleasure
of the text, than two policemen are ready to jump on you: the
political policeman and the psychoanalytical policeman; futility
and/or guilt, pleasure is either ideal or vain, a class notion or an
illusion.

Roland Barthes, *The Pleasure of the Text*

My reading of Abigail's story, found in 1 Samuel 25, is
concerned with woman as reader of male-produced literature,
and with the way the hypothesis of a female reader changes
our understanding or vision of a text[1] by exploring the significance of its sexual codes.[2] Formerly, in analyzing biblical texts, it
was *de rigueur* to present scholarly interpretations as objective
or neutral descriptions; some critics now recognize that such a
'neutral reading' is no more innocent than any other. All this
time scientific scholars have been telling it slant, reading from
the male point of view. The typical reader response to female
characters has held them in thrall to the dominant male figures,

---

* This article first appeared in A. Bach (ed.), *The Pleasure of Her Text:
Feminist Readings of Biblical and Historical Texts* (Philadelphia: Trinity Press
International, 1990), pp. 25-44.

1. For our ongoing exploration of woman as reader and for providing
pleasure in analyzing texts, I am grateful to J. Cheryl Exum.

2. For a feminist literary delineation of the difference between women
reading male-authored texts and women reading books written by women
('gynocritics') see E. Showalter, 'Feminist Criticism in the Wilderness', in
idem (ed.), *The New Feminist Criticism: Essays on Women, Literature, and
Theory* (New York: Pantheon Books, 1985), pp. 243-70.

who are accepted as the keystone of each narrative unit. Female character is defined by male response. Often the perception of female characters as 'flat' results from scholars' crushing assumption that male authors have created male characters to do the bidding of their male god. A hermeneutical version of the old-boy network.

In this paper I consider the story of Abigail as a self-contained narrative unit which achieves its dramatic effect by the skillful interweaving of dialogue and by contrasts of character.[1] By examining the sexual code, I am presenting an unabashedly subjective reading.[2] Instead of evaluating and praising Abigail as a suitable partner for David, reading the text as it has been controlled by codes of male dominance, I adopt a revisionary approach, in order to explore female influence in a male-authored work. Understanding Abigail to be the focus of her own narrative, I award her an opportunity to break free of the traditional plot of love and marriage. The text lends itself to this interpretive strategy since all the other characters, the young outcast David, Abigail's landowner husband Nabal, and the peripheral male and female servants, interact only with Abigail. No other character in the episode interacts with all the other characters. Thus, even though the story appears to be about male authority, female presence shines through.

A closer examination of the sexual codes in the text shows Abigail to be more subversive than her male authors have understood. During the time and space of her narrative, she has used her wise good-sense to control her life verbally while appearing socially dependent and compliant. The moment she encounters David, she speaks. Her determination is reflected in the series of active verbs (v. 23) which rapidly move the narrative: *wattᵉmahēr, wattēred, wattippōl, wattištaḥû*.

---

1.   Flaubert, in a letter to Louise Colet, Oct. 12, 1853, thus defined his own aspirations in attempting to write the perfect artistic novel.

2.   Mieke Bal in *Murder and Difference* (Bloomington: Indiana University Press, 1988) has illustrated the effectiveness of a reading strategy that employs a combination of codes, 'a transdisciplinary approach'. The advantage of Bal's method is that one avoids privileging one code, allowing it the voice of authority, obscuring social realities. This article owes much of its understanding of examining codes to Bal's perceptive work.

> She *hastened* and *got down from* the donkey
> and *fell* before David on her face and *bowed* to the ground.

The first speech is hers. Before David can articulate the anger which the reader has heard him express to his men as Abigail was riding toward him, she delivers a series of beseeching demands, orchestrated to absorb the insults her husband has spoken. Well-chosen words will wash away the villainous words spoken earlier.

> 'upon me, my lord, be the guilt', v. 24
> 'let your maidservant speak', v. 24
> 'hear the words of your maidservant', v. 24
> Let your maidservant arrange for the gift to be given, v. 27
>   [loose rendering]

Calling herself 'maidservant', *'ªmāt^ekā* or *šip̄āt^ekā*, synonyms delineating a lower-class woman of no power, Abigail reflects the opposite in her actions: the text has informed us that Abigail is a wealthy woman, and now we see her in charge, comfortably issuing orders, while at the same time deflecting male anger. One suspects she has spoken equally soothing words to her husband to still his rages. There is no reply from David. The scene continues to belong to Abigail. After offering the gift of nourishment for him and his men, she proffers a greater gift: spiritual nourishment in the form of the prophecy endorsing David's destiny to reign as the chosen one of God.[1] Once she is assured that David has no further violent intentions toward Nabal, she dissociates herself from this husband, who she concedes has no hope of survival (vv. 25-26), and seeks to link herself with David. 'When YHWH has made good his promises to my *lord*, may your remember your *maidservant*' (v. 31). Throughout her speech, Abigail continues to emphasize a power

---

1.   In this central scene, vv. 14-35, Kyle McCarter's sensitive translation reads with Vaticanus against Alexandrinus and Venetus and against the MT, eliminating the name of Nabal. Thus, the name Nabal is not spoken by either the servants, Abigail, or David, until the potentially violent situation has been resolved. The loss of his name reflects the loss of his status, as well as his importance to the story. By removing his name, McCarter has emphasized the loss of the power Nabal possessed at the beginning of the narrative. See P.K. McCarter, Jr, *I Samuel* (AB, 8; Garden City, NY: Doubleday, 1980).

hierarchy, repeatedly calling David *'ªdōnî* and herself *'ªmāt^eka/šiphāt^ekā*. While her actions show that she is accustomed to controlling situations, her words assure David that she is handing over power to him. Abigail's cloying humility is a result of her belief in her own words of prophecy. Her deference to the landless pauper underscores David's position as prince in disguise. We are in no doubt that Abigail would not herald a rogue with words suited to royalty.

Abigail's ability to act halts the negative progress of the story. The young men, who reported the foul acts of Nabal (vv. 14-17), are incapable of reversing their master's action. Abigail, the woman, acts swiftly. Nabal had refused to give David *bread and wine and meat* (v. 11); Abigail gathers up extravagant amounts of those items and more. 'Two hundred *loaves,* two skins of *wine,* five dressed *sheep,* five seahs of parched grain, one omer of raisins, and two hundred fig cakes' are brought to David (v. 18).

A central illustration of her verbal power is provided in Abigail's prophecy. Her words echo and elaborate Saul's acknowledgment (ch. 24) that David will become the next king of Israel. But her words have a more powerful effect on David than Saul's had; they stop him from committing a violent act. In the previous episode in the cave, David had spared Saul's life *before* Saul extracted David's promise of protection. Abigail's words to David change the course of his action toward Nabal, and possibly the echo of her prophecy in ch. 26 guides David's hand when he so flamboyantly seizes, then returns, Saul's spear.

One impression of the patrician landowner's wife is that she is the maternal wife of order and control. She sets limits on her husband's refusal to comply with David's request; she brings calm to David's fury. The biblical author does not consider Abigail merely as the good mother. If she were, she would have been rewarded with a long life (in the text) and a top-rated male heir, a common patriarchal convention for conferring praise on a biblical woman. For a moment Abigail steps outside the bounds of convention: a woman succeeds in stopping the future king from committing bloodguilt. But in exercising power and speaking in her own distinctive voice, perhaps Abigail has been guilty of the crime of female ambition. In order for male power to be restored, her voice must be stifled. Her recorded moment of prophecy is not to be repeated.

Scholarly readings of Abigail's story have often reduced it to '1 Samuel 25', that is, the commentators' somewhat mechanical explanation of how David annexed his second wife and the valuable territory south of Jerusalem. Perhaps that is why Abigail has no passionate admirers. Few have taken pleasure in her text.

Suppose we befriend for a moment this woman, brave enough to ride out from the closed security of her home to face the storms of her husband's enemy. Instead of imprisoning her in the language of *wife*, let her break those restraints and relate to other women. We know she is strong and decisive; might she be capable of sustaining friendships, perhaps with Michal and Bathsheba? As Elizabeth Abel discovered in her study of women's friendships, 'through the intimacy which is knowledge, friendship becomes a vehicle of self-definition for women, clarifying identity through relation to an other who embodies and reflects an essential aspect of the self'.[1] Might Abigail comfort Bathsheba on the death of her baby? Did Michal return as 'primary wife'; or had that position been claimed by Ahinoam, mother of Amnon, David's eldest son? Was Abigail's gift for pronouncing the right words at the right time necessary to keep peace among the wives of the monarch?

As the story unfolds, we can contrast Abigail's behavior with the men's actions; by holding our literary mirror at another angle, we can contrast her with the other women within the Davidic cycle. When Abigail is placed at the center of her drama, she emerges as a redeemer whose action and prophecy are necessary in assuring the future role of David, the divinely chosen monarch of Israel. Is it surprising to find that the historical code, strengthened with added muscle from the theological code, inscribes a woman in the role of God's helper? Permitting a woman to pronounce a crucial prophecy remains well within the Deuteronomistic Historian's narrative program. The prophecy is supportive, highlights the role of the deity in the selection of

---

1. E. Abel, '[E]merging Identities: The Dynamics of Female Friendship in Contemporary Fiction by Women', *Signs* 6 (1981), pp. 413-35.

David as king, and 'emphasizes David's success in avoiding any action that would later jeopardize the integrity of his rule'.[1]

Among the thematic threads that bind together chs. 19–28 one can identify the depiction of Saul as the seeker and David as the vulnerable one whose life is sought. Holding the thread, like Ariadne guiding the reader through the Deuteronomist's maze, is Abigail, who makes explicit the connection between the 'seekers after David' and Nabal. At the center of the maze, the minotaur is Saul/Nabal. Abigail's action is 'providential persuasion', part of the larger pattern within chs. 24–26 of God's active protection of David.[2] Like Ariadne rescuing Theseus, Abigail keeps David safe from the devouring minotaur. Comparing Abigail with Ariadne is not frivolous; both women figure as a trajectory in a story about men; both women rescue/protect the questing hero and then follow him to a different land. Once in David's land, Abigail is left out of David's story. Theseus deserted Ariadne on the island of Naxos. As a figure of the process of solution Abigail/Ariadne rewards the hero (as well as the reader who makes her/his way to her) with a way out of the story. When we grasp Abigail/Ariadne's thread, we follow a different path through the labyrinth. Instead of admiring the man who entered the arena to do violence, we admire the woman who led him out alive.

Neglecting to put Abigail at the center of her drama, as a primary actor, weakens her role as God's helper. Adele Berlin does not regard Abigail's words of prophecy (vv. 28-31) as crucial to the narrative, claiming the insertion is 'hardly relevant to the events of the Abigail story'.[3] Many scholars agree,[4]

---

1. R. Polzin, *Samuel and the Deuteronomist* (New York: Harper & Row, 1989), pp. 213-15. Although Polzin does not characterize his approach as a reading of the theological-historical code active in the text, his strategy of tracing allusions and repetitions within the History results in laying bare this code.

2. Polzin, *Samuel and the Deuteronomist*, pp. 206-207.

3. A. Berlin, 'Characterization in Biblical Narrative: David's Wives', *JSOT* 23 (1982), p. 77. Incorporated in *Poetics and Interpretation of Biblical Narrative* (Bible and Literature Series, 9; Sheffield: Almond Press, 1983), pp. 23-43.

4. See D.M. Gunn, *The Fate of King Saul: An Interpretation of a Biblical*

however, that the primary theological function of Abigail is to speak the word of YHWH to David. While Nabal is ignorant of David's true identity, Abigail recognizes David as the future king of Israel. Her prescience is a clear indication that Abigail is God's chosen prophet-intermediary.[1] Abigail's assurance to David that he is YHWH's intended ruler and must remain innocent to do God's will is the link between the anointing prophecy of Samuel and the dynastic prophecy of Nathan.[2] In an ironic twist, the fate about which YHWH's prophet Abigail has warned David, that of shedding innocent blood, prophesies his downfall while it connects this episode of David acquiring his good-sense wife with that future episode of David acquiring another wife (2 Sam. 11.1-25). Possibly Abigail's words reveal a latent subtextual desire for connection with Bathsheba, for a community of women.

Inevitably Abigail must join Michal and Bathsheba, the other

Story (JSOTSup, 14; Sheffield: JSOT Press, 1980); McCarter, *I Samuel*; Polzin, *Samuel and the Deuteronomist*.

1.   J.D. Levenson ('1 Samuel 25 as Literature and as History', *CBQ* 40 [1978], p. 20) acknowledges that Abigail is the first person to announce that David will be chosen *nagid 'al yiśrā'ēl*, 'ruler over Israel' (v. 30) and that her assertion that YHWH will build David a *bayit ne'emān*, 'secure house' (v. 28) is an 'undeniable adumbration of Nathan's prophecy which utilizes identical language'. Levenson, however, decides that 'the narrator does not present Abigail as a prophetess [*sic*] in the narrower sense; she is a person who from intelligence rather than from special revelation senses the drift of history, and who endowed with the highly valued initiative and efficiency of the "ideal woman" (see Prov. 31.10-31) rides the crest of the providential wave into personal success'. It seems highly speculative to assume Abigail does not possess special revelation. At best Levenson's tone indicates that Abigail's intelligence is a gift secondary to prophecy.

2.   Splitting the impact of Abigail's prophecy (vv. 28-31) by concluding that these verses are a later Josianic addition to the earlier story of David's meeting with Abigail is another way to diminish the female role in the story. McCarter falls victim to this approach by calling the later redaction 'a vehicle for an early reference to the promise of dynasty to David' (*I Samuel*, p. 402). McCarter does not mention that the Josianic historian has chosen to put the prophecy on the lips of Abigail, nor does he suppose any connection between the Josianic addition of v. 1, the report of the prophet Samuel's death, and the addition of the proleptic prophecy within the chapter.

wives of David who experience moments of narrative power. A clear illustration of gender politics is found in the biblical portrayal and scholarly interpretation of David's wives. Seen through the stereotyping lens of male authority, each of these women typifies a particular aspect of *wife*; Michal is the dissatisfied daughter/wife of divided loyalties; Abigail is consistently the good-sense mother-provider, and Bathsheba the sexual partner. There is no interdependence of the wives of David, although in their actual lives there might well have been.[1] Nor is any of the three women portrayed as a woman with depth or timbre. In the text as traditionally interpreted, as well as in their lives, the wives of David cede to male domination, and in ladylike fashion allow biblical literature to privilege male gender and to demystify their own. However, by rerouting the circuits of conventional comparisons, we can clarify and restore the identity to each woman through her relation to an other who embodies and reflects an essential aspect of the female self. We can imagine alliances based upon affiliation instead of kinship and filiation.

As the only female character in her story, Abigail's isolation is apparent. When, however, we join her story to and make it part of and a link with Michal's story (Michal is essentially erased from David's life when Abigail is inserted into it) and then link Bathsheba's story to the previous two, we see female power, or self-identity, asserting itself. We can bring the women together by altering our usual chronology of reading with a Lacanian moment of mirroring. This strategy allows the women to reflect one another as whole bodies, and deflects the bits-and-pieces views we get from glimpsing a shard of each woman in the Davidic mirror, where she appears as a distortion of the male image. Such revisioning provides the reader with a method to probe the ideological assumptions which have resulted in the

1. See C. Gilligan, *In a Different Voice: Psychological Theory and Woman's Development* (Cambridge, MA: Harvard University Press, 1982). Gilligan argues that women typically develop different moral languages and decision-making styles from those of men. Gilligan has concluded from her female informants that women embrace an ethic of responsibility, nurturance and interdependence, which differs from the male ethic of autonomous individual entitlement.

polarized 'good wife, bad wife' stereotypes, the popularly held view of the women within the Davidic narratives.

Abigail: The Good-sense Wife

Abigail is labeled the good-sense wife, the embodiment of *śēkel* in contrast to her husband *nābāl*, the fool. The connection to the book of Proverbs where the use of the word *śēkel* is the most extensive in the Bible is immediate. The portrait of Abigail at first glance seems to be a narrative interpretation and expansion of the qualities attributed to the good wife of Proverbs 31, who provides food for her household, and 'opens her *mouth* with wisdom, and the teaching of kindness is on her *tongue*' (v. 26).

Providing us with some of the details of the life of an upper-class wife, Proverbs offers a clue to Abigail's many accomplishments. She considers a field and buys it; she perceives that her merchandise is profitable; she spins, she takes care of the poor, she makes all manner of garments and sells them. Clearly she does not eat of the bread of idleness (when would she have time!), while her husband sits in the gates of the city. Not surprisingly her children call her blessed. She is rated far more precious than jewels. Perhaps Nabal thought his good-wife Abigail was a glittering gem until the morning she told him that she had appeased the greedy son of Jesse. Discovering that his precious jewel had sided with the young brigand struck the undefended hungover Nabal in his heart with the force of a stone.

Traditional interpretations of 1 Samuel 25 have consistently focused upon Abigail's good-sense works as advantageous to the men in the story: as appeasing David in his anger, thus saving the lives of her husband's workers; preventing David from committing bloodguilt by killing her husband, and of course providing quantities of food for David and his men. The moral code reflects patriarchal values: a woman's personal payoff for virtue is connecting herself to a 'better' husband, one as beautiful, pious, and pleasing to God as she is herself. The rabbinic view of Abigail expands and escalates her biblical goodness.[1] In *b. Megillah* she is considered the most important wife of David, equal with Sarah, Rahab, and Esther, as the four most beautiful women in biblical history.[2] In the women's Paradise, Abigail supervises the women in the fifth division, her domain bordering those of the matriarchs, Sarah, Rebekah, Rachel, and Leah.[3] Josephus also emphasizes Abigail's goodness and piety, referring to her as *gynaikos d'agathēs kai sophronos*.[4] This description of Abigail is close to that of the ethical paragon par excellence, Joseph, a model of *sophrosynē*, 'self-control', for both Josephus and Philo. In both stories, of course, there is the motif of sexual restraint bringing divine rescue. It is understood by the rabbis also that Abigail's moral goodness and self-control cools David's ardor, thus distinguishing her from Bathsheba. The mere sight of Bathsheba enflames David to sin, whereas encounter with Abigail cools David's fervor to kill Nabal.

Kyle McCarter's summary of the narrative unit is typical of the traditional patriarchal response to the portrayal of Abigail as necessary piece in the grander Davidic mosaic: 'the partnership of such a wife bodes well for David's future, not only because of her good intelligence and counseling skills, but also because she is the widow of a very rich Calebite landowner'.[5] Jon Levenson characterizes Abigail as one who 'rides the crest of the providential wave into personal success'.[6] His view of her as an opportunistic surfer is no more complete than McCarter's wife of mergers and land deals. The pleasure of her text comes from acknowledging both these aspects of Abigail and celebrating her subtleties and contradictions.[7]

1. But see Valler's article in this volume, esp. pp. 134-36.

2. There were apparently only four women of perfect beauty. In *b. Meg.* 15a Sarah, Rachel and Abigail are consistently mentioned although there is no agreement as to the fourth beauty. Vashti, Esther, Rahab, Michal and Jael are all competitors.

3. When it comes to describing women, the rabbis seem to suffer from narrative exhaustion, since they describe Michal also as a woman of entrancing beauty, who was a model of the loving wife (*Beit HaMidrash* III, 136).

4. Josephus, *Ant.* 6.296.

5. McCarter, *I Samuel*, p. 402.

6. Levenson, '1 Samuel 25', p. 20.

7. Adele Berlin describes the wives of David with phrases that prolong

Although the biblical author describes Abigail as *yᵉpat tō'ar*, her beauty is apparently not the sort to inspire sexual desire (*pace* the ancient aggadists who have dreamed on paper of her) since there is no hint of a sexual relationship between Abigail and either husband. We are not told of any children from her marriage to Nabal, indeed if Abigail had had children with Nabal, they, not David, would have inherited their father's important estate. The biblical narrators/writers are not interested in Abigail's son from her marriage to David, referring to him as Chileab (2 Sam. 3.3) or Daniel (1 Chron. 3.1).[1] The text emphasizes Abigail's importance as the wife with the goods, the flocks and herds, detailing the quantity of every delicious item of food and drink she brings to the outcast David. His sexual hunger will be satisfied by another wife.

To illustrate the textual denial of sexuality to Abigail we might compare how the themes of sexuality, nourishment and death are developed in another story, that of Judith, a different story to be sure, but one with striking similarities. A woman rushes from the security of home to halt the destructive action of a male. Unlike Abigail, Judith spends a long time dressing to please the male, to seduce him into helplessness. Once in the presence of Holofernes, Judith tantalizes him with possibility. She stays in a tent adjoining his for three days, offering words that are sharply double-edged, meant to fool her enemy into

gender stereotyping: e.g., Michal as 'unfeminine' for declaring her love for David, and 'aggressive and physical' (apparently negative qualities) for helping him to escape through the window. Collaborating with the patriarchal agenda, Berlin describes Abigail as an exaggerated stereotype of the 'model wife and modest woman'. See Berlin's chapter, 'Character and Characterization', in *Poetics*, pp. 23-43.

1. There is a rabbinic tradition that claims Chileab was so named because he resembled physically and in his mental powers his father David (*kil'āb*, like [his] father). The name, according to L. Ginzberg, *Legends of the Jews* (Philadelphia: Jewish Publication Society of America, 1968), VI, p. 275, silenced any misunderstanding about David's hasty marriage to Abigail. The son is clearly the son of David because he resembles him physically. For similar explanation see *Targ. 1 Chron.* 3.1. David's marriage to Abigail seems implicitly to be connected with the marriage to Bathsheba. Although both marriages were impulsive, one was born of improper sexual desire; one was proper. Abigail's good name is protected by the name of her son.

believing that she is preparing for a sexual banquet and that she has come to lead him to victory, when the audience understands she plans the opposite. Taking with her the same items as Abigail does, a skin of wine, barley cakes, loaves from fine flour, and dried fruit (Jdt. 10.5), Judith brings the food to nourish herself, not to appease the appetite of Holofernes. Food in the book of Judith functions as a symbol of impending death; Abigail's vast amounts of the same food serve the opposite function. The gift of food comforts David and permits him to accept her words of prophecy. Abigail does not deceive David with words or with food. Judith serves tempting words and is herself the tasty dish.

Another textual silence concerns Abigail's lineage, for she is not the wife of important bloodlines. That connection with Saul's house is achieved by David's marriage to Michal. After Abigail's prophecy, assuring David that his own house is secure, v. 28, the mosaic is altered, the royal connection to Saul is no longer necessary. As if to underscore his awareness of David's relentless rise to power, Saul, flailing in his own impotence against the challenger, gives Michal to Paltiel (v. 44).[1] From the chronological order of wives in David's life, one can posit a setting of priorities of male ambition. First, the connection with the royal house, then the acquisition of personal wealth and the assurance of kingship, and finally a pleasurable sexual liaison.

Casting Abigail in the role of mother-woman represents a view of woman as a respite or dwelling place for man. She functions 'as a kind of envelope [for man] in order to help him set limits to things'.[2] In its positive aspect, as we have noted,

1.   Although Michal is returned to David (2 Sam. 3.13), their relationship is anything but harmonious. When David orders Abner to bring Michal to him, he refers to her as 'Saul's daughter'; in the following verse in speaking to Ishbosheth, Saul's son, David refers to Michal as 'my wife'. Once again the occasion of Michal's becoming David's wife is surrounded by male violence. Soon after she has been returned, Abner is killed by Joab.

2.   See L. Irigaray, 'Sexual Difference', in T. Moi (ed.), *French Feminist Thought* (Oxford and New York: Blackwell, 1987), pp. 118-30. Irigaray argues that 'the relationship between the envelope and the things represents one of the aporia, if not the aporia, of Aristotelianism and the philosophical systems which are derived from it'. She concludes that man, in fear of leaving the mother a subject-life of her own, in a dynamic

Abigail helps David set limits to his fury. While this envelope or place sees the female body as offering a visible limit or shelter, it also views her place as dangerous: the man risks imprisonment or murder within the villainous other unless a door is left open. Thus, to protect himself from the possibility of her engulfing him, the man must distance himself from her, and place limits upon her that are the equivalent of the place without limits where he unwittingly leaves her. After acknowledging that Abigail has stilled his murderous sword, 'unless you had hurried and come to meet me, truly by the dawning of day not a single man would have been left to Nabal' (v. 34), he must limit her power. Serving David's unconscious will, the narrator turns down the heat of the female hero. Our last image of her is as she is riding subdued toward David's house, in the company of female servants, playing her role as traditional wife, obeying the will of her husband. How different from that passionate ride down the mountainside in the company of male servants! Shut away from the action of the story, Abigail is no longer a threat.

Mieke Bal has noticed a similar framework expressing the unconscious fear of woman in the story of Abimelech by connecting six motifs (identified by Fokkelman): death, woman, wall, battle, shame, folly. Bal interprets the linking of these images as a strong chain of warning from male to male to keep his distance, to proceed with caution. 'One dies a shameful death as soon as one is so foolish as to fight woman when she is defending her wall/entrance from her mighty position as the feared other'.[1] Abigail has defended her entrance with words instead of violence. By offering David all her goods, she keeps her own body secure. Ironically David does not risk imprisonment in her house, indeed does not even show curiosity about what might be within. Instead he sends messengers to her in conventional fashion to define her as *wife*, as though her

subjective process, remains within a master–slave dialectic. 'He is ultimately the slave of a God on whom he bestows the qualities of an absolute master. He is secretly a slave to the power of the mother woman, which he subdues or destroys'.

1.   M. Bal, *Lethal Love* (Bloomington: Indiana University Press, 1987), p. 33.

moment of power and prophecy had never occurred.

As Abigail's absence in the subsequent text of the Davidic narrative proves, David is more successful than Nabal in keeping Abigail shut up in his house, within her own limits.[1] Only when she breaks free of the container of Nabal's house does she become all-powerful, simultaneously saving and threatening the men in the story. The story is resolved when the narrator serving the male characters puts Abigail in her place.

A feminist reading intent on restoring dimension to flattened characters must account for pieces that do not fit. Abigail the woman resists being dismissed as a literary type, 'the exemplum, the perfect wife'.[2] Nor is equating Abigail with mother-provider congruent if we understand Mother to be the Earth Mother, the well-spring of fertility. Abigail, the good wife of Nabal, is the mother of none. As the wife of David, she is the mother of a son, whose name Chileab, 'like [his] father',[3] removes him from her influence and control. Abigail is clearly the mother-provider of transformation. She turns the raw material provided by her destructive husband into salvific nourishment. She is not the tender of lambs, but of dressed sheep; she does not offer grain, but baked loaves. Model wife? She refers to her husband as a fool (v. 25), sides with his enemy, and does not even mourn his death.

The Women

In introducing the character of David, Meir Sternberg has observed that the biblical author provided a complete, formal and ordered portrait of David through 'summary epithets' in the glowing report Saul's servant makes about 'the young son of Jesse, skillful in playing, able in deed, a man of war, wise in counsel, a man of good presence, and the Lord is with him'

1. For a convincing argument of the silencing of Michal within the Davidic story, especially the metonymic function of the house as agent of silence and confinement, see J.C. Exum, 'Murder they Wrote: Ideology and the Manipulation of Female Presence in Biblical Narrative', *USQR* 43 (1989), pp. 19-39; repr. in Bach (ed.), *The Pleasure of Her Text*, pp. 45-67.

2. Berlin, *Poetics*, pp. 30-31.

3. Another interpretation of Chileab is, 'yes, the father is mine'.

(16.18).[1] Most biblical portraits, unlike this one, are the product of the reader's gap-filling activity; one collects shards of information as the narrative unfolds. Usually the biblical text provides the reader with only a partial picture of each character. This is certainly the way in which interpreters have read the relevant texts in the Davidic cycle in which female characters are present. Critics consistently define women as foils for David's development. As we have noted, female characters tend to have their identity stolen.[2] Traditional commentary has failed to fill out the identity of Abigail, Michal and Bathsheba, binding them by their gender to the overpowering portrait of David. In Sternberg's schema the entire personality of marginal characters gets telescoped into one or two words: churl and paragon.[3] Thus, he robs the story of elements of paradox. A reading that lingers over the collisions and conflicts between characters adds pleasure to the text.

Assigning to each of David's wives her summary epithets provides us with a male-produced map of each woman's place in the larger landscape. Michal's summary epithet states that she loved David, a fact not revealed about his other wives. Next

1. M. Sternberg, *The Poetics of Biblical Narrative: Ideological Literature and the Drama of Reading* (Bloomington: Indiana University Press, 1985), p. 326.

2. By reducing the story to slogans, Sternberg's reading does not acknowledge Abigail as the initiator of action. While there are tropes of folktale in Abigail's story—the wicked husband, the good and faithful wife—outcast David makes an odd Prince Charming. His threat of violence is not intended to rescue the fair maiden but rather to increase his own wealth. For a stimulating 'caution' against reading folktale or myth without expressing its ideological bias, see M. Bal, 'Myth à la Lettre: Freud, Mann, Genesis and Rembrandt, and the Story of the Son', in S. Rimmon-Kenan (ed.), *Discourse in Psychoanalysis and Literature* (London: Methuen, 1987), pp. 57-89; repr. in A. Brenner (ed.), *A Feminist Companion to Genesis* (The Feminist Companion to the Bible, 2; Sheffield: Sheffield Academic Press, 1993), pp. 343-78.

3. Sternberg, *Poetics*, pp. 325-28. Even though biblical texts reflect such formulas, I do not agree with Sternberg's conclusion that the reason for verbal shorthand is to discourage further inquiry into makeup and motivation. He sees omitted features as blanks rather than gaps to be filled in by the reader. While Nabal by his very name is to be thought of as a churl, one can fill in the gaps within the text by comparing his behavior with that of his wife.

the narrator tells us that Saul gave Michal 'as a snare for him' (18.21). The language of her epithets is clear. Described as daughter of Saul and snare, she is to spell death for David, although her love for him keeps her from snapping the trap. Abigail, as we noted earlier, is the good-sense wife. She is also wise and beautiful. But neither her name nor her epithets are presented until after a description of her husband's flocks. Nabal is mentioned first. David hears that Nabal is shearing his sheep and sends his men to ask for the payoff. David seems unaware of or uninterested in the beautiful wife inside the landowner's house. In contrast is a later David, inactive, no longer a fighter or outlaw, watching a beautiful woman in her bath. In this case Bathsheba is mentioned before Uriah. Immediately after identifying Bathsheba as the daughter of Eliam, the wife of Uriah, David[1] sends for this other man's wife and lies with her. In this narrative the biblical author develops themes of sexual power: in contrast to his earlier stories of David's marital alliances, which are really male power struggles.

Bathsheba's epithets are the most telling of the three products of male fantasy. For her creators, Bathsheba certainly provided pleasure in her text. Through the eyes of the focalizer David we see beautiful Bathsheba bathing: we observe her having sex with him. Then the narrator takes over, revealing that she is at the beginning of her menstrual cycle and then that she has just conceived a child. Bathsheba's first spoken words, 'I am with child', could serve as her summary epithet. But the language of sexual intimacy continues. We learn that Uriah will not have sex with her. After his death she mourns Uriah, is brought to David's house, becomes his wife, lies with him (again), and bears him a son. The explicit details of Bathsheba's sexual life stand in sharp contrast to the absence of any sexual language in the story of Abigail. Thus, the biblical author exposes private matters to paint the portrait of Bathsheba as the wife who inspires improper desire; he uses the language of prophecy and deference to describe Abigail, the wife of legitimacy and public acquisitions.

1. The text of 2 Sam. 11.3 reads *wayyōmer hᵃlô' zō't bat sheba'*. The identity of the male speaker who identifies Bathsheba is not clear. It could refer to David.

Examining these summary epithets provides major clues about the fate of each woman. The daughter of death inherits death (in a woman figured as barrenness) from her father; she does not pass on death to her husband. In the concluding episode about Michal (her stories are split as are her allegiances), she is scornful of David, uncovering himself before maidservants. David, Michal's husband, triumphant in his sexuality, is a sharp contrast to the dispirited figure of Saul, Michal's father, holding in his hand his spear, a symbol of male potency, and failing to kill David with his ineffectual shaft (1 Sam. 19.10). As Saul's life force wilts, David's grows stronger. Deprived of David's sexual energy, Saul's household is powerless: in the first episode, Saul cannot stop David from playing his lyre until Saul hurls his spear at him; in the second Michal cannot stop David from ecstatic dancing. Since there is no sexual life between Abigail and David, Abigail enjoys no further textual life either. Only Bathsheba, the wife of sexual intimacy, participates in the ongoing story of David's reign. The length of female textual life seems to be directly connected to the extent of sexual pleasure she provides her male creators.

Another contrast among the women is the way in which David wins each of them: within the consistent framework of fragmented episodes about the women, there are full reports of how David gains these wives: Michal through violence against the Philistines; Abigail through withholding violence against Nabal; Bathsheba through violence against Uriah. While Abigail prevents David from acting against Nabal, Michal has no part in the deal struck between her father and David. She is the reward of a struggle between men doing violence to men. Bathsheba, a casualty of David's sexual imperialism, has no part in David's death-dealing plan. Only Abigail actively opposes David's violence.[1] In her story, David refrains from the

1. *Contra* R. Alter, *The Art of Biblical Narrative* (New York: Basic Books, 1981), p. 61. Alter sees a progression of violence in each of the three 'discriminated premarital episodes', i.e., Michal, Abigail, Bathsheba. Alter reads each text with David at its center, missing the critical difference in interpretation when Abigail is placed at the center of her story. Her actions stop violence; the other women are not participants in the episodes which lead to their alliances with David; they are the prizes.

impetuous act of killing the unpleasant Nabal and so gains Abigail through YHWH's will; in the episode of Bathsheba, after he has gained the power of kingship, David arranges the death of Uriah in order to assure with his own actions that he may possess Bathsheba. When Saul set the bride price of Philistine foreskins for his daughter, he hoped the violent encounter would kill his enemy David (20.21). Rather, David triumphed through sexual slaughter. David himself sent his enemy Uriah into battle, again the prize being a woman. David kills the Philistines with the sword; Uriah is also killed by the sword. In Abigail's story, David and his men strap on their swords but never unsheath them in battle. It is the only one of the three stories in which sexual violence does not lead to marriage. It is also the only one of the three in which there is no allusion to sexual union, or non-union in the case of Michal. After Nabal's death, David sends his messengers to collect Abigail, 'to make her his wife' (v. 42). After Bathsheba's period of mourning for Uriah was over, 'David sent and brought her to his house, and she became his wife, *and bore him a son*' (2 Sam. 11.27). Saul gave Michal to David as a snare for him, but with the help of the wife who loved him, David escaped the snare and fled. And Michal was left with an empty bed, stuffed with *t^erāpîm*, an imitation man. David escapes Michal's bed; Bathsheba is ensnared in his.

Fathers and Son

In his vigorous examination of the literary history constructed by the Deuteronomistic Historian, *Samuel and the Deuteronomist*, Robert Polzin uses a strategy of 'allusive readings' to make interbiblical connections among episodes within 1 Samuel.[1] Through his comparisons of Saul and Nabal, he makes a convincing case for Nabal's death as proleptic of Saul's. Earlier David Gunn concluded that 'one of the important functions of Abigail's speech, in the context of the story as a whole, is to foreshadow Saul's death'.[2] But it is Abigail herself who first made this connection explicit in telling David, 'Let your enemies and those who seek to do evil to my lord be as Nabal' (v. 29).

1.   Polzin, *Samuel and the Deuteronomist*.
2.   Gunn, *The Fate of King Saul*, p. 96.

Following their lead, let us test connections between foolish men.

As Polzin notes, one of the major themes of the first book of Samuel is the establishment of kingship in Israel. Read through a psychoanalytic lens, this translates into a taut chain of fathers and sons, tensions of male power. Beginning with the birth of Samuel, spiritual father to both Saul and David, and ending with the death of Saul and his sons, and the kingship or coming of age of David, 1 Samuel can be read as a record of war games of slaughter and betrayal. The cycle of doom is compressed into a question in a Margaret Atwood poem:

> Aren't you tired of killing
> those whose deaths have been predicted
> and who are therefore dead already?[1]

But the struggle is inevitable. Until the father is vanquished, the son cannot flourish. David Jobling sees the motif of heredity as the most important aspect of continuity between the books of Judges and Samuel.[2] The sins of Eli's sons lead to the rise of Samuel as Eli's surrogate son; David, the one who can soothe Saul when the dark spirit comes upon him, becomes a surrogate son to Saul and a brother to Jonathan. Jobling understands the rise of the monarchy under Saul as a move toward continuous and hereditary government. There is, however, no mention of kingship as hereditary in 1 Sam. 8.4–12.25. As Jobling recognizes, the theological code supports monarchy in circumstances much like those of the judge-deliverers. The king unifies Israel and does not appear as a dynast.[3] For a dynasty is 'a direct negation of divine initiative in the raising of Israel's leaders'.[4]

Struggles between fathers and sons abound throughout the biblical narratives. Within the scope of this paper we can only glance at those that involve David as son. As we have noted earlier, the son of Jesse refers to himself as son to two

---

1.   M. Atwood, 'Circe/Mud Poems', in *Selected Poems* (New York: Simon & Schuster, 1976), p. 59.

2.   D. Jobling, *The Sense of Biblical Narrative*. II. *Structural Analyses in the Hebrew Bible* (JSOTSup, 39; Sheffield: JSOT Press, 1986), p. 53.

3.   Jobling, *Sense of Biblical Narrative*, p. 64.

4.   Jobling, *Sense of Biblical Narrative*, p. 85.

surrogate fathers: Saul and Nabal. This self-designation underscores the liminality of David's situation. No longer the child-shepherd guarding his father's flocks in the hills of Bethlehem, not yet ready to discard the time of sonship.[1] We can contrast another son connected to David, his 'brother', Jonathan, who struggles against his father, but dies alongside Saul, never to escape the role of son.

From the time David flashes his sword against the Philistines to capture the bride price for the daughter of Saul, assuring himself sonship to the king, the woman-mother is the prize for the murder of the father. Michal never quite achieves this status; she remains a transitional figure, the link between Saul and his successor. Her divided loyalties mirror the difficulties of the reader in deserting Saul and taking up emotional residence with David. Although David may be the ultimate Father's chosen son, the biblical author's ambiguous feelings toward him remind the reader that David is not always the popular choice. Abigail like Michal stands between David and a father figure. On first reading, the author's response to Nabal's wife appears to be different from his response to Saul's daughter. After all Abigail is the subject of an entire chapter in the narrative. And she is rewarded with a son, even if an 'unimportant' one. David flees the daughter of Saul, and neither her husband nor the biblical authors praise her for her courage in helping David escape her father. Michal, the companion of David's liminal period, is discarded like an outgrown garment. She remains childless, a daughter until the day of her death.

However, there is a similarity between the two women David has taken from older men: he seems to lose interest in them after he has possessed them and overcome the fathers their husbands represent. They are his public wives, as he publicly wrenched power from their husbands. Bathsheba, the wife of his bed, with whom he mourns the death of his infant son, is the

---

1. I understand the term 'liminality' to refer to important boundaries of the hero's life. Thus, David's rite of passage is bounded by the slingshot stone at one and the stone-dead Nabal at the other. This liminal or transitional period ends with the marriage to Abigail, who marks the beginning of the portrait of the adult David, who soon after this 'adult' marriage is anointed king of Judah.

wife of adulthood and privacy. David's victory over Uriah was born in an act of concealment. The only benefit from that marriage was Bathsheba herself. No kingship, no land, no wealth. Of course there is a future benefit for David from Bathsheba herself. From her womb comes the son Solomon, who will rule after his father.

Mother-women are at the center of the father and son battle from the first chapter of the book of Samuel through Elkanah's question to his wife Hannah, 'Am I not more to you than ten sons?'. It is also possible to imagine the question posed to Abigail by the young man who has introduced himself to her husband as *bin^{e}kā*, 'your son'. Standing as intercessor between him and the father, she answers his question with resounding affirmation. Presenting him with the goods of the father, she tells him that his house will be secure, unlike the houses of his predecessors, Saul and Nabal. And she plans to follow him into the house. Lest he be overcome with her devouring power, she calls herself *'āmāt^{e}kā / šipḥāt^{e}kā*, signalling that he will be the ruling father, and she will be his obedient mate. David acknowledges this transfer of power by telling Abigail that he has heard her voice and granted her petition (v. 35).

Earlier in the narrative David instructs his men to ask Nabal for a payoff because they had not harmed his shepherds. In other words David wants a reward because he behaved correctly. He had not invaded the older man's territory; he requests recognition from the father: 'give whatever you have [in] your hand to your son' (v. 8). At the rejection of the father, David responds in anger and pain and threatens to kill him. Abigail holds up the mirror to the son David in this episode, assuring him that he is good. It is the father Nabal who is evil and who must die.

The death of Nabal marks the end of this liminal period for David begun with the death of Goliath, also felled by a stone. In the next chapter, in what is to be their final meeting, David possesses Saul's spear, the metonymic weapon of sexual power, and receives acknowledgment from the father, 'Blessed be you, my son David'. Not believing Saul's words, David flees the borders of Israel, but the record of Saul's pursuit of David has ended. The transitional time of David's struggle to overtake the older king, which began with his battling Goliath in Saul's name, concludes with another scene of displaced victory, the death of Nabal. During this liminal period, David has depended on women to assure him that he is better than the father. In the episode with Bathsheba, he has become the man in charge. Bathsheba's announcement, 'I am with child', proclaims that David is no longer a son. No longer does he need a woman to defend him from the threatening father. No longer does he depend on the ultimate Father to do his killing for him. In this story he takes control from the Father God and proves that he can kill in his own name. And, thus, with this supreme act of disloyal sonship, he incurs the wrath of the Father, who takes the life of David's infant son.

Abigail 'Almānâ

After Nabal's death, Abigail becomes a widow, *'almānâ*.[1] The word is derived from the root *'lm*, meaning dumb, without speech. From the same root comes the noun *'ēlem*, meaning silence.[2] In Akkadian, *lēmūn*, a cognate word, means 'it is bad'. In spite of her marriage to David, Abigail remains a widow, that is, she survives without speech in the text. Her name is mentioned twice to remind the reader that she lives. Although she has a son, he is Chileab, like (his) father, and thus not connected with his mother. We do not hear her wise voice again. Ironically, in spite of the textual insistence that Abigail was improperly paired with the fool, that marriage gave her the power of speech as well as the power to ride down a mountainside, emboldened by her mission to stop David from killing her husband. In spite of the implication that Abigail lived happily ever

---

1.   Abigail is not called *'almānâ* in the text, perhaps because she is already considered David's wife. From the moment David tells her to return to her house, for 'I have granted your petition', the reader links Abigail with him and not with the drunken Nabal, whose life seems to drizzle out of him like the previous night's wine.

2.   I am indebted to Edward L. Greenstein of the Jewish Theological Seminary of America for his etymological acumen as well as for his careful reading and valuable discussion about many of the issues and suggestions raised in the article.

after with her Prince Charming, the vibrant, verbal Abigail seems to have functioned better as the wife of Nabal. While he lived, she demonstrated bravery. She had the power of prophecy. After his death, Abigail's voice is absorbed into David's, much as she is absorbed into his household. Once inside his house, she is no longer a threat or a redeemer to men.

Living on in the echo of her story as widow, isolated by the tradition as the good-sense wife, the Paragon, Abigail is denied political agency and her own identity. At the moment at which readers conceive of Abigail as agent, as actor, as subject, they restore dimension to her. And delight in the pleasure of her text.

KING DAVID AND 'HIS' WOMEN:
BIBLICAL STORIES AND TALMUDIC DISCUSSIONS

Shulamit Valler

The concepts of masculinity and femininity in rabbinic literature are quite different from their equivalents in the Bible. The roles fulfilled, actions carried out and discourses articulated by figures of men and women undergo various shifts when we move from the Bible to the Talmud and Midrash. This can be illustrated by comparing the biblical narratives about the women in King David's story with the interpretations of these same narratives in rabbinic literature.

The Bible presents David, the king of Israel, as a complex character who gradually evolves from a soft, delicate and sensitive boy into (when a grown man) a powerful and lustful king and, finally, into a weak old man. Sentimentality and sexuality are the notable characteristics ascribed to him and depicted in the Bible many times. One gets the impression that, since David is presented as an emblem of maleness and masculinity, his story exemplifies—for better or for worse—male behaviour. There are narratives about women's reactions to David's demonstrations of heroism (such as the killing of Goliath [1 Sam. 11]). There are stories about David's valiant fights for women (such as Merab [1 Sam. 17–18], Michal [18.17-28], Ahinoam [25.43] and Abigail [most of ch. 25]). And there are many episodes which reflect David's toughness when dealing with men, as opposed to his softness or weakness when dealing with women (the latter shown for instance in the episodes with Abigail [1 Sam. 25], Bathsheba [2 Sam. 11–12] and the wise woman of Tekoah [2 Sam. 14]). All in all, and despite his weaknesses, the biblical David is a masculine symbol which conforms to the most prevalent biblical concept of masculinity. He is a great warrior, yet also a poet and lover; a cruel yet sensitive king, wild and greedy in his relationships with women, yet also a man of high principle in the domain of law and order.

The women who are linked to the biblical stories that narrate King David are, indeed, secondary characters. However, they are presented in a way which not only does not deride the female gender but, on the contrary, almost flatters it. For instance, Michal is an independent and daring woman. She is the one who initially falls in love with David. She later dares to despise and criticize him when she does not like his actions (2 Sam. 6). Abigail (1 Sam. 25) and the wise woman of Tekoah (2 Sam. 14) are intelligent and enterprising women who undertake political missions. And even Bathsheba, whose voice is never heard at the beginning of her affair with David, is not afraid to send David—the king—word of her unexpected pregnancy (2 Sam. 11), and shows a great deal of courage when she fights for the rights of her son Solomon (1 Kgs 1).

The sages who created rabbinic literature had their own vision, their own understanding, of masculinity and femininity, of men and women. In the Bible, King David functions as an epitome of manhood; therefore, the talmudic exegetes altered some of David's traits in order to present him as an ideal man according to their own concepts of manhood. By the same token, they altered the features and deeds attributed to the women associated with him and presented them too according to their own ideas of femaleness and femininity.

In the talmudic interpretations of the biblical story, David is an exceedingly spiritual man, whose faith in God surpasses all his other interests in life. All his actions are interpreted as evidence of his great faith and willingness to sacrifice himself for the glory of God.

In order to create this mutation of David's character, the talmudic interpreters do not hesitate to distort the actions and words ascribed to the female characters involved in his life. These alterations are motivated by their wish to create another David as well as by concepts of women and womanhood, according to which women are materialistic, sexual and cunning human beings who try to seduce men and to obtain control over them.

In order to establish my claims I shall present, one by one, the talmudic interpretations of biblical narratives about David and women. First, I will discuss interpretations that deal with David himself or, more precisely, with David's marriages, without concentrating on any individual woman.

Marital Relations and David

Tractate *Sanhedrin* in the Mishnah (*Sanh.* B.3) presents three interpretations of the biblical word 'multiply', which is used in the law of the king in Deut. 17.17: 'Neither shall he *multiply* (ירבה) wives unto himself'. The first interpretation concludes that the usage of the word 'multiply' in this specific instance refers to a number of wives that exceeds 18. The Babylonian Talmud (*Sanh.* 21a) tries to establish a reason for this seemingly arbitrary number through complicated arithmetical computations, which are based on an artificial homily. The sage Rabina does not accept the lesson of this homily, and presents proof from Tannaitic sources for other numbers (24 or 48 wives). However, Rav Kahana explains again the reason for the number 18, and the Gemara cites sayings of other sages in order to sustain this number. A rendering of the talmudic passage (*Sanh.* 21a) would read as follows:[1]

> What is the reason, then, for the Tanna in our Mishna? R. Kahana said, He compares the second *kāhēnnâ*[2] with the first. Thus, just as the first *kāhēnnâ* ('like those') indicates an addition of six [wives], so does the second.[3] But there was Michal too! Rav said, Eglah[4] is Michal. And why was she called Eglah? Because she was beloved by him [David] as an Eglah [heifer] by its mother. And thus is it

1. Square brackets enclose clarifications of the talmudic text.
2. Hebrew כהנה, literally 'like those' (in the feminine mode). The reference is to 2 Sam. 12.8, where the prophet Nathan says to David regarding the appropriation of Bathsheba and Uriah's death: 'And I gave you your master's house, and I put your master's wives in your bosom, and I gave you the house of Israel and Judah, and [as] if it were too little, I would add [have added] on *like those and like those* for you'.
3. All in all, then, the number of wives—6 mentioned in 2 Sam. 3.2-5; 6 + 6 of the twice 'like those' in 12.8—becomes 18. Only Michal disturbs that reckoning, hence the ensuing discussion.
4. Literally 'heifer'; mentioned as a wife of David in 2 Sam. 3.5.

said, 'Had you not ploughed with my heifer' etc.[1] But did Michal have children? Is it not written, 'And Michal the daughter of Saul had no child until the day of her death'[2]? R. Hisda said, She had no child until death but on the day of her death she did [she died in childbirth].

Let us see, then. His children are listed as born in Hebron, whereas the incident with Michal occurred in Jerusalem, as it is written, 'And Michal the daughter of Saul looked out of the window and saw King David leaping and dancing before the Lord, and she despised him in her heart'.[3] And Rav Judah or, according to others, R. Joseph said, Michal received her due punishment. But we might argue thus. Prior to that incident she did have [children] but after it she did not.

The efforts that the talmudic exegetes invest in showing that David had no more than 18 wives illuminate their determination to present him as an exemplary man, who conducts his sexual life in perfect harmony with the sacred rabbinic law. Another expression of this tendency is the saying of Rav Judah in Rav's name (*Sanh.* 107a):

> Rav Judah said in Rav's name, Even during David's illness he fulfilled the conjugal rights [literally the 'eighteen marital duties'] of his eighteen wives, as it is written, 'I am weary with my groaning; every night make I my bed to swine; I water my couch with my tears'.[4]

When applied and interpreted literally, the biblical passage cited (Ps. 6.7) may describe King David's religious sense. But Rav links this religious sense to David's relations with women in order to show that these relations were not simply motivated by sex. Rather, they were inspired by David's strong will to carry out the religious commandment concerning matrimony.

To this trend of changing David into a devout man belong also Rabbi Yossi's and Rabbi Yehoshua Ben Karha's attempts to explain the story of David's marriages to the sisters Merab and Michal (*Sanh.* 19b). The biblical narrative (1 Sam. 18.17-28) about these marriages is ambiguous. We are not told whether Adriel

---

1. The reference is to Samson's words about his wife, Judg. 14.18. An erotic or love connotation is attached to 'heifer' there too.
2. 2 Sam. 6.23.
3. 2 Sam. 6.16; cf. 1 Chron. 15.29.
4. Cf. Ps. 6.7.

(Merab's husband, 18.19) had taken David's place in Merab's life before her marriage to David or after it (like Palti in Michal's case, 25.44). In the Babylonian Talmud (*Sanh.* 19b) there is a dispute over this point. Rabbi Yossi maintains that Merab was married to David. His students ask: 'Is it possible that David married two sisters during their lifetime?' (which is forbidden by the Torah [cf. Lev. 18.18] and rabbinic law). Rabbi Yossi answers, 'Michal married David *after* the death of Merab'. R. Yehoshua Ben Karha does not agree with Rabbi Yossi and says that David's marriage to Merab was a false marriage.[1] These two sages try to show that David's marriage to the loving Michal was properly executed in accord with rabbinic law.

As the biblical story about David and Michal unfolds, another question ensues. Michal is brought back to David after she has been taken from him by her father and given to Palti. A Torah law (Deut. 24.1-4) forbids a man to remarry his divorced wife if she marries another man after the divorce. In Samuel, though, there is no mention of Michal's being divorced from David, or of her being given to Palti as, specifically, his *wife*. It is merely stated that Saul 'gave his daughter Michal, wife of David, to Palti' (1 Sam. 25.44). In fact, in the narrative about Michal's being handed over to Palti the Bible calls her 'David's wife'. However, in the composite narrative about her delivery back to David (2 Sam. 3.13-16), the Bible tells that Ishbosheth took her 'from *a man*, from Paltiel Ben Laish'. Hence it is not clear whether 'a man' means a husband, or just any male. Finally, at the end of this passage we are actually told that Palti *was* Michal's husband: 'her husband (אישׁ) followed her all the way to the town of Bahurim, crying as he went' (v. 16a).

The Babylonian Talmud (*Sanh.* 19b) contains a long discussion on this biblical phrase (2 Sam. 3.16a), with the apparent intention of proving that Palti was *not* Michal's husband but only her guardian:

1. He maintains that the marriage was not valid because Saul wanted to give Merab to David in lieu of his promise of riches for the man who killed Goliath (1 Sam. 17.25). According to rabbinic law, one cannot have a woman in exchange for a debt. If the riches promised are regarded as a debt, it is impossible for Saul to give his marriageable daughter as a substitute.

> R. Yohanan said, His name was actually Palti. But why was he
> called Paltiel? Because God saved him from transgression.[1] What
> did he do [to be delivered from sin]? He planted a sword
> between her [Michal] and himself and said, Whoever [first]
> attempts this thing [i.e. forbidden indulgence] shall be pierced
> with this sword. But is it not stated, 'And her *husband*[2] went with
> her'? This means that he was to her like a husband [i.e.
> maintaining and loving her, but no more]. But is it not written
> that he followed her, weeping? This was for losing the good deed
> [self-restraint]. Hence [he followed her] to Bahurim, implying that
> they both had remained like unmarried young people, without
> tasting the pleasure of marital relations.

To sum up so far: all the talmudic interpretations mentioned
above present David's relationships with women as if they were
properly conducted, in keeping with both ancient (Torah) and
rabbinic law. The women do not have any role in these sayings
and homilies created by the sages. Even Michal, who is very
active in the biblical story, vanishes in the Talmud, in the sense
that she is transformed from a subject to a token or object.[3]

Having discussed the reactions of the sages to the biblical narratives about David's relationships with women in general, I
would like to move on to examine their responses to the biblical
narratives about specific women in David's life.

Abigail

The Bible describes Abigail as beautiful and intelligent
(1 Sam. 25.3). In the biblical narrative Abigail is an extraordinary
woman who is ready to take risks in order to save her husband
and household members from David's wrath. She tries very

---

1.   The Hebrew word פלטיאל is a theophoric name composed of two
elements: פלט, 'escape', 'release' or 'discharge' (also in the sexual sense) and
אל, 'God'.

2.   Italics mine.

3.   Michal falls in love with David (1 Sam. 18.20, 27). She helps him to
escape from her father's anger (19.11-17), and mocks him when he dances
with the Ark of the Covenant (2 Sam. 6.16-23; this is only briefly mentioned
in the greatly expanded account of Chronicles, 2 Chron. 15.29). There is a
long Midrash about Michal's conversation with David after his dancing with
the Ark of the Covenant in *Numbers Rabbah* (which is a relatively late
anthology of homilies about the book of Numbers), ch. 4.

hard to prevent bloodshed and, although she speaks critically of her husband Nabal, her efforts to save his life seem fairly sincere. The Babylonian Talmud draws quite a different portrait of her. She is presented as a 'femme fatale' who toys with David's lust and seduces him but, at the same time, hinders him from touching her. She is far from innocent and tries to gain control over David by using erotic tricks. Here is a rendering of the first part of the dialogue between Abigail and David, as it is recounted in the Babylonian Talmud (b. Meg. 14a-b):

> Abigail...as she rode on her ass and came down 'by the cover of the mountain'. By the 'cover'[1] of the mountain? It should say 'from the mountain'. Rabbah b. Samuel said, It means that she came with reference to blood and showed it to him [to David]. He said to her, Is blood to be shown by night? She replied, Are capital cases tried at night? He said to her, He [Nabal] is a rebel against the King, and no trial is necessary for him. She replied, Saul is still alive, and your fame is not yet spread abroad in the world. Then he said to her, Blessed be your discretion and blessed be you that have kept me this day from blood guilt [דמים].[2]

The first paragraph of this dialogue shows Abigail's wisdom. Like the wise woman of Tekoah (2 Sam. 14), she supports her argument by using a concrete example. However, unlike the wise woman of Tekoah, her example is taken from the realm of sex. It seems as if Rabbah (the sage to whom the dialogue is attributed) wants to say that sex is women's domain, the only subject they really know about and employ in argument, even when they are as intelligent as Abigail. The Talmud transforms the biblical narrative of the meeting between Abigail and David to a story of temptation, and in so doing it presents Abigail as a woman who illustrates the notions characteristic of its era.

1. The reference is to 1 Sam. 25.20, where Abigail rides under cover or 'secret' (סתר) of the mountain to meet David.
2. Cf. 1 Sam. 25.26. The word דמים, 'blood' and also 'blood guilt', is in the plural, thus used to indicate *two* kinds of 'blood'. In order to prevent David from touching her Abigail says she is menstruating. This is based on the biblical story about David and Bathsheba, according to which Bathsheba came to David when 'she had just finished her [monthly] ritual of purification' (2 Sam. 11.4). The Talmud links the two biblical stories and draws analogies between them.

Here is how the talmudic dialogue proceeds:

> The passage teaches that she bared her thigh and he went three
> parasangs by light of it [because of his desire for her]. He said,
> 'Listen to me'. She replied, 'Let not this[1] be a stumbling block to
> you'. The word *this* implies that something else would occur, and
> what was that? The incident of Bathsheba: and so it eventually
> was. 'The soul of my Lord shall be bound up in the bundle of
> life'.[2] When she left him she said to him, 'and when the Lord shall
> have done good to my Lord...then remember your handmaid'.[3]
> R. Nahman said, This bears out the popular saying, While woman
> talks she spins. Some adduce the saying, The goose stoops as it
> trots along, but its eyes peer afar.

In the biblical passage the word 'this' (זאת) means 'this revenge
that you are going to take on Nabal'. However, in the Talmud
the meaning of the word becomes 'this time of seducing a
married woman'. Thus the subject of the dialogue is altered—
from bloodshed and blood guilt to sex. Ultimately, although
Abigail is presented as a prophet, or at least as a woman who
has the ability to see beyond time, she is also portrayed as a
dishonest and scheming woman.

The Talmud interprets Abigail's words to David—'When the
Lord has blessed you, sir...please do not forget me' (25.30-31)—
as an expression of feminine tricks, and utilizes the opportunity
for attributing intrigue and falsehood to the whole female
gender. It is worth noting that the Jerusalem Talmud attributes
scheming and machinations to Abigail only, without concluding
by a generalized reference aimed at the whole female gender.

Bathsheba

The story of David's love affair with Bathsheba is imagined by
many readers as one of the most passionate in the Bible. The
main characters of the biblical narrative are David and Uriah.
Bathsheba's role is secondary and very small, and there is no
mention of her feelings or initiatives. It seems as if the prime
interest of the Bible is to present extreme opposites: Uriah, an

---

1.   זאת (relative pronoun in the feminine singular mode), 25.31.
2.   Cf. 25.29.
3.   25.31.

honest and reliable officer, stands in stark contrast to David, the devious and decadent king.

The Talmud focuses on just one character, that of David king of Israel, whom it mutates from a plain adulterer into a great believer. According to the interpretation of the Babylonian Talmud (*Sanh.* 107a), David asked God to test him so that he could be included in the assembly of the ancestors of Israel. The story goes on like this:

> ...He [David] said unto him [God], Sovereign of the Universe! Why do we say [in prayer] The God of Abraham, the God of Isaac, and the God of Jacob, but not the God of David? He replied, They were tried by me, but you were not. Then replied he [David], Sovereign of the Universe, examine and try me—as it is written, 'Examine me O Lord, and try me'.[1] He answered, I will test you, and yet grant you a special privilege, for I did not inform them [of the nature of their trial beforehand], yet I inform you that I will try you in a matter of adultery. Straightaway, 'And it came to pass in an eveningtide, that David arose from his bed' etc.[2] R. Yohanan said, He changed his night couch to a day couch, but he forgot the halakha: There is a small organ in man; when he satisfies it, it is hungry; when he starves it, it is satisfied. And he walked upon the roof of the king's house, and from the roof he saw a woman washing herself; and the woman was very beautiful to look at.[3] Now Bathsheba was cleansing her hair behind a screen when Satan came to him, appearing in the shape of a bird. He shot an arrow at her, which broke the screen. Thus she stood revealed, and he saw her. Immediately, 'And David sent and enquired after the woman. And one said, Is not this Bathsheba the daughter of Eliam, the wife of Uriah the Hittite? And David sent messengers, and took her, and she came unto him, and he lay with her, for she was purified from her uncleanliness; and she returned to her house'.[4] Thus is it written, 'You have tested my heart; You have visited me in the night, You will not transgress'.[5] He [David] said thus, Would that a bridle had fallen into the mouth of mine enemy [i.e. my own mouth], that I had not spoken thus. [i.e., I wish that I had not asked God to try me].[6]

1. Ps. 26.2.
2. 2 Sam. 11.2.
3. 2 Sam. 11.2.
4. 2 Sam. 11.3-4.
5. Ps. 17.3.
6. This is a wordplay. The biblical זמתי (Ps. 17.3, possibly 'I intended' or

The moral of this whole passage is that David is not to blame for having an affair with a married woman. The moment Satan is introduced into the story, it changes into a story about God and Satan; hence, David can have no influence on the sequence of events.

Four homilies of the sage Raba are attached to the story about David and Satan in this talmudic *sugia* (issue). The first homily deals with David's plea for forgiveness; the other three constitute an attempt to eliminate or at least diminish his culpability. Here is a rendering of the three homilies concerning David's transgression.

> Raba expounded, What is meant by the verse 'Against you, only You, have I sinned, and done this evil in Your sight, that You might be justified when You speak, and be clear when You judge'.[1] David pleaded before the Holy One, blessed be He: You know full well that had I wished to suppress my lust, I could have done so, but though I [could], let them [the people] not say, The servant triumphed over his Master.

> Raba expounded, What is meant by the verse 'For I am ready to halt and my sorrow is continually before me'?[2] Bathsheba, the daughter of Eliam, was predestined for David from the six days of Creation although she came to him with sorrow, 'For I am ready for my rib',[3] [i.e. Bathsheba is David's rib]. And the school of R. Ishmael taught likewise. She was worthy [i.e. predestined] for David from the six days of Creation, but that he enjoyed her before she was ripe [i.e. before she was his legitimate wife].

> Raba expounded, What is meant by the verse, 'But my adversaries they rejoiced, and gathered themselves together, they did gather themselves together against me, and I knew it not; they did tear me, and would not stop'?[4] David exclaimed before the Holy One, blessed be He: Sovereign of the Universe! You know full well that had they torn my flesh, my blood would not have flowed.[5] Moreover, when they are engaged in studying the four

'was destined') is linked with the phonetically similar זמם, 'bridle', and the second half of the verse is seen as explanatory of the first.

1.   Ps. 51.6.
2.   Ps. 38.18.
3.   Translating the biblical כי אני לצלע נכון (Ps. 38.18a) as 'I am ready for my rib', 'woman' (Gen. 2).
4.   Ps. 35.15.
5.   By reason of the shame to which he was put. Cf. *B. Mes.* 58: the red

deaths inflicted by בית דין [a court of law] they interrupt their
studies and taunt me [saying], David, what is the death penalty
for him who seduces a married woman? I reply to them, He who
commits adultery with a married woman is executed by strang-
ulation, yet he has a portion in the world to come. But he who
publicly puts his neighbour to shame has no portion in the world
to come.

The first homily eradicates David's sin altogether. Whatever he
did he did for the glory of God, not for his own gratification.
The second homily reduces David's sin by teaching that
Bathsheba was predestined for him from the very beginning of
the creation and, in taking her from Uriah, David put things
back into their natural order (even though much pain was
involved). And the third homily reduces David's guilt by
showing that adultery with Bathsheba was the only sin he had
committed during his whole lifetime.

The most extreme attempt of the Babylonian Talmud to exon-
erate David from his guilt in the Bathsheba affair is to be found
in tractate Šabbat 56a:

R. Shemuel b. Nahman said in R. Jonathan's name, Whoever says
that David sinned is plainly mistaken, for it is said, 'And David
behaved himself wisely in all his ways: and the Lord was with
him'.[1] Is it possible that sin came to his hand yet the Divine
presence was with him? Then how do I interpret 'Why have you
despised the word of the Lord, to do that which is evil in his
sight'?[2] He wished to do (evil) but did not. Rav observed [that]
Rabbi, who is descended from David, seeks to defend him,
and expounds (the verse) in David's favour [thus]: The 'evil'
[mentioned] here is unlike every other evil [mentioned] elsewhere
in the Torah. For of every other evil in the Torah it is written,
'and he did'; whereas here it is written, 'to do'. [This means] that
he [David] desired to do but did not. 'You have smitten Uriah the
Hittite with the sword', you should have had him tried by the
Sanhedrin, but did not; 'And have taken his wife to be your
wife',[3] you have marriage rights in her.[4] For R. Shemuel B.

colour of the face disappears because of shame, and white takes its place.
1.   1 Sam. 18.
2.   2 Sam. 12.9.
3.   The verse expounded is 2 Sam. 12.9.
4.   לקח, which is the verb employed here, denotes 'taking in marriage'.
Cf., for instance, Deut. 24.1, 4.

Nahman said in R. Jonathan's name, Every one who went out for
the wars of the house of David wrote a bill of divorce for his wife,
for it is said, 'and bring these ten cheeses unto the captain of their
thousand, and look how your brothers fare, and take their
pledge'.[1] What is meant by 'their pledge'? R. Joseph learned, The
things which pledge man and woman [to one another].[2] 'And
you hast slain him with the sword of the children of Ammon'.[3]
Just as you [David] are not [to be] punished for the sword of the
Ammonites, so you are not [to be] punished for [the death of]
Uriah the Hittite. What is the reason? He [Uriah] was rebellious
against royal authority, saying to him [to David], 'and my Lord
Joab, and the servants of my Lord are encamped in the open
field' (etc.).[4]

The sages cited in the Gemara quoted above entirely annul
David's grave sin of adultery with a married woman. As for his
sin of murder, they change it into a procedural mistake. The
attitude of these sages to David's acts is a sharp contrast to the
attitude of the prophet Nathan, as it appears in the Bible
(2 Sam. 12.1-14).

Nathan does not concentrate on the erotic part of David's
crime, possibly because for him the appropriation of a woman,
and even a married one, might have been recognized (if not
necessarily approved of) as a royal prerogative. He does say, 'I
[the Lord] gave you his [Saul's] kingdom and his wives' (2 Sam.
12.8); nevertheless, this is of less weight in comparison to the
moral crime committed against Uriah.

Unlike the Bible, the Talmud deals mainly with the erotic
aspect of the story. According to the sages' thought, having an
affair with a married woman is a mortal sin. They are therefore
very persistent in trying to prove that David had not committed
adultery with Bathsheba, and they do not pay much attention
to his other sins. The fact that the sages' response to David's
affair with Bathsheba is more intense than their reaction to
Uriah's murder shows that, within their idea of the emblematic

1. 'Their pledge': Hebrew ערובתם; 1 Sam. 17.18.
2. That is, the 'pledge' is a bill of divorce, a conditional cancellation of
marriage.
3. 2 Sam. 12.9.
4. Uriah disobeyed David's order to go home to his (pregnant by
David) wife: 2 Sam. 11.11.

man, sexual mores is an extremely important component. This marginalization of Uriah's framework may perhaps seem paradoxical in the framework of the whitewashing attempts reviewed.

Abishag

It is nonetheless important to remember that the sages do not denounce physical needs. They only confine them to the boundaries of marriage. Sex within the lawful limit is legitimate, and viewed as a commandment. Thus the Gemara (*Sanh.* 22a) asks about Abishag, the last woman in David's life, 'What are the facts regarding Abishag?'[1] And the answer is:

> She [Abishag] said to him, Let us marry; but he [David] said, You are forbidden to me [since he already had the allotted number of eighteen wives, see above]. When courage fails the thief, he becomes virtuous [so taunting him with impotence], she gibed. Then he said to them [his servants], Call Bathsheba for me, and we read, 'And Bathsheba went to the king into the chamber'.[2] Rav Judah said in Rav's name, On that occasion Bathsheba dried herself thirteen times [i.e., they had intercourse thirteen times].

The lesson Rav's interpretation derives from the biblical story is very clear: lust for a woman is an extremely positive force, as long as it is limited to the beloved, legitimate wife.

Concluding Remarks

The talmudic pieces reviewed above focus on David. However, they also recount the figures of Michal, Abigail, Bathsheba and Abishag, female characters who—according to Scripture—played their parts in David's life. In their effort to present David, the king of Israel, as an ideal man and a symbol of masculinity according to their own vision, the sages find justifications for all his peccadilloes. In so doing they sometimes change the women's narrative roles, and present them in a way that

---

1. Because, according to the Bible, although Abishag became a companion to the king, she was not a formal wife (1 Kgs 1.1-4).
2. 1 Kgs 1.15.

corresponds to *their* idea of femininity. The talmudic sages ignore Michal's and Bathsheba's independent acts and initiatives, and turn them into subdued, legitimate wives. They also change Abigail into a sexual and scheming woman, and attribute her imagined characteristics to all women.

THE BEARING OF WISDOM ON THE SHAPE OF
2 SAMUEL 11–12 AND 1 KINGS 3*

Carole R. Fontaine

The definition and depth of 'wisdom influence' to be found in
2 Samuel 9–20, 1 Kings 1–2, along with the material which may
be properly included for consideration as part of the story of
David's court and succession, have been argued for some time.
In 1926 Leonhard Rost argued for the stylistic and thematic
unity of the piece whose intent was the legitimation of the
Solomonic succession.[1] While many have preferred the name
'Court History' to 'Succession Narrative', seeing a subtle
weaving of pro- and anti-monarchic (or Solomonic) sources from
different periods,[2] R.N. Whybray's monograph on these texts
raised the possibility that the intent of this work is that of
didactic illustration of themes found in the book of Proverbs.[3] In

*   This article first appeared in *JSOT* 34 (1986), pp. 61-77.

1.   L. Rost, *Die Überlieferung von der Thronnachfolge Davids* (BWANT, 3.6;
Stuttgart: Kohlhammer, 1926).

2.   See L. Delekat, 'Tendenz und Theologie der David-Salomo-
Erzählung', in F. Maass (ed.), *Das ferne und nahe Wort* (BZAW, 105; Berlin:
Töpelmann, 1967), pp. 22-36; J.W. Flanagan, 'Court History or Succession
Document: A Study of 2 Sam. 9–20 and 1 Kings 1–2', *JBL* 91 (1972), pp. 72-
81, who understands an earlier substrate, David's 'Court History', lacking
the Solomonic materials in 2 Sam. 11.2–12.25 and 1 Kgs 1–2, to underpin the
text as it presently stands; E. Würthwein, *Die Erzählung von der Thronfolge
Davids—theologische oder politische Geschichtsschreibung?* (Theologische
Studien, 115; Zürich: Theologischer Verlag, 1974), among others, raises the
possibility that the work is anti-Solomonic. T.C.G. Thornton, however, sees
the work as Solomonic apologetics ('Solomonic Apologetic in Samuel and
Kings', *CQR* 169 [1968], pp. 159-66).

3.   *The Succession Narratives: A Study of 2 Sam. 9–20 and 1 Kings 1 and 2*
(SBT, 2.9; London: SCM Press, 1968).

tone and method his study shared much with Gerhard von Rad's suggestive essay on the Joseph Cycle.[1] While not necessarily endorsing Whybray's conclusions, other commentators have found wisdom in motif and theme to occupy a significant unitive role in these materials.[2]

Biblical critics within and without wisdom studies have demonstrated considerable distaste with the term 'wisdom influence'. Does this refer to authorship, inclusion of motifs and elements typical to concerns of wisdom tradents, function of the text as 'illustrating' wisdom, or to some other movement within the text?[3] The story of David's Court History is certainly peppered throughout with an inordinate number of elements found in the wisdom tradition. Clear wisdom motifs are noticeable, such as the importance of counsel (2 Sam. 13; 15; 16–17; 1 Kgs 1.12), the high estimation of the societal roles of wise men and women (2 Sam. 14; 15; 20; 16.23), and the occasionally ambiguous nature, from an 'ethical' point of view, of the designation of a person as a possessor of wisdom (2 Sam. 13; 15.32-37; 1 Kgs 1.12; 2.6). Within the sophisticated world of court intrigue, these are all natural elements, suitable for advancing the plot. Vocabulary and generic items found with the wisdom literature also abound.[4] While the authorship of the narrative need not

1.   'The Joseph Narrative and Ancient Wisdom', in *The Problem of the Hexateuch and Other Essays* (Edinburgh: Oliver & Boyd, 1966), pp. 292-300.

2.   The studies of R.A. Carlson (*David, the Chosen King: A Traditio-Historical Approach to the Second Book of Samuel* [trans. E.J. Sharpe and S. Rudman; Stockholm: Almqvist & Wiksell, 1964]), J. Blenkinsopp ('Theme and Motif in the Succession History [2 Sam. xi 2ff] and the Yahwist Corpus', in J.A. Emerton *et al.* [eds.], *Volume du Congrès International pour l'Etude de l'Ancien Testament* [VTSup, 15; Leiden: Brill, 1965], pp. 44-57) and D.M. Gunn (*The Story of King David: Genre and Interpretation* [JSOTSup, 6; Sheffield: JSOT Press, 1978]), among others, have all looked at the role of wisdom in the materials under discussion.

3.   For a discussion of these difficulties, see J. Crenshaw, 'Method in Determining Wisdom Influence upon Historical Literature', *JBL* 88 (1969), pp. 129-42.

4.   See 2 Sam. 12; 13.12; 14.14; 16.9; 18.18; 1 Kgs 2.1-9, for example. Also see H.-J. Hermisson, 'Weisheit und Geschichte', in H.W. Wolff (ed.), *Probleme biblischer Theologie: Gerhard von Rad zum 70. Geburtstag* (Munich: Chr. Kaiser Verlag, 1971), pp. 136-54.

necessarily be ascribed to a wisdom tradent, nor the text owe its major interest in composition to the illustration of wisdom's principles of observation and prudence in action, it may be argued that such occurrences give support for the contention that wisdom undoubtedly occupies a signal role as motivator of action and evaluator of deed.

It is the thesis of the present study that wisdom forms a critical link not simply within the Court History itself, but also between the Bathsheba incident of 2 Samuel 11–12 and the Deuteronomistic introduction of Solomon's reign in 1 Kings 3. The use of wisdom as a narrative connective in two pivotal passages, each of which introduces important phases in the reigns of David and Solomon, is accomplished in two ways. First, the clustering of typical wisdom motifs in vocabulary and theme may be seen at the surface level of the text. Here may be found such items as the use of antithetic contrasts (father/son, rich/poor, righteous/wicked, father/mother, *ṭôb/raʿ*). The occurrence of literary forms drawn from the repertoire of wisdom genres, and the themes of royal wisdom, illicit sexual activity, wisdom in judgment, 'the woman who brings death',[1] and Wisdom who brings life also belong to this use of wisdom in the text. Secondly, at the deeper level of compositional structure, the choice of wisdom/folly figured in the actions of the dramatis personae yields an analogous sequence of 'functions' (that is, units of action performed by the characters)[2] underlying each story.

Syntagmatic analysis[3] adapted from that done on the plot

---

1. Blenkinsopp, 'Succession History', pp. 52-56; Gunn, *King David*, p. 43.

2. This method of analysis is drawn from Russian formalism and structural folkloristics. See V. Propp, *Morphology of the Folktale* (Austin: University of Texas Press, 2nd rev. edn, 1968), p. 20; A. Dundes, *The Morphology of North American Indian Folktales* (Folklore Fellows Communications, 195; Helsinki: Suomalainen Tiedeakatemia, 1964), and P. Maranda (ed.), *Soviet Structural Folkloristics: Texts by Meletinsky, Nekludov, Novik, and Segal with Tests of the Approach by Jilek and Jilek-Aall, Reid and Layton* (Approaches to Semiotics, 43; The Hague: Mouton, 1974), I.

3. For a very different structural analysis dealing with paradigmatic units in the Court History, see E. Leach's 'The Legitimacy of Solomon: Some Structural Aspects of Old Testament History', *European Journal of Sociology* 7 (1966), pp. 58-101, reprinted in M. Lane (ed.), *Introduction to*

composition of folk narrative shows that the texts under discussion may each be subdivided into three gross constitutive episodic 'moves' or units of action:[1] (1) an act of choice (whose object is wisdom or folly), 2 Sam. 11.1-3; 1 Kgs 3.3-9; (2) the consequences of the choice, 2 Sam. 11.4-27; 1 Kgs 3.10-15; and (3) an evaluation of the act and consequence in the form of a court judgment scene, which issues in a living or dead child, 2 Sam. 12.1-25; 1 Kgs 3.16-28.[2] Correlation of the syntagmatic patterns in each story along the paradigmatic axis[3] reveals a thematic treatment of the ideals of Yahwistic kingship, with the folly of David providing a dramatic contrast and occasional negative parallel to the wisdom of Solomon.

A comment might be made on the application of methodology drawn from structural folkloristics to the texts under discussion.

Structuralism (New York: Basic Books, 1970), pp. 248-92. For rejoinders by biblicists, see A. Malamat, 'Comments on E. Leach: "The Legitimacy of Solomon—Some Structural Aspects of Old Testament History"', *European Journal of Sociology* 8 (1967), pp. 165-67, and R. Culley, 'Some Comments on Structural Analysis and Biblical Studies', in J.A. Emerton *et al.* (eds.), *Congress Volume Uppsala 1971* (VTSup, 22; Leiden: Brill, 1972), pp. 129-42.

1.   A 'move' is a sequence of functions which proceeds from Villainy or Lack through the resolution of the misfortune. An 'episodic move' is a semantically linked series of functions which interrupts the major move. New moves or reduplication of episodic moves may begin before previous moves have been resolved, or several moves may intertwine in a variety of ways (Propp, *Morphology*, pp. 92ff.).

2.   These gross syntagmatic units correspond roughly to C. Bremond's 'elementary sequence' for narrative, a triad of the functions of 'virtuality' (goal to be attained), 'actualization' (act necessary to attain goal), and 'conclusion' (attained result). See 'The Logic of Narrative Possibilities', *NLH* 11 (1980), pp. 387-88.

3.   For discussion of paradigmatic analysis of tale syntagmata (i.e. functions and episodic moves), see R. Barthes, 'Introduction à l'analyse structurale des récits', *Communications* 8 (1966), pp. 1-27; C. Lévi-Strauss, 'L'analyse morphologique des contes russes', *International Journal of Slavic Linguistics and Poetics* 3 (1966), pp. 122-49; A.-J. Greimas, *Structural Semantics: An Attempt at a Method* (trans. D. McDowell, R. Schleifer and A. Velie, with an introduction by R. Schleifer; Lincoln: University of Nebraska Press, 1983); and E. Meletinsky *et al.*, 'Problems of the Structural Analysis of Fairytales', in Maranda (ed.), *Soviet Structural Folkloristics*, I, pp. 73-139.

The materials presented here are 'historical' narratives, but ones whose style bears witness to a number of underlying literary genres, from the traditional story and tale to Egyptian royal novellas and Ugaritic epic.[1] A successful synchronic analysis of such varied subject matter must attempt to discover and employ categories (such as those of structure) which facilitate comparisons across the diversity of literary forms and textual history. Secondly, evidence of the impact of the conventions of traditional (oral) composition on the structure and content of individual episodes within the Court History has been convincingly argued by D.M. Gunn and H.A. Kenik.[2] R.A. Carlson's traditio-historical study of the Deuteronomistic group of editors sees similar principles at work at the redactional level,[3] thus making the use of folkloristic categories more apt than might be supposed, given the historical orientation of the texts.[4]

1.   See Gunn, *King David*, pp. 19-65, on the genre designation 'traditional story'; on the folkloric character of 1 Kgs 3.16-28, see J. Gray, *I and II Kings: A Commentary* (OTL; Philadelphia: Westminster Press; London: SCM Press, 2nd rev. edn, 1970), pp. 24, 127-28, and B.O. Long, *1 Kings—With an Introduction to Historical Literature* (FOTL, 9; Grand Rapids: Eerdmans, 1984), pp. 68-70. S. Herrmann suggests that the genre here is the Egyptian 'Königsnovelle', or political novel used to legitimate, glorify and introduce new innovations in the reign of Pharaoh ('Die Königsnovelle in Ägypten und Israel', in *Wissenschaftliche Zeitschrift der Karl-Marx Universität, Leipzig* [Gesellschafts- und Sprachwissenschaftliche Reihe, 3; Leipzig: Karl-Marx Universität, 1953–54, Part 1], pp. 51-62). More recently, Manfred Görg proposed that 1 Kgs 3.4-15 is an 'imitation' of the 'Prinzennovelle', a variant of the Königsnovelle (*Gott–König-Reden in Israel und Ägypten* [BWANT, 105; Stuttgart: Kohlhammer, 1975]), showing parallels with the Sphinx Stele of Tuthmosis IV (*idem*, 'A Divine Oracle through a Dream', in *ANET*, p. 449). For Court History parallels to the Epic of King Keret, see Carlson, *David*, pp. 190-93; see also C.-L. Seow, 'The Syro-Palestinian Context of Solomon's Dream', *HTR* 77.2 (1984), pp. 141-52.

2.   Gunn, *King David*, pp. 38-50; H.A. Kenik, *Design for Kingship: The Deuteronomistic Narrative Technique in 1 Kings 3.4-15* (SBLDS, 69; Chico, CA: Scholars Press, 1983).

3.   Carlson, *David*, pp. 16-22, 35-36.

4.   The compositional patterns displayed in the plot structure of 2 Sam. 11 bear a marked similarity to Propp's sequence of tale functions (Absentation, Violation, Reconnaissance, Delivery, Villainy, etc.), although the sophisticated literary treatment of the story has transferred some

Reading together the texts of act, consequence and evaluation
of the choice of Folly and Wisdom in 2 Samuel 11–12 and 1 Kings
3 (see the table below), one finds a wide range of events portrayed. Moving out of David's and his son's attempts to deal
with dynastic threats, the Ammonite War (2 Sam. 10–12) is presented, and with it the birth of Solomon, whose kingship is vali-
dated in the giving of wisdom at Gibeon celebrated before the
Ark of the Covenant in Jerusalem.[1] The war narratives contain
the seeds of David's ruin in the overt origin of the curse on the
king's house—the foolish king's affair with Bathsheba. By the
closure of the Court History in 1 Kings 2, Solomon's claim to
kingship has been solidified by the removal of the last potential
claimant Adonijah, and his supporter Joab, whose death has
been sealed, at least in David's mind, since the death of
Absalom. Here also Bathsheba, an example of the woman who
brings death,[2] plays a role in bringing about the final success of
her son Solomon, as well she might. This queen is not only the
favorite, but in a sense, Wisdom's own 'granddaughter': her
father Eliam,[3] one of David's trusted men, is the son of the
counselor Ahithophel, wisdom's greatest practitioner and suicidal failure. Wisdom and folly in action, outside the confines of
collections of 'scholarly' discourse on the virtues of Lady

functions of the hero to Uriah the Hittite, for the purpose of highlighting
David's villainy and Uriah's inadequacy. The impact of folkloric plot
constraints on presentation of 'historical' (and other) literature in Samuel–
Kings deserves a good deal more study.

1. See P.R. Ackroyd, 'The Succession Narrative (so-called)', *Int* 33
(1981), pp. 388, 392, on the difficulties of delimiting the materials. Note the
important role which narratives including the theme of the Ark and
priesthood play, from 2 Sam. 6 through 1 Kgs 31.

2. Blenkinsopp, 'Succession History', pp. 47-49.

3. Whybray's comments on Bathsheba's role as a 'good-natured, rather
stupid woman who was a natural prey both to more passionate and to
cleverer men' (*Succession Narrative*, p. 40) are apt with respect to the
function played in the incident concerning Adonijah and Abishag only if we
suppose her stupidity at the outset. The fact that the Samuel sources prefer
the name 'Bath-sheba' to the 'Bath-Shua' traditions of the Chronicler, thus
connecting the queen mother with Eliam (2 Sam. 11.2; 23.34), the revolt of
Sheba in 2 Sam. 20, and the 'sevenfold' restitution for theft (and, by
implication, adultery) in Prov. 6.20-35 (Carlson, *David*, pp. 154-69) suggests
that the texts evaluate Bathsheba's role more highly than does Whybray.

Wisdom over against sly Dame Folly, is amply portrayed here in a story which finds its denouement not simply in Solomon's success politically, but in his ultimate pragmatism[1] in seeking legitimation in his prayer for wisdom at the high place of Gibeon. Adding 1 Kings 3 to the customary designation of the textual limits of the materials telling the story of David's successor Solomon, we find wisdom and folly in Israel forming handsome inclusions of motif and action in this narrative of vice and victory among viceroys and kings.

David's act of choosing folly occurs when he denies his duty during the siege of Rabbah (hence fulfilling Samuel's acerbic prophecies to the people who rejected Yahweh as king in 1 Sam. 8), to remain in Jerusalem (2 Sam. 11.1-2). If heroes are most especially known by their willingness to marry well, go on quests and accomplish difficult tasks which lead to the liquidation of the 'lack' or insufficiencies felt at their stories' outset,[2] than David's unwillingness to set out from Jerusalem foreshadows the less than heroic actions of the king which follow. The scene begins with a surplus of 'lacks'—the people and the Ark lack rest, for they are still surrounded by enemies; Joab and all Israel lack their commander-in-chief (2 Sam. 11.1). David, without the wisdom to meet these difficulties,[3] turns aside to address insufficiencies in the area of dynastic succession caused by Michal's barrenness (2 Sam. 6.23). An important group of motifs ties together the episode of folly's act and consequence: those of 'dwelling' (*yôšēb*, v. 1), 'walking' (*yithallēk*, v. 2), 'king's house' (*bêt-hammelek*, vv. 2, 8-9, 27) later to be contrasted to the house of Uriah the Hittite (vv. 4, 8-11, 13), and 'lying' (*miškābô*, v. 2; *wayyiškab*, vv. 4, 9; *wᵉliškab*, v. 11; *liškab bᵉmiškābô*, v. 13).

The thick procession of verbal actions gives texture to the picture of the potentate who unwisely assumes that his power

---

1. M. Noth, 'Die Bewährung von Salomos "Göttlicher Weisheit"', in M. Noth and D. Winton Thomas (eds.), *Wisdom in Israel and in the Ancient Near East* (VTSup, 3; Leiden: Brill, 1955), pp. 225-37.

2. Propp, *Morphology*, pp. 50, 80; P. Maranda, 'Introduction', in *idem* (ed.), *Soviet Structural Folkloristics*, I, pp. 10-11.

3. See W. Brueggemann, *In Man We Trust* (Richmond, VA: John Knox, 1972), pp. 32-45, 64-68 for a discussion of David's wisdom.

places him above the Torah. It is the king who sends armies and messengers (vv. 1, 3, 4, 6, 14), 'inquires' after the identity of the vision of loveliness sighted from his rooftop (*wayyidrōš*, v. 3), takes another wife (v. 4), interrogates (vv. 7, 10), and orders (vv. 8, 12, 15, 25). Responses to this autocratic figure are servile (v. 10) and shielded, making use of the indirection of the rhetorical question which protects its user by involving the party addressed (v. 3).[1]

Joab's assessment of David's anger when he hears the bad news of a battle heightens this reading of the king's character. The wily commander's cautious instruction to his subordinate in the art of safe message delivery (2 Sam. 11.19-21) betrays a typical concern of wisdom over the difficulties of dealing with kings.[2] His 'proverbial' reference to the death of Abimelech, the son of Jerubbesheth, at the hands of another woman who brings death, provides us with an incidence of 'proverb performance', that is, the purposeful transmission of a saying in a social interaction in order to evaluate or affect.[3] Although this

1. C.R. Fontaine, *Traditional Sayings in the Old Testament: A Contextual Study* (The Bible and Literature Series, 5; Sheffield: Almond Press, 1982), pp. 41, 83, 192-93. Obviously, not every rhetorical question makes use of indirection to achieve its goal (see, for example, 2 Sam. 11.21 for Joab's hypothetical interrogation of his messenger by David, or Job 38 and Papyrus Anastasi I [*ANET*, pp. 475-79] for strings of rhetorical questions designed to intimidate and insult). The technique of indirection is operative most often in contexts where the questioner is inferior in status to the hearer(s).

2. The 'ways of a king' and Yahweh's response to them have always been of close interest to the tradents of wisdom, since their lives and reputations so often depended on their efforts in discerning such matters. See Prov. 14.35; 16.9-15; 19.12; 20.2; 21.1; 23.1-3; 24.21-22; 25.1-10; 28.16; 29.4; 14; Qoh. 4.13; 5.8-9; 8.2-6; 10.16-17; 20.

3. For a full discussion of the correlation of structural elements when a saying is applied to a social context in an interaction in proverb performance, see Fontaine, *Traditional Sayings*, pp. 57-62, 139-70. 2 Sam. 11.14-21 presents an interesting case, since Joab, by projecting what David *might* say to his messenger, adds another level of meaning to the transmission of the proverbial reference to Abimelech's death. The 'saying' is a simple identifical statement (A = B), in the form of a rhetorical question, with nuances of positive causation (A →B), but carries two metaphorical associations when applied to Uriah: (1) his death was caused by going near the city wall

proverbial reference is only hypothetical ('...and *if* he says to you, "...Who killed Abimelech, the son of Jerubbesheth? Did not a woman cast an upper millstone upon him from the wall, so that he died at Thebez?"', 2 Sam. 11.20aα, 21aα) since it is Joab's conjecture of the king's response, it highlights commander's and king's knowledge for the real reason behind Uriah's demise. Unlike Wisdom at the gate, bringing life through her teachings (Prov. 1.20ff.; 8.1ff.), the woman at the wall of Thebez brings death, and the allusion to the incident conjures up a feminine shadow of death hovering over Uriah at the gate of Rabbah (2 Sam. 11.23b), all because of his failure to stand father to David's child. To the king's final question in this theoretical exchange, 'Why did you go so near the wall?', the context yields the unspoken answer David already knows too well: 'Because of the woman who brings death—Bathsheba'.

The consequences of David's choice round out his abuses of power by adding deceit, trickery and murder to neglect of duty and adultery. When the attempted deception concerning the parentage of Bathsheba's child fails, the father David is scarcely distinguishable from the sinners and fools of Proverbs who lure the innocent on to their deaths (cf. e.g. Prov. 1.10-12). Gratifying the desire conceived as he walked about on his palace roof (*wayyithallēk*, 11.2), David lies with the wife of a trusted and trusting servant (*wayyiškab 'immāh*, 2 Sam. 11.4), thereby rejecting the teachings of wisdom on adultery in Prov. 6.22, teachings which 'will lead you when you walk (*behithallekā*)' and 'watch over you when you lie down (*bešokbekā*)'. The king's wicked judgment of death is pronounced on the duped Uriah at the gate of Rabbah (2 Sam. 11.23-24), allowing David to add the pregnant Bathsheba to his house (2 Sam. 11.27a), thus liquidating his dynastic lacks.[1] Act and

(David's interpretation); and (2) his death was caused by a woman (Joab's interpretation). David's assessment, made by use of 'proverbial' reference to the events of Judg. 9, occurs *before* he learns of Uriah's death, and questions the choice of such dangerous location for battle. Joab's placement of this question in the mouth of David is made *after* Uriah's death, and reflects David's complicity in ordering Uriah into danger (2 Sam. 11.15) on account of Bathsheba's predicament.

1. So with Carlson (*David*, pp. 147-48, 154), who compares the use of

consequence are explicitly evaluated as *ra'*, as the text comments in 2 Sam. 11.27b that 'the thing which David had done displeased the Lord' (*wayyēra' haddābār 'ăšer 'āśâ dāwid bᵉ'ênê YHWH*).

Evaluation continues in a judgment scene where wisdom indicts folly, finding no pity (2 Sam. 12.6) in the actions of the king. Nathan uses a parable replete with imagery of rich and poor, righteous and wicked, and human greed. Concern for retribution for the ewe lamb who used to lie in the bosom of her owner (*ûbᵉḥêqô tiškāb*, 2 Sam. 12.3) forces the king to reveal and judge himself. Later, the wise woman of Tekoa will fill the prophet's role in using a similar ploy to bring David to a realization of the claims of justice (2 Sam. 14) The devouring sword that slew Uriah is now turned against the king's own house for all Israel to see (2 Sam. 12.10, 12). Though David himself is spared, his folly leads to the death of his child, as restitution begins.

In the story of the giving of wisdom at Gibeon, the pattern of action (act of choice, consequences, evaluation) remains the same, but matters arrange themselves differently, with a rhetorical shape that suggests how different son is to be from father, wise from foolish king. Strong Egyptian parallels to Solomon's dream in 2 Kgs 3.3-14 suggest that this passage also attempts to address a felt insufficiency, that of proper legitimation for the accession of an untried ruler who is not the first born.[1] The Deuteronomistic introduction (vv. 1-2) to the incubation-dream at a high place important in pre-monarchic times[2] raises familiar

hithallēk and *bayit* here to that in Dan. 4.

1.   Herrmann, 'Königsnovelle', pp. 51-62; Gray, *I and II Kings*, p. 21. Görg (*Gott–König–Reden*, pp. 62-63) cites the following elements in the Sphinxstele of Tuthmosis IV and 1 Kgs 3 which he feels allow the differentiation of these texts as representative of the *Prinzen*- rather than the *Königsnovelle*: (1) introduction of a neighboring place of pilgrimage; (2) visit of a royal guest; (3) time approximately before a true regency; (4) encounter with a deity in a dream; (5) divine speech; (6) absence of a promulgation; and (7) act of worship with subordinates.

2.   On the importance of the location of the dream, Görg comments: 'Dafür hat das Aufsuchen einer traditionsbestimmten Wallfahrtsstätte einen gewichtigen Stellenwert. Der Prinz erhält hier für seine spätere Regentschaft entscheidende Impulse. In dieser Perspektive hat der Traum

themes in the lack of a house for the name of the Lord (1 Kgs 3.2), and the mention of a 'foreign woman' par excellence, Pharaoh's daughter, in the King's house. Here David presents a parallel with Solomon, for his affair with Bathsheba, perhaps herself a foreigner,[1] brought death to the royal house, and it is Solomon's association with foreign women which leads to the downfall of house and kingdom, at least in the Deuteronomist's opinion (cf. 1 Kgs 11.1-8).

In the episode of Solomon's choice, the foolish father who walked about on the palace roof is evoked in the introduction of his son in v. 3, 'Solomon loved the Lord, walking (*lāleket*) in the statutes of David his father' (cf. v. 6). David, who stayed behind in Jerusalem in 2 Samuel 11, is replaced with Solomon, 'a son to sit (*yôšēb*) on his throne this day' in v. 6. The reader is told that God appeared, rather than the sight of an appealing diversion for a languid afternoon while the troops are away. It is Yahweh who instructs the 'good' king to 'Ask what I shall give you' (*šeʾal mâ ʾetten-lāk*, v. 5b), recalling this beneficent donor's itemization of gifts to the ungrateful David in 2 Sam. 12.8 (*wāʾettenâ lekā ʾet-bêt ʾadōnêkā*, etc.). In contrast to his father, humility and an understanding of his proper place before God characterize Solomon's responses. The new king exclaims over his lack of knowledge and the size of the task of ruling, making use of the hyperbole of proverbial phrase in v. 8 (the people cannot be numbered). In an action perhaps reminiscent of Pharaoh's title as 'Lord of Maʾat' and the Egyptian royal ideology that hails this goddess or principle of cosmic justice and order as the foundation of rulership,[2] the good king requests, instead of riches or downfall of enemies, a 'discerning mind',

---

seine besondere Funktion, weil er Zukunftsorientiert ist' (*Gott–König-Reden*, p. 62).

1.   Blenkinsopp, 'Succession History', pp. 52-54.

2.   See W. Westendorf, 'Ursprung und Wesen der Maat, der altägyptischen Göttin des Rechts, der Gerechtigkeit und der Weltordnung', in S. Lauffer (ed.), *Festgabe für Dr Walter Will, Ehrensenator der Universität München zum 70. Geburtstag am 12. November 1966* (Cologne: Carl Heymanns, 1966), p. 208; H. Brunner, 'Gerechtigkeit als Fundament des Thrones', *VT* 8 (1958), pp. 426-28.

wisdom's *lêb šōmēa'* or 'listening heart'.[1] The great people who cannot be numbered or counted for multitude (1 Kgs 3.8) may only be served by one possessed of proverbial wisdom and largeness of mind (*rōḥab lēb*) like the sand on the seashore (1 Kgs 5.29 [English versions 4.29]). Solomon's desire for the ability to discern between good and evil (*lᵉhābîn bên-ṭôb lᵉrā'*, v. 9) ends with a motivating expression of his dilemma in a rhetorical question addressed to superior, Yahweh, from inferior, petitioning king, 'For who is able to govern this thy great people?' While the foolish, power-mad father's choice had displeased the Lord, the text comments on the son's act of choice that 'It pleased the Lord that Solomon has asked this thing' (*wayyîṭṭab haddābār bᵉ'ênê 'ᵃdōnāy kî šā'al šᵉlōmōh 'et-haddābār hazzê*, v. 10), completing the antithetical contrast between *ṭôb* and *ra'* in the actions of father and son.

The consequences of Solomon's choice (vv. 10-15) are those things which Wisdom normally confers upon her seekers: riches, honor, long life and right relationship with God.[2] Returning to Jerusalem, which David in our texts never left, Solomon bears back not another woman who brings death, but wisdom who brings life. Closeness to God is celebrated in sacrifice before the Ark of the Covenant;[3] harmony between the king and his servants is visible in the feast Solomon gives, one which is in contrast to his father's ignoble dinner with Uriah, where the king attempted to compromise his officer's ritual asceticism to serve the ends of his deception (2 Sam. 11.13).

The evaluation of Solomon's choice of wisdom comes in another judgment scene at court in the dispute of the two *zōnôt* in 1 Kgs 3.16-28. Yahweh's wisdom, absent in David's liaison with Bathsheba, now implicitly benefits the most reviled and helpless of women, the prostitute so often cast in the role of

1.   H. Brunner, 'Das hörende Herz', *TLZ* 11 (1954), cols. 698-99.
2.   R.E. Murphy, 'The Kerygma of the Book of Proverbs', *Int* 20 (1966), pp 3-14. Görg (*Gott–König-Reden*, p. 114) suggests that the various elements in Yahweh's gift to Solomon parallel the Egyptian 'life! health! prosperity!' ascribed to Pharaoh.
3.   If we are to believe Uriah, the Ark was present with Joab and the troops at the siege of Rabbah (2 Sam. 11.11), thus emphasizing David's distance from God, in contrast to Solomon's presence before the Ark.

Folly, Wisdom's foil. Here then is a different sort of wisdom from the kind which planned the rape of Tamar and the death of Joab. The zōnôt of 1 Kings 3 are functional 'widows', since they have no husbands or male protectors willing to intervene in disputes, and for the same reason, their children are 'orphans'. They also stand before the king as a kind of 'resident alien', since it is likely that they have little or no reason to expect legal protection from a society to whose indifferent fringes they cling.[1] Like the inhabitants of Sodom in Genesis 18, if God is not their justice—here in the aspect of Wisdom to the delegated monarch—where shall they find it? If Solomon's bureaucracy and marriage to Pharaoh's daughter is indeed the true origin of wisdom in Israel,[2] it is unlikely that the Egyptian princess saw in the courts of her father such intensive functionality of Wisdom operant on behalf of the oppressed and degraded.

As the distraught harlot begins her story in v. 17, we learn that she and her disputant dwell in the same house (yōšᵉbōt bᵉbayit 'eḥād), and as with the king's house in 2 Samuel 11–12, it is there that the action takes place. The theme of the woman who brings death is combined ironically with the šākab motif: the child of the second harlot dies 'because she lay on it' (šākᵉbâ 'ālāyw, v. 19). Deception over parentage is once again attempted, as the harlot lays the living child of the first in her bosom (wattaškîbēhû bᵉḥêqāh) and her dead child in the bosom of the other (hiškîbâ bᵉḥêqî, v. 20), recalling the slain ewe lamb of Nathan's parallel. Wisdom in theme and action once again plays a critical role in the giving of judgment, as the guilty party is cleverly revealed. 'All Israel' witnessed the outcome of David's choice or folly in the curse upon his house (2 Sam. 12.12); in 1 Kgs 3.28, 'all Israel heard of the judgment which the king had rendered, and they stood in awe of the king, because they perceived that the wisdom of God was in him, to render justice'.

The pattern of act, consequence and evaluation in Solomon's story in 1 Kings 3 is retrospective of that found in the Bathsheba incident of 2 Samuel 11–12, but the outcome is

1. F.C. Fensham, 'Widow, Orphan and Poor in Ancient Near Eastern Legal and Wisdom Literature', *JNES* 21 (1962), pp. 129-39.

2. R.B.Y. Scott, 'Solomon and the Beginnings of Wisdom in Israel', in Noth and Winton Thomas (eds.), *Wisdom in Israel*, pp. 262-79.

entirely different, with the relationship to Yahweh and the choice of wisdom appearing as constituent transforming elements. It is God who initiates the action at Gibeon, though perhaps as suggestively solicited by the king's sacrifice in hope of obtaining an oracle as Bathsheba is solicited by the king's desire. The comparison of striking oppositions in the activity of father and son reveals a dramatic contrast. This is precisely the sort of didactic antithesis which the Hebrew Bible's wisdom literature loves to portray (see, for example, the juxtaposition of Lady Wisdom and Dame Folly in Prov. 1–9). Solomon has his dream at night, away from the capital, with God's express consent. The sluggard David sleeps by day in his capital, and desires what is abhorrent to God, though God has given him much already (2 Sam. 12.7-10). David inquires after the object which ends in fulfillment of his desire as an individual; Solomon requests the means to fulfill his duty to the people. The good king is given wisdom to judge; the wicked king takes (*wayiqqāḥehā*, 2 Sam. 11.4) another's wife—which brings a curse upon his house, but which ultimately issues in the birth of the wise, good Solomon. Wisdom and Woman exchange function and place in the royal action. Duty, not pleasure, is to be the first concern of Yahweh's ideal ruler.

The good/bad evaluations of the actions of the two kings are made tangible in the judgment scenes which conclude each text, externalizations which typify wisdom's act–consequence relationship.[1] In the royal household, the first child of Bathsheba dies, but the second, Solomon, born of a licit union and loved by the Lord, lives (2 Sam. 12.24-25). In the tale[2] of the house of

1. Blenkinsopp, 'Succession History', p. 48; G. von Rad, *Wisdom in Israel* (New York: Abingdon Press, 1974), pp. 124-37.

2. This 'clever judgment' motif is found around the world, and seems to be especially prevalent in Indian folklore (see Motif J1171.1, J1171.2, J1171.4, and Tale Type 653 in S. Thompson, *Motif-Index of Folk Literature* [Bloomington: Indiana University Press, rev. edn, 1975]). H. Gressmann believes the Indian version, where both women are widows of the same man, to be the original version (*Die älteste Geschichtsschreibung und Prophetie Israels* [Göttingen: Vandenhoeck & Ruprecht, 2nd edn, 1921], p. 198). If so, then the change in the text from 'wives' to 'harlots' makes the argument for deliberate wisdom shaping of these materials (here, prostitutes [= Folly] versus wisdom of vv. 3-15) even stronger.

harlotry, the first child lives and the second child dies. Indeed, the first child lives 'twice', since its mother's compassionate response[1] (*nikm^erû rh^amêḥā 'al-b^enāh*, 1 Kgs 3.26) spares it in the mock death scene designed as a trial to determine the truth of the women's claim. In the king's house where God's wisdom is unwelcome, not even a royal father's atypical response can spare the child of sin (2 Sam. 12.15-23), because 'he did this thing and had no pity' (2 Sam. 12.6).

Interestingly enough, the cluster of motifs of efficacious wisdom, monarch at court, and 'severing' also occur together in the 'Tales of Wonder' at the court of Pharaoh Khufu, set in the Fourth Dynasty (2613–2494 BCE), found preserved in the Westcar Papyrus.[2] Here we meet a noted wisdom tradent, one Prince Hardedef, who is credited with the authorship of the Instruction bearing his name.[3] Taking his turn at telling tales to amuse his father Khufu (tales also set in the context of birth-narratives!) with the prospect of finding hidden treasures, Hardedef relates the remarkable powers of the sage Djedji. Khufu is intrigued but obviously subscribes to the maxim that 'seeing is believing'. Hence, the ailing wise man is summoned to the court to demonstrate his wisdom and prowess with a sword to the august ruler of the Two Banks. After first quoting a proverb to soothe the angry monarch for the wise man's omission in not having appeared at Court previously ('"He who comes is he who is summoned", my sovereign!'), Djedji gives a modest affirmative when he is quizzed about his reputed ability

---

1.   P. Trible, *God and the Rhetoric of Sexuality* (Philadelphia: Fortress Press, 1978), pp. 32-33, but *contra* G.W. Coats ('Parable, Fable, and Anecdote: Storytelling in the Succession Narrative', *Int* 35 [1981], pp. 377-80), who see 1 Kgs 3.16-28 as an anecdote (parallel to 2 Kgs 6.26-29) whose only content and function consist of its emphasis on the king's wisdom.

2.   W.K. Simpson (ed.), *The Literature of Ancient Egypt: An Anthology of Stories, Instructions and Poetry* (New Haven: Yale University Press, 2nd edn, 1973), pp. 22-30. The tale is set in Dynasty IV, but manuscripts date to the Twelfth Dynasty (1991–1786 BCE).

3.   Simpson (ed.), *Literature of Ancient Egypt*, p. 340; G. Posener, *REg* 9 (1952), pp. 109-20. This work is cited in the Instruction of Ptahhotep, and has been found in New Kingdom tomb inscriptions (M. Lichtheim, *Ancient Egyptian Literature* [Berkeley: University of California Press, 1975], I, pp. 5-9).

to join a severed head to its body. Pride in his craft turns to dismay when Pharaoh orders a criminal brought in and beheaded for a demonstration. In this scene, monarch demands, and wise man decries, the need to use a human being in the operation ('Lo, not to the people, O sovereign my lord [life! prosperity! health!])! It is not commanded to do the like of this to this noble herd!'[1]) Subsequently a goose, waterfowl, ox and lion act as experimental animals to the court of Pharaoh, and the real intent of the narrative, disclosure of the placement of the treasure trove, moves on. In both narratives, the severing motif is used to accentuate the wisdom and cleverness of the sage, but in 1 Kings 3, the king acts to preserve life, whereas in the Egyptian tale, the monarch's interest in human life is minimal. Even so, wisdom, seen in the deft arguments of its bearer Djedji, still operates in positive fashion to shield others from the whim of a ruler who can hardly be characterized as a humanist.

The roofs of Jerusalem (2 Sam. 11.2; 16.22), the high places of Gibeon, and the courts of Pharaoh all serve as life settings for the use of Wisdom, whose 'theological goal' is not simply craft, but the craft of preserving the simple from wanton power and dreams of pleasure which obscure the vision of duty. In the 'judgment' scenes which follow the stories of each king's act of choice and its consequences, the parable of Nathan and the narrative of the harlots' dispute act to verify the bad/good judgments upon foolish and wise king, as they themselves are shown coping with judging. The outcome for the wise king is a living child; the fool loses children and kingdom when he loses sight of the role of the chosen king. Later, his wise son Solomon would, in another parallel to his father's negative action, also become blinded to the requirements placed upon Yahweh's king as he catered to phantoms of imperial power which ran so contrary to the early roots of Israel's traditions. In this great

1.   Note a similar usage in a hymn to wisdom found in the Instruction for King Meri-ka-re (Lichtheim, *Ancient Egyptian Literature*, I, p. 222; Simpson [ed.], *Literature of Ancient Egypt*, p. 191): '...God is aware of whoever serves Him. Provide for men, the cattle of God, for He made heaven and earth at their desire. He suppressed the greed of the waters, He gave the breath of life to their noses, for they are likenesses of Him which issued from His flesh'.

rejection of Yahweh's wisdom by refusal to rule justly, Solomon and his successors lose the wisdom to hold the kingdoms of Judah and Israel together (1 Kgs 12.6-20) The United Monarchy—a harlot's child (Ezek. 16.44-52) in the hands of foolish statesmen—is divided forever, when God's wisdom is absent from the judgments given. Wisdom is capacity to act effectively, based on discernment, as is shown in a variety of ways throughout the Court History and in 1 Kings 3. The texts, though not from the same hand, are held together neatly in their final form by repetition of action episodes, vocabulary and themes of folly, wisdom and judgment. The question has been, then, not simply 'Who will succeed David, why and how?' but 'What kind of king will it be, fool or wise man?'

Wisdom and Folly in 2 Samuel 11–12 and 1 Kings 3

Motifeme (unit of action)	2 Sam. 11–12	1 Kgs 3
Act (C. Bremond:* 'Virtuality')	2 Sam. 11.1-3 choice of folly (adultery)	1 Kgs 3.3-9 choice of wisdom
Consequences (Bremond: 'Actualization')	2 Sam. 11.4-27 illicit pregnancy deceit trickery murder v. 27b: *wayyēra'* *haddābār 'ªšer 'āśâ dāwid* *bᵉ'ênê YHWH*	1 Kgs 3.10-15 *lēb ḥākām* riches honor long life v. 10: *wayyîṭab haddābār* *bᵉ'ênê 'ªdōnāy kiśā'al* *šᵉlōmōh 'et-haddābār* *hazzeh*
Evaluation (Bremond: 'Conclusion')	2 Sam. 12.1-15 Judgment scene father's child dies Evil is brought on David's house before 'all Israel' (vv. 10-12)	1 Kgs 3.16-28 Judgment scene mother's child lives 'All Israel heard of the judgment which the king had rendered…' (v. 28)

* C. Bremond, 'La logique des possibles narratifs', *Communications* 8 (1966), pp. 60-76, translated in *NLH* 11 (1980).

Yahweh's gift to Solomon acts as the mediating factor which transforms the negative example of a foolish ruler into the paradigmatic example of the 'wise king'—Solomon. It is likely that a larger study of the traditions dealing with Solomon's wisdom would confirm this aspect of wisdom as mediator between father and son, providing a more thorough contrast between David's political and familial failures and the triumphs of his son.[1] The hand of the redactor, concerned both with justifying Solomon's accession and laying the ground for the future demise of the kingdom, is visible in the arrangement of 1 Kings 3 into a syntagmatic structure which recalls 2 Samuel 11–12.

How, then, does one account for the ambiguity inherent in the presentation of David? In our reading, he is a foolish deluded king, but it is David who nevertheless becomes the paradigmatic Yahwistic 'servant'-monarch[2] against which later kings will be measured (1 Kgs 15.9; 2 Kgs 18.1-3; 22.2). From the perspective of 1 Kings 3, and the materials in the Court History, it is David's choice of Solomon, the son loved by the Lord who asks for Wisdom, which redeems that ruler. In a similar interpretive movement, Solomon's appeal to the idealized portrayal of David and other elements of the Torah and royal traditions in 1 Kings 3 attempts to mediate and justify the choice of this successor.[3] The portrait of Solomon is incomplete without reference to the mediation of David the servant who appoints this son to follow him; the reading of David is laden with nuances which must be interpreted in the light of Solomon's story. Wisdom, the mediator given by Yahweh and negated by David (cf. 2 Sam. 15.31), stands in the middle of the complex relations between father and son.[4]

1. See, for example, the interchange between Hiram and Solomon in 1 Kgs 5.15ff. (English versions 5.1-12), where the latter is hailed as 'a wise son' of David, now able to build a house for the Lord.

2. Kenik, *Design for Kingship*, p. 101.

3. Kenik, *Design for Kingship*, pp. 57-119.

4. The author wishes to thank Claudia Camp, Roland Murphy, Barbara Geller Nathanson and Choon-Leong Seow for their helpful comments on this study.

A RESPONSE TO 'THE BEARING OF WISDOM'

Carole R. Fontaine

It is both a delightful and delightfully strange assignment to be asked to respond to one's earlier work from the perspectives one now occupies. The first thing that struck me as I reread 'The Bearing of Wisdom' for this exercise was the impression that younger scholars—those without tenure in the US educational system—intrinsically understand how to shield themselves behind secondary scholarship and footnotes, rather than allowing their true perspectives to be discerned easily. In a sense, the young author of this article simply adopted the strategy of the Deuteronomistic Historian (DH) who was probably responsible for the redaction of her texts: by speaking neutrally and impersonally, she hardly lets the readers know that there is an author with a point of view of her own. Rather, she masquerades, and allows the impression that the text itself is her point of view. Feminist theory addresses this neutral 'scholarly' style well when it points out that there is *indeed* an author behind such 'objective' language, and the author's point of view ought to be made explicit—a dangerous prospect to one who has not yet been received into the Guild's tenured few.

This study began as an attempt to explore the perceived surface literary and deep structural similarities of two texts, the Court History of David and DH's introduction of the wise Solomon. While these texts are generally granted by scholars to be covering similar subject matter, they nevertheless are not always brought into close juxtaposition. This is because our scholarly perception of the differences in time, place and point of view of the supposed 'source' documents or authors often blinds us to the places of contact and tension which are apparent to any lay reader who comes to the text. Reading texts as biblical scholars used to do, that is, through the strict categories of source analysis and historical criticism, allows one only to see what the methods predispose us to see. The limits of the methods in question set the limits of the critics' vision. In shifting away from the fragmented, historically over-determined readings young scholars were trained to make toward a more holistic, literary apprehension of the text, I took a deliberate step in the direction of feminist literary criticism. While such a method certainly has its own historical concerns and political suspicions which must be put to the text in a thoroughgoing analysis, it also leaves space for the readerly imagination which receives the text and completes it. Although I hid behind the mask of more established secondary scholarship on these two texts, the impetus that led me to juxtapose these texts was the radical revisioning of the artist who saw different authors from different times working in a markedly similar way.

Since completing this study, I have continued to mull over the technical problems of the scholarly guild, such as the method for determining the elusive 'wisdom influence' that wisdom scholars (mainly) sometimes see in texts outside the wisdom movement proper (Proverbs, Job, Ecclesiastes). Like a good form critic— we are makers of charts *par excellence*—I eventually established a paradigm which allows a critic to 'graph' the incidence of wisdom elements in the text under consideration (see Figure 1). Wisdom influence may be said to be at work when a text shows a preponderance of motifs drawn from the following categories: items, characters and functions. Motifs may be 'items'— distinctive vocabulary, woven into distinctive wisdom genres, which illustrate particular wisdom themes (a bundle of motifs appearing together). Generally speaking, these items make up the category of 'form'. The motifs of wisdom 'characters' performing wisdom 'functions' or actions work together with the skeleton provided by vocabulary and genres to further flesh out the wisdom themes, thus creating the 'content'. The advantage of this approach to 'calculating' the presence of wisdom influence is that it is entirely text-oriented, and need not depend on the ascription of authorship to a member of ancient Israel's class of sages and wise women. The text we always have before us; authors of the text are elusive at best.

Obviously, the more elements there are in a given text drawn from all categories making up form and content, the more likely it is that wisdom influence is present. In particular, scholars have tended to discount 'wisdom themes' (a bundle of wisdom motifs, which themselves may be represented by actions, characters or items) and 'wisdom functions' as indicative of wisdom influence. It was felt that these constellations of components were too subjective, or at least, more subjective than the occurrence of standard wisdom vocabulary and forms. As this study shows to good effect, however, when all of these elements occur together, wisdom in action, whether through the vehicle of narrative focus on issues important to wisdom tradents or in the fulfillment of the social roles played out by wisdom practitioners (wise kings giving just judgments), carry their own weight in assessing the occurrence of slippery 'wisdom influence'. Given the probable association of those responsible for transmitting and editing these texts with the practitioners of the wisdom tradition—the educational, bureaucratic and literary elite of their day—we ought not to be amazed to find wisdom at all levels providing a strategy for yoking together two texts such as we have here. For someone such as myself, who sees the presence of wisdom alive and well in the lives of the non-elite, the fact that wisdom so easily lends itself to the support of the privileged few and a form of government, the monarchy, which cuts at the heart of Israelite tribal organization—presumed by some to be somewhat more egalitarian[1]—is an unpleasant one, but a fact of the tradition nevertheless. Wisdom will serve whatever ends her masters determine; in the hands of some, she will serve justice; in other hands, she is a powerful instrument for the preservation of the status quo. It is a tool as much as it is a point of view, or cosmically ordained source of world order.

The greatest omission from 'The Bearing of Wisdom' is an understandable one, given my limited acquaintance with feminist literary criticism at the time the study was written. What is not included is a clear statement about the way women's bodies and their children's bodies are traded like pieces on the game board

1. Cf. N.C. Gottwald, *The Tribes of Yawheh: A Sociology of Liberated Israel 1250–1050 BCE* (London: SCM Press, 1979).

of patriarchal power relations, a game at which the male god plays as well as his 'chosen' male followers. All the questions that the most untutored reader might ask about such texts have 'disappeared' from the scholar's narrowly focused gaze: what kind of god strikes down an innocent child to pay for the crimes of a parent (2 Sam. 12.14-19)? What kind of king, even for noble purposes—much less for purposes of plot development and personal aggrandizement!—plays at the execution of a blameless infant (1 Kgs 3.15-28)? From a humanistic point of view, there is not so great a difference between the court of Pharaoh (Exod. 1–2) and the royal courts of Jerusalem, once we look from the perspective of women and children.

The juxtaposition of the two texts before us offers once again a telling insight into the ways that patriarchal ideology cracks and breaks open under the weight of its own assumptions. The ignominious King David who walks the roof of his palace while engaging in voyeurism in 2 Sam. 11.2 resurfaces in 1 Kings 3 as DH's 'ideal king' who 'walked before [God] in faithfulness, in righteousness, and in uprightness of heart before [God]' in v. 6, a noble path followed by his son, so the editor tells us in v. 3. The shameful appropriation of Bathsheba and the consequent murder of Uriah the Hittite have vanished so thoroughly in the royal ideology of the sycophant editor that David's behavior can actually be used to legitimate Solomon's! More of this ideology emerges in 1 Kgs 3.1-2, where we are notified of Solomon's marriage to a Strange Woman (cf. Prov. 1–9) *extraordinaire*, an Egyptian princess. This notice sets up a convenient patriarchally-approved reason—the woman who brings death—for Solomon's eventual failures. The habitual abuses of power at court which are so amply catalogued in the Court History and beyond go almost unremarked as sources for the social upheavals to come, yet there they stand boldly outlined in the text for those who have eyes to see.

If we compare 1 Kgs 11.1-13 to 1 Kgs 12.1-20 we see the wisdom theme of the woman who brings death (in the form of Solomon's foreign wives) in explanatory conflict with the wisdom functions of counsel given by wily old counsellors to an unwise young king, Solomon's son Rehoboam. Here, at last, wisdom sides with the plight of the people oppressed by a burden of royal ostentation that the economics of Israel and Judah could never quite afford. When the people cry out to Rehoboam for relief, the 'old men who had stood before Solomon' advise the young man, 'If you will be a servant to this people today and serve them, and speak good words to them when you answer them, then they will be your servants for ever' (1 Kgs 12.7). But Rehoboam will have none of them, forsakes their counsel, and listens to the machismo of his young cohorts (vv. 10-11), thereby sealing the split between north and south. Though the people of that time do not realize it, they are only reaping the harvest of royal patriarchy: where women and children, the lowest ranking members of the patriarchal power pyramid of social organization (see Figure 2), can be used and viewed as pawns of regal power, the status and well-being of lower ranking men are also at risk. DH's attempt to convince us—and the ancient kingdom of Judah—of the rightness and efficacy of its royal ideology fails miserably: David's 'righteous' walk produced a murder and a dead child; Solomon's glorious meander down the same path produced a murdering child who split the people of God into two hostile, warring nations. Regardless of their relative powerlessness within the text, the fate of the women and children in these two wisdom dramas signals the symbolic fate of the whole people, and therein, perhaps, our readings reclaim for them a dignity and power denied them by the text itself.

Figure 1

*Categories of Wisdom Motifs
Contributing to Wisdom Influence*

Wisdom Items	*Wisdom Characters*	*Wisdom Functions**
Vocabulary:	Sage/Fool	Teaching
wise/foolish	Righteous/Wicked	Counselling
righteous/wicked	Rich/Poor	Managing
wisdom/folly	Woman Wisdom	Judging
rich/poor	Goddess figures	Writing
counsel/teaching	Wife/Mother	Editing
'blessed—'	figures	Nurturing
tree of life	Prophetic figures	Healing
etc.	Woman Stranger	Conflict Resolution
	Foreign Woman	Writing
Forms:	Prostitute	Editing
proverbs	Adulteress	
admonitions	King/Commoner	
prohibitions	Court Counsellor	
instructions	Wise Woman	
wisdom poems	Author/Redactor	
parables	Teacher/Student	
numerical sayings	Economic Manager	
'better than' sayings	Tree of Life*	
'blessed/happy'		
sayings		

Themes:
Duality of all kinds:
    good/evil
    wise/foolish, etc.
Wise King
Woman Who
    Brings Death
Wisdom Who
    Brings Life
importance of:
    choice, counsel,
    teaching
deft use of language
    etc.

* Because of the Tree of Life's close association with Woman Wisdom in her goddess aspect, I view her as a character and not an inanimate object.

* I note here only socially 'positive' functions; each might be balanced with foolish, 'negative' functions, such as wastefulness, seduction, failure to judge, etc.

Figure 2
*The Patriarchal Pyramid: Social Organization
in the Ancient Near East*

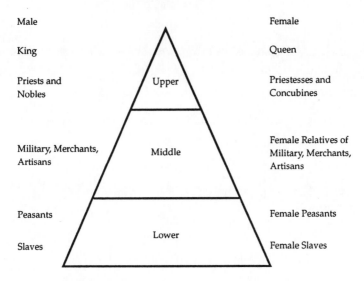

Male		Female
King		Queen
Priests and Nobles	Upper	Priestesses and Concubines
Military, Merchants, Artisans	Middle	Female Relatives of Military, Merchants, Artisans
Peasants		Female Peasants
Slaves	Lower	Female Slaves

Males outrank females of the same class
Elite females outrank males of lower classes
Females' status is usually dependent on the status of their male relatives

Part IV
QUEEN MOTHERS?

THE STATUS AND RIGHT OF THE $G^E B\hat{I}R\hat{A}$*

Zafrira Ben-Barak

Many scholars have assumed that the $g^e b\hat{i}r\hat{a}$ or queen mother in ancient Israel resembled her sisters elsewhere in the ancient Near East, as regards both her official position in the realm and her attainment of significant power in the kingdom ruled by her son.[1] Three principal meanings attach themselves to the term $g^e b\hat{i}r\hat{a}$: (1) mother or wife of the reigning sovereign (1 Kgs 11.19; 2 Kgs 10.13; Jer. 29.2; 1 Kgs 15.13; 2 Chron. 15.16; Jer. 13.18);[2] (2) female ruler, governess (Isa. 47.5, 7); (3) mistress in relation to maidservant (Gen. 16.4, 8, 9; 2 Kgs 5.3; Ps. 123.2; Prov. 30.23; Isa. 24.2).[3] The most common and frequently applied of these three meanings is that of queen mother. This meaning is

*   This article originally appeared in *JBL* 110.1 (1991), pp. 23-34.

1.   On the $g^e b\hat{i}r\hat{a}$, see J. Pedersen, *Israel: Its Life and Culture* (London: Cumberlege, 1953), III, IV, pp. 71-72; G. Molin, 'Die Stellung der Gebira im Staate Juda', *TZ* 10 (1954), pp. 161-75; H. Donner, 'Art und Herkunft des Amtes der Königinmutter im Alten Testament', in *Festschrift Johannes Friedrich zum 65. Geburtstag* (Heidelberg: Carl Winter, 1959), pp. 104-45; G.W. Ahlström, *Aspects of Syncretism in Israelite Religion* (Lund: Gleerup, 1963), pp. 57-88; T. Ishida, *The Royal Dynasties in Ancient Israel* (BZAW, 142; Berlin: de Gruyter, 1977), pp. 155-60. N.-E. Andreasen, 'The Role of the Queen Mother in Israelite Society', *CBQ* 45 (1983), pp. 179-94.

2.   Only once does the term $g^e b\hat{i}r\hat{a}$ refer to the king's wife: Tahpenes, Pharaoh's wife (1 Kgs 11.19). The LXX, however, reads here $g^e d\bar{o}l\hat{a}$; see J. Gray, who considers this term a gloss (*I & II Kings: A Commentary* [OTL; repr.; Philadelphia: Westminster Press; London: SCM Press, 2nd rev. edn, 1975 (1970)], pp. 28 n. h).

3.   For the meaning of the term $g^e b\hat{i}r\hat{a}$, see R. de Vaux, *Ancient Israel: Its Life and Institutions* (London: Darton, Longman & Todd, 1962), p. 117; Ahlström, *Aspects*, pp. 61-63; *HALAT*, p. 166; A. Even-Shoshan, *A New Concordance of the Bible* (Hebrew; Jerusalem: Kiryat Sefer, 6th edn, 1977), I, pp. 409-10.

confirmed by parallel usages that refer to the same event and persons: 'And he carried away Jehoiachin...and the *king's mother*' (2 Kgs 24.15); '...into exile...this was after King Jeconiah and the *g^ebîrâ'* (Jer. 29.2); 'he also removed Maacah his *mother* from being *g^ebîrâ'* (1 Kgs 15.13).

This, then, is the sense we have taken over in considering the person of the *g^ebîrâ*, that is, the queen mother.[1] Some scholars regard the *g^ebîrâ* as a survival of the matriarchal period.[2] Others have argued that the *g^ebîrâ*'s political station in the realm was second only to that of the king himself.[3] There are those who hold that she exercised her power primarily in cultic matters,[4] and some have made a case for attributing to her the function of the king's chief counselor.[5] There are scholars who even speak of an institution of the *g^ebîrâ*[6]—which in the view of some was confined entirely to the kingdom of Judah,[7] whereas others believe it to have arisen under the influence of neighboring kingdoms.[8]

1. According to Ahlström, to be *g^ebîrâ* thus meant more than simply being the king's mother (*Aspects*, p. 61). See Molin, who distinguishes between the term *g^ebîrâ* and queen mother ('Die Stellung', p. 165).

2. See R. Kittel, *Die Bücher der Könige* (HKAT, 1.5; Göttingen: Vandenhoeck & Ruprecht, 1900), p. 18; see also Molin, 'Die Stellung', pp. 172-73.

3. Molin, 'Die Stellung', p. 161; Donner, 'Art und Herkunft', p. 107; cf. Ahlström, who concluded from certain passages that the position of the Israelite queen mother was virtually equal to that of the king (*Aspects*, pp. 61-63).

4. Ahlström suggests that the office of the *g^ebîrâ* in Israel was primarily religious in its motivation and was based on some cultic function (*Aspects*, pp. 57-88, esp. p. 75). He suggests also that in other lands in the Near East the position occupied by the queen mother was based on religious considerations.

5. See Andreasen, 'Role of the Queen Mother', pp. 189-90. His main idea is that the chief function of the queen mother was that of senior counselor to the king and the people; cf. Ahlström, *Aspects*, pp. 64-65.

6. Ahlström, *Aspects*, p. 63.

7. See de Vaux, *Ancient Israel*, p. 118.

8. Hittite influence was especially marked; see de Vaux, *Ancient Israel*, p. 118; A.A. Kampman, 'Tawannamans, der Titel der hethitischen Königin', *JEOL* 2.6-7 (1939–42), pp. 432-42; Molin, 'Die Stellung', pp. 172, 173-75; cf. Donner, who emphasizes the direct political influence of the political

I

None of these assumptions, however, is based on any known law or other direct evidence furnished by either the OT or extrabiblical sources. Rather, they depend entirely on a very small number of instances of indirect evidence contained in the Hebrew Bible. The queen mother's name is mentioned in connection with the ascent to the throne of each of the kings of Judah.[1] This may doubtless be regarded as merely an introductory formula. Since queen mothers are nowhere mentioned in the same way in the kingdom of Israel[2] or any other monarchy in the region, we can assume that the hand of the Deuteronomistic redactor has intervened here in order to mark the ascent of the kings of Judah to the throne with fitting solemnity—possibly with an eye to stressing the uninterrupted dynastic continuity of the house of David.[3]

In backing their claim, scholars have primarily relied on examples contained in the historiographical biblical sources— namely, that of Bathsheba, mother of Solomon; Maacah, mother of Abijah; Hamutal, mother of Jehoahaz and Zedekiah; and Nehushta, mother of Jehoiachin.[4]

Bathsheba, the daughter of Eliam (2 Sam. 11.3). Bathsheba was the first *gᵉbîrâ*, and her case furnishes the basic premises concerning the senior status enjoyed by the queen mother.[5] These

system of Syria, Canaan and Egypt ('Art und Herkunft', pp. 123-30).
    1.   Except in the cases of Jehoram (2 Kgs 8.16-18) and Ahaz (2 Kgs 16.2-3); see de Vaux, *Ancient Israel*, pp. 117-18; Andreasen, 'Role of the Queen Mother', pp. 179-80; cf. Ahlström, *Aspects*, p. 62.
    2.   Only once in 2 Kgs 10.13 we find the term *gᵉbîrâ* referring to the kingdom of Israel. This can only be Jezebel, but, as de Vaux noted, the word is put in the mouth of the princes of Judah (*Ancient Israel*, p. 118). He also drew attention to the rare term *šēgal* (Ps. 45.10) and suggested that it can be the Israelite equivalent of the *gᵉbîrâ* of Judah.
    3.   See Andreasen, 'Role of the Queen Mother', pp. 179-80.
    4.   Andreasen, 'Role of the Queen Mother', pp. 179-94; see also de Vaux, *Ancient Israel*, pp. 117-18; Ahlström, *Aspects*, pp. 57-88.
    5.   On Bathsheba and her high status, see R.N. Whybray, *The Succession Narrative: A Study of II Samuel 9–20 and 1 Kings 1 and 2* (SBT, 2.9; London: SCM Press, 1968), p. 40; Ishida, *Royal Dynasties*, pp. 155-58; A. Berlin, 'Characterization in Biblical Narrative: David's Wives', *JSOT* 23 (1982),

premises rely on the account of Bathsheba petitioning her son Solomon on behalf of Adonijah (1 Kgs 2.13-25). The high status of the *g^e̱bîrâ* is thought to be demonstrated in this episode by the behavior toward her on the part of the king, who rises to meet her, bows to her[1] and seats her on his right side. Some have gone so far as to argue that her position is equal to that of the king. In any event, the story of Adonijah's petition is the source of the hypothesis that the queen mother was chief counselor to the king and that she represented the interests of the people and the members of the court.[2]

Maacah, the daughter of Abishalom (1 Kgs. 15.2). Maacah is the second major instance that is cited in evidence of the high position held by the queen mother.[3] According to 1 Kgs 15.13 (cf. 2 Chron. 15.16), Asa removed his mother, Maacah, from being *g^e̱bîrâ* because she had had an abominable image made for Asherah.[4] This is the only instance in which the term *g^e̱bîrâ* is applied directly to the queen mother, and it is the basis for assuming that she was vested with enormous power, especially in regard to cultic matters. According to G.W. Ahlström, this is the single source containing information about the office of the

pp. 70-76; J.W. Flanagan, 'Succession and Genealogy in the Davidic Dynasty', in H.B. Huffmon, F.A. Spina and A.R.W. Green (eds.), *The Quest for the Kingdom of God: Studies in Honor of George E. Mendenhall* (Winona Lake, IN: Eisenbrauns, 1983), pp. 48-49.

1. For a similar custom in Ugarit, where the king bows to his mother, see M. Dietrich, O. Loretz and J. Sanmartín, *Die Keilalphabetischen Texte aus Ugarit* (Neukirchen–Vluyn: Neukirchener Verlag; Kevalaer: Butzon & Bercker, 1976), II, p. 13 ('At the feet of my mother I bow down'); C.H. Gordon, *Ugaritic Textbook* (Rome: Pontificium Institutum Biblicum, 1965), Text 117.5; cf. E. Lipiński, 'Ahat-Milki, reine d'Ugarit et la guerre du Mukiš', *OLP* 12 (1981), pp. 92-94.

2. Andreasen, 'Role of the Queen Mother', pp. 189-90.

3. On Maacah and her high position as queen mother, see S. Yeivin, 'Social, Religious and Cultural Trends in Jerusalem under the Davidic Dynasty', *VT* 3 (1953), pp. 162-64; Ahlström, *Aspects*, pp. 57-88.

4. See J. Morgenstern, 'The Oldest Documents of the Hexateuch', *HUCA* 4 (1927), pp. 106, 113; A. Malamat, 'Aspects of the Foreign Policies of David and Solomon', *JNES* 22 (1963), p. 9; *idem, Israel in Biblical Times: Historical Essays* (Hebrew; Jerusalem: Bialik Institute, 1983), pp. 208-209.

gᵉbîrâ, which only the king could revoke; this also reveals its cultic associations.[1]

Hamutal, the daughter of Jeremiah of Libnah (2 Kgs 23.31).[2] Hamutal's being the mother of two kings, Jehoahaz and Zedekiah, and her association with Ezekiel's lamentation on the mother,[3] are regarded as further evidence that the queen mother was a personage of considerable power and status in the realm.

Nehushta, the daughter of Elnathan (2 Kgs 24.8).[4] The case of Nehushta is perhaps the outstanding instance cited in connection with the office of the queen mother. In the passage concerning the exiles sent into captivity to Babylon (2 Kgs 24.15), the queen mother is mentioned immediately after her son, King Jehoiachin. This implied order of precedence, in conjunction with Jer. 13.18 ('Say to the king and the *gᵉbîrâ*: "Take a lowly seat, for your beautiful *ᵃṭārâ* has come down from your head"'), has been cited as evidence of the high station and importance of the *gᵉbîrâ*. Like the king, she too wore an *ᵃṭārâ* ('crown'), and so great was her power that the enemy regarded her as dangerous to the point of meriting banishment together with the sovereign.[5]

Two additional cases have been adduced in support of this claim.

Jezebel, the daughter of Ethbaal, king of the Sidonians, and wife of King Ahab (1 Kgs 16.31).[6] The assumption here is grounded in

---

1. Ahlström, *Aspects*, p. 61.

2. On Hamutal, see Gray, *I & II Kings*, pp. 749, 762; Ishida, *Royal Dynasties*, pp. 156, 169; Malamat, *Israel in Biblical Times*, p. 251.

3. See G. Fohrer, *Ezechiel* (Tübingen: Mohr [Paul Siebeck], 1955), pp. 104-106; W. Zimmerli, *Ezechiel* (Neukirchen–Vluyn: Neukirchener Verlag, 1969), pp. 420-28; M. Greenberg, *Ezekiel 1–20* (AB, 22; Garden City, NY: Doubleday, 1983), pp. 354-59.

4. See Malamat, *Israel in Biblical Times*, pp. 251-52.

5. See W.F. Albright, 'The Seal of Eliakim, and the Latest Preexilic History of Judah, with some Observations on Ezekiel', *JBL* 51 (1932), p. 91; Ahlström, *Aspects*, pp. 62-63; Donner, 'Art und Herkunft', p. 109; J. Bright, *Jeremiah* (AB, 21; Garden City, NY: Doubleday, 1965), p. 95; W. Rudolph, *Jeremia* (Tübingen: Mohr [Paul Siebeck], 1985), p. 95.

6. On Jezebel and her high position as queen consort in the realm, see Donner, 'Art und Herkunft', p. 168; Ishida, *Royal Dynasties*, pp. 156-57; *idem*, 'The House of Ahab', *IEJ* 25 (1975), pp. 135-37; O.H. Steck, *Überlieferung und Zeitgeschichte in den Elia Erzählungen* (WMANT, 26; Neukirchen–Vluyn:

2 Kgs 10.13, which relates the visit of the kinsmen of Ahaziah to the royal princes and the sons of the *gᵉbîrâ*. This is the only reference to the *gᵉbîrâ* that occurs in connection with the kingdom of Israel, and it is assumed by scholars that the implied bearer of the title is Jezebel. The fact that her sons are being visited on apparently equal terms with those of the king is taken as an indication of her high station.[1] Some have proposed that she also ruled the kingdom in 2 Kgs 9.15.[2] Finally, 2 Kgs 9.30, 'She painted her eyes, and adorned her head', is offered in evidence of her also having worn a crown.[3]

Athaliah, the daughter of Ahab (2 Kgs 8.18) or the daughter of Omri (2 Kgs 8.26).[4] The destruction of the entire royal family of the house of David and Athaliah's seizure of the government of the realm have been cited as attesting to the considerable power that had accrued to the station of the queen mother, since only the possession of enormous power would have made it possible for her to take control of the kingdom.[5]

Neukirchener Verlag, 1968), pp. 62-68; S. Timm, *Die Dynastie Omri: Quellen und Untersuchungen zur Geschichte Israel im 9 Jahrhundert vor Christus* (FRLANT, 124; Göttingen: Vandenhoeck & Ruprecht, 1982), pp. 288-94; F.I. Andersen, 'The Socio-Juridical Background of the Naboth Incident', *JBL* 85 (1966), pp. 46-57; A. Brenner, *The Israelite Woman: Social Role and Literary Type in Biblical Narrative* (The Biblical Seminar, 2; JSOT Press, 1985), pp. 20-28.

1.   Steck, *Überlieferung*, pp. 55, 62-65; Timm, *Die Dynastie Omri*, pp. 288-94.

2.   Andreasen assumed that Jezebel functioned as queen mother in Samaria while Joram stayed in Jezreel ('Role of the Queen Mother', p. 186).

3.   Ahlström, *Aspects*, p. 63; Steck, *Überlieferung*, pp. 57-59.

4.   See S. Herner, 'Athalja: Ein Beitrag zur Frage nach dem Alte des Jahwisten und des Elohisten', in *Vom alten Testament: Festschrift Karl Marti* (BZAW, 41; Berlin: de Gruyter, 1925), pp. 137-41; J. Begrich, 'Atalja, die Tochter Omris', *ZAW* 53 (1935), pp. 78-79; H.J. Katzenstein, 'Who were the Parents of Athalia', *IEJ* 5 (1955), pp. 194-97; Ishida, *Royal Dynasties*, pp. 159-61.

5.   Ahlström, *Aspects*, pp. 63-64; Molin suggests that Athaliah wanted to bring Judah under the rule of Phoenicia ('Die Stellung', p. 164). Cf. H. Reviv, 'On the Days of Athaliah and Joash' (Hebrew), *Bet Miqra* 47 (1970–71), pp. 541-48.

II

Let us begin with a consideration of the last two instances. Neither Jezebel nor Athaliah is relevant to our concern, since nothing regarding their activity or status has any connection with the function of the queen mother.

Jezebel's status and involvement in the life of the realm pertain to the time when she was the wife of Ahab, and the honors she enjoyed came to her by right of her father.[1] It should be kept in mind, moreover, that her prominence depends on the prophetic sources,[2] whose intention it is to stress the prophet Elijah's conflict with her. Nowhere is there any reference to her status or actions in the capacity of queen mother—and certainly not that she actually ruled during the period of Joram's reign. As for the phrase 'the sons of the $g^e b\hat{i}r\hat{a}$',[3] no single term can of itself constitute sufficient grounds for any assumption concerning the position of the $g^e b\hat{i}r\hat{a}$ in the kingdom of Israel—let alone for developing a fully articulated theory regarding such an office. The term $g^e b\hat{i}r\hat{a}$ was in common use among the members of the court of Judah, possibly because this was the title that was ordinarily used by them in reference to the queen mother.[4] J. Gray may well be right in arguing that $b^e n\hat{e}\ hammelek$ means the royal family in general and $b^e n\hat{e}\ hagg^e b\hat{i}r\hat{a}$ the actual sons of the queen and the late king.[5] Besides, it would be more reasonable to assume that Ahaziah's visit to the sons of the $g^e b\hat{i}r\hat{a}$ had the character of a private visit with blood relations rather than a gesture of appropriate respect to the $g^e b\hat{i}r\hat{a}$'s high station in court. Finally, the phrase 'she adorned her head' concerns her

---

1. See Jehu's words: '...bury her, for she is a king's daughter' (2 Kgs 9.34).

2. See B. Uffenheimer, 'The Stories of Elijah; the Stories of Elisha', in *Ancient Prophecy in Israel* (Hebrew; Jerusalem: Magnes, 1973), pp. 186-277.

3. Steck, *Überlieferung*, pp. 55, 62-65; Timm, *Die Dynastie Omri*, pp. 288-94.

4. De Vaux points out that the word $g^e b\hat{i}r\hat{a}$ is put in the mouth of the princes of Judah (*Ancient Israel*, p. 118).

5. See Gray, *I & II Kings*, p. 556.

preparations to meet with Jehu and has nothing to do with her wearing a crown.[1]

Concerning Athaliah, her assumption of the throne cannot be regarded as evidence of the political power of the queen mother,[2] and it furnishes no firm ground for a general hypothesis about the high status of the *gᵉbîrâ*. More likely, this was an act of desperation to which she had been compelled as a descendant of her family. Athaliah's rage and her fears regarding her own destruction at the hands of the God-fearing people of Judah (which did in fact take place seven years later) are entirely understandable in the light of the annihilation of the royal family of the northern kingdom and the murder of her son and all of the brothers of the king.[3]

Turning now to the remaining and principal instances that form the basis for the assumptions of scholars concerning the status and power of the *gᵉbîrâ*, two arguments can be adduced to counter the hypotheses in this regard.

First, out of all the queen mothers in Judah and Israel, only in the case of four do the historiographic texts go into any detail concerning the person of the *gᵉbîrâ*. Moreover, each of them is connected with the house of David—Bathsheba, Maacah, Hamutal and Nehushta. It is puzzling, therefore, that scholars should have arrived at their conclusions regarding the *gᵉbîrâ* on the basis of so sporadic and insubstantial a sample of instances in kind. Rather than being regarded as isolated exceptions to the rule, this handful of cases has furnished the occasion for a general assertion concerning the character of the *gᵉbîrâ*. Moreover, even these few scattered examples offer very little material for conjecture. For example, the passage concerning Bathsheba's petition on behalf of Adonijah is extremely brief, consisting of only a few verses (1 Kgs 2.19-20). Nevertheless, this same passage has served as the basis for elaborate hypotheses concerning the prestige and power of the *gᵉbîrâ*, her role

1. See n. 3, p. 175; see also Jer. 4.30; Ezek. 23.40, 42. From these passages it clearly follows that these preparations were commonly practiced by women who tried to look beautiful.

2. See n. 5, p. 175.

3. See Reviv, 'On the Days of Athaliah', pp. 541-48; Ishida, *Royal Dynasties*, p. 160.

as an institution of state and her function as chief counselor to the king and intercessor. In the case of Maacah, the entire theory concerning her also relies on a single verse—1 Kgs 15.13—which has been spun out to support a broad hypothesis about the high authority vested in the office of the $g^e b\hat{\imath}r\hat{a}$, especially in cultic and religious matters.[1] Finally, the hypotheses regarding Hamutal and Nehushta depend on indirect evidence and interpretation of reported material only.[2] We must conclude, therefore, that no general rule can be made from so small a sample and such meager evidence as compared with the total number of known queen mothers. Certainly no comprehensive theory can be developed on these inadequate grounds in regard to the position of the $g^e b\hat{\imath}r\hat{a}$ as an office of the state.

The second counter-argument is that each of these four chief instances of queen mothers represents a unique case. Bathsheba's son Solomon was a younger son, and Adonijah was his older brother.[3] It was the practice in Israel and other monarchies in the lands of the Bible that the royal succession should devolve upon the firstborn or eldest son.[4] Solomon therefore had no claim to the kingship, which was by right Adonijah's.[5] From the

1. See n. 4, p. 173.

2. Hamutal, from the very evidence that she was the mother of two kings, and mainly from the interpretation of Ezekiel's lamentation; Nehushta, only from the fact that she went into exile with her son the king, and from Jeremiah's prophecy (Jer. 13.18).

3. After the death of Ammon and Absalom, Adonijah, the son of Haggith, was now in line. He was the fourth son of David from the Hebron period, whereas Solomon, Bathsheba's son, was from the Jerusalem time (1 Chron. 3.1-5).

4. For the right of the firstborn to the throne, see H. Lewy, 'Nitokris-Naqi'a', *JNES* 2 (1952), p. 271 n. 39; she claims that the right of the male firstborn to the throne is undisputed. Z. Ben-Barak concludes that the succession to the throne proceeded according to an accepted order—the order of primogeniture ('Succession to the Throne in Israel and in Assyria', *OLP* 17 [1986], pp. 85-100). The firstborn had the right to the throne. If the firstborn died, this privilege passed to the brother next in line. From Assyria we learn about the rights of the firstborn from the term for heir apparent: *mār šarri rab ša bit ridūti*, 'the eldest son of the king of the house of succession'.

5. About the Adonijah–Solomon conflict (1 Kgs 1–2), see J.A. Soggin, *Das Königtum in Israel* (Berlin: Töpelmann, 1967), pp. 77-79; S. Zalevski,

biblical texts it is evident that Solomon's accession came as a consequence of his mother's energetic efforts on his behalf. Bathsheba's presence in Jerusalem and her close association with the prophet Nathan give us some idea of how she managed successfully to obtain the support of ambitious Jerusalemites recently arrived to positions of power, such as Nathan himself and Zadok the priest from among religious circles, and Benaiah the son of Jehoiada from within the military.[1] Bathsheba's intercession on behalf of Adonijah should therefore be regarded as part of her machinations in advancing the cause of her son.[2] It was she who was instrumental in eliminating Adonijah, who remained a threat to Solomon as long as he was alive.

Maacah's son Abijah was also a younger son and had brothers older than he who were in the line of succession (2 Chron. 11.18-23). Rehoboam's love for her and her own domineering personality were the major factors accounting for Rehoboam's choice of Abijah as his successor.[3] It is reasonable to assume that by the force of her strong and dynamic personality Maacah was able to obtain for herself a position of significant power during the three years of her son's kingship,[4] most particularly in the religious sphere. She also tried unsuccessfully to maintain her influence during the reign of Asa (1 Kgs 15.9-13), who was either her son or grandson.[5]

Solomon's Ascension to the Throne (Hebrew; Jerusalem: Marcus, 1981), pp. 39-144, 208-30; T. Ishida, 'Solomon's Succession to the Throne of David: A Political Analysis', in *idem* (ed.), *Studies in the Period of David and Solomon and Other Essays* (Tokyo: Yamakawa-Shuppansha, 1982), pp. 175-87; Ben-Barak, 'Succession to the Throne', pp. 85-89.

1. See Ishida, *Royal Dynasties*, pp. 157, 158.

2. And not, as some scholars think, as evidence of her naïve nature. See Ahlström, *Aspects*, pp. 64-65; Andreasen, 'Role of the Queen Mother', pp. 188-90; Whybray, *Succession Narrative*, p. 40.

3. S. Yeivin, *Studies in the History of Israel and its Country* (Hebrew; Tel Aviv: Newman, 1960), p. 204; de Vaux, *Ancient Israel*, p. 101.

4. See Andreasen, 'Role of the Queen Mother', p. 181; Ahlström, *Aspects*, pp. 57-88.

5. According to 1 Kgs 15.10 and 2 Chron. 15.16 Asa was the son of Maacah, but according to 1 Kgs 15.2 and 2 Chron. 11.22 Maacah was the mother of Abijah, Asa's father (1 Kgs 15.8)—that is, Maacah was the grandmother of Asa. See Gray, *I & II Kings*, pp. 347-49; Malamat, *Israel in*

Hamutal's son Jehoahaz was crowned before his elder brother Jehoiakim, who was the legitimate successor to the title (2 Kgs 23.31, 36). The fact that Hamutal belonged to a well-connected Judahite family from the outskirts of the kingdom and could therefore claim a superior lineage to that of the Galilean mother of Jehoiakim (2 Kgs 23.36)[1] was undoubtedly critical in determining Jehoahaz's precedence in the succession. She was therefore able to effect her son's accession to royal power by successfully exploiting the anti-Egyptian orientation in the kingdom and—what is especially significant—by obtaining the support of 'the people of the land'.[2] That such was indeed the case is amply attested to in Ezekiel's lamentation (Ezek. 19.1-4): 'What a lioness was your mother among lions' (v. 2)—which gives evidence as well of the high dignity of her position in the kingdom. The same passage confirms and bears witness to her singular role in placing her son on the throne: 'And she brought up one of her whelps: he became a young lion' (v. 3). Nor does it appear that her involvement in the affairs of state ended with Jehoiakim's death and Jehoiachin's exile; she continued her political activities by seeing to it that another of her sons, Zedekiah, would assume the title of king—a circumstance that is reflected also in Ezekiel's lamentation (Ezek. 19.5-9): 'She took another of her whelps and made him a young lion' (v. 5).[3]

Nehushta was the daughter of one of the most distinguished families in Jerusalem.[4] Two traditions were preserved concerning the accession of her son, Jehoiachin, to the throne. According

Biblical Times, pp. 208-209; Yeivin, *Studies*, pp. 236-39.

1. For the place and status of Jehoiakim's mother, see Yeivin, *Studies*, p. 290; Malamat, *Israel in Biblical Times*, pp. 251-52; Z. Ben-Barak, 'The Religious-Prophetic Background of the "Law of the King" (Deuteronomy 17.14-20), in J. Greenfield and M. Weinfeld (eds.), *Shnaton: An Annual for Biblical and Ancient Near Eastern Studies* (Hebrew; Jerusalem: Newman, 1975), p. 42.

2. On the link between the queen mother, who came from the provinces, and 'the people of the land', see Ihromi, 'Die Königsmutter und der Amm Ha'arez im Reich Juda', *VT* 24 (1974), pp. 421-29; Ishida, *Royal Dynasties*, pp. 160-66. Cf. A. Malamat, 'The Historical Background of the Assassination of Amon, King of Judah', *IEJ* 3 (1953), pp. 26-29.

3. See n. 3, p. 174.

4. See Yeivin, *Studies*, pp. 279, 296.

to one of these (2 Chron. 36.9-11), Jehoiachin was at that time a minor and only eight years of age, whereas his older brother Zedekiah was in his majority, twenty-one years old. To Nehushta must go the credit for having obtained the crown for her son while he was still a minor, in place of the older Zedekiah. This she was able to accomplish by the combined virtues of her lineage, character and pro-Egyptian orientation.[1] To the extent that the second part of the lamentation of Ezekiel refers to Nehushta (Ezek. 19.5-9), what it says concerning her involvement in her son's accession to royal office is illuminating. But even according to the account contained in the second and more widely accepted tradition (2 Kgs 24.8-18)—namely, that Jehoiachin became king at the age of eighteen and Zedekiah was his uncle—Zedekiah would still be senior and first in line of succession. Zedekiah was the surviving son of King Josiah and the brother of two kings who had preceded him, Jehoahaz and Jehoiakim. The practice of succession to the throne of brothers in Judah and Israel is seen in earlier cases. Thus, after the death of Rehoboam's son Abijah, the throne was occupied by Asa, who according to one tradition was the brother of Abijah (1 Kgs 15.10).[2] Following the demise of Ahab's son Ahaziah, the succession passed on to his brother Jehoram (2 Kgs 1.17).[3] The same applied to the sons of Josiah. After Jehoahaz was exiled, it was his brother Jehoiakim who succeeded (2 Kgs 23.33-34). When Jehoiakim died, his brother Zedekiah was certainly next in line of succession—and not his nephew, who was younger than he and was crowned only as a consequence of Nehushta's exertions on his behalf.

The foregoing analysis of the cases of Bathsheba, Maacah, Hamutal and Nehushta has shown that they all have in common the following two characteristics: (1) each of these queens was the mother of a younger son who was without right to the succession, which legitimately belonged to an older brother; (2) they each succeeded in recruiting a powerful following of ambitious adherents who helped make it possible to place a

1. Allbright, 'Seal of Eliakim', p. 91.
2. See n. 4, p. 180.
3. According to a biblical source, the reason was that Ahaziah had no son (2 Kgs 1.17).

younger son at the head of the kingdom, although this was in contradiction to accepted practice in regard to the royal succession. The particular nature of the cases we have been examining gives us an insight into the way in which these queen mothers were able to obtain positions of influence and power in their sons' realms. These were ambitious and strong women who were prepared to use every available means in order to obtain the royal succession for their offspring. This they were eminently successful in accomplishing, and their sons, being aware of their mothers' enormous power, granted them broad authority in the realm in gratitude and continued dependence. This is what accounts for Solomon's gesture of respect toward Bathsheba in bowing to her and having her sit at his right side. It explains also how Maacah was able to assume so high a station during the reign of Abijah and how Nehushta rose to a position of such eminence and power when her young son, aged eight or eighteen, was king that Nebuchadnezzar felt constrained to include her among the principal captives who were sent into exile. And if *ʿaṭārâ* has the meaning of crown, then only Nehushta would have worn a crown, as did her son, during her tenure as regent ruling on his behalf. Indeed, this particular instance would demonstrate that the queen mother did not customarily wear a royal diadem.

III

Some of the scholars who considered that the queen mother ranked high in the realm of her son have adduced instances of queen mothers in the ancient Near East, apart from the biblical examples, who attained significant political power in kingdoms ruled by their sons.[1] The plentiful extrabiblical documentation that is available concerning the region indicates that the situation in other states in the Near East was very much the same as that which obtained in the biblical kingdoms—namely, that the cases of queen mothers who achieved significant power were relatively few and far between among the vast numbers of queen mothers throughout the kingdoms of the ancient Near

1. See Ahlström, *Aspects*, pp. 65-69; Andreasen, 'Role of the Queen Mother', pp. 182-83.

East. What is especially illuminating in this regard, however, is that even these rare cases follow a pattern that is close to the one found in the OT: they are mothers of younger sons who became kings without being legitimately in line for succession; and these queens were responsible for their sons' attainment of sovereign power.

Personal ambition and intrigue accounts for their success in establishing a fully developed system that served to place the royal crown on their sons' heads, and it was only by this circumstance that they were themselves able to achieve power in their child's realm. What follows is a chronological listing of queen mothers in this category.

1. Aḫatmilku, the wife of Niqmepa, king of Ugarit (fourteenth–thirteenth century BCE), helped her young son Ammistamru II to succeed to the title, although he had older brothers.[1]

2. Puduḫepa, the wife of Hattushili III, king of Hatti (thirteenth century BCE), assisted her husband's seizure of power and thereby ensured that her sun, Tudḫaliya IV, would be king.[2]

3. Tm, the wife of Hayyah, king of Y'dy-Sam'al (ninth century BCE), was behind the accession of her young sons, Kilamuwa, who had an older brother.[3]

4. Sammuramat, the wife of Šamši-Adad V, king of Assyria (ninth–eighth century BCE), helped her son, Adad-nirari III,

---

1. See J. Nougayrol, *PRU IV* 17, pp. 121-22. For her power in the kingdom, see her seal in *PRU III* 16, pp. 197, 150-51. See Lipiński, 'Aḫat-Milki', pp. 79-115; M. Heltzer, *The Internal Organization of the Kingdom of Ugarit* (Wiesbaden: Reichert, 1982), p. 183.

2. See O.R. Gurney, *The Hittites* (Harmondsworth: Penguin, 1954), pp. 9, 36, 37, 140, 176, 199; S.R. Bin-Nun, *The Tawananna in the Hittite Kingdom* (Heidelberg: Carl Winter, 1975), pp. 171-74, 178-83, 203-206; E. Laroche, 'Le Voeu de Puduhepa', *RA* 43 (1949), pp. 55-78.

3. F. Rosenthal, 'Kilamuwa of Y'dy-Sam'al', *ANET*, pp. 654-55; T. Ishida, 'Solomon who is Greater than David: Solomon's Succession in 1 Kings I–II in the Light of the Inscription of Kilamawa King of Y'dy-Sam'al', in J.A. Emerton (ed.), *Congress Volume: Salamanca 1984* (VTSup, 36; Leiden: Brill, 1985), pp. 145-53; F.M. Fales, 'Kilamuwa and the Foreign Kings: Propaganda vs. Power', *WO* 10 (1979), pp. 6-22.

take possession of the kingdom, although he was a younger son without claim to the crown.[1]

5. Naqi'a-Zakûtu, the wife of Sennacherib, king of Assyria (eighth–seventh century BCE), was behind the decision of her husband to choose their younger son, Esarhaddon, as his royal heir, notwithstanding the fact that he had an older brother. After her son's accession, she acquired enormous influence in the realm and was consequently able to intervene in behalf of her grandson, Ashurbanipal, who succeeded as king rather than his older brother, Šamaš-šum-Ukin.[2]

6. Adad-Guppi of Babylon (sixth century BCE) acted as the motive force in setting her son, Nabonidus, on the throne of Babylon—although he was not of royal blood. She herself attained considerable influence in the kingdom.[3]

7. Atossa, the wife of Darius I, king of Persia (sixth–fifth century BCE), was able by virtue of her distinguished lineage to place her son, Xerxes, on the nation's throne, although he had older brothers who preceded him in the line of succession.[4]

---

1.   See W.W. Hallo, 'From Qarqar to Carchemish: Assyria and Israel in the Light of New Discoveries', *BA* 23 (1960), pp. 2, 42; Lewy, 'Nitokris-Naqi'a', pp. 264-65, 278-79; W. Schramm, 'War Semiramis Assyrische Regentin', *Historia* 2 (Wiesbaden: F. Steiner, 1972), pp. 513-21; W. Röllig, 'Semiramis', in *Der kleine Pauly* (Stuttgart: A. Druckenmüller, 1975), V, pp. 94-95; cf. D.D. Luckenbill, *Ancient Records of Assyria and Babylonia* (New York: Greenwood, 1968), I, 260, 231, 264-65, 745.

2.   On Naqi'a Zakûtu and her great influence and deeds in the rule of Sennacherib her husband, and especially in the rule of her son Esarhaddon, see Lewy, 'Nitokris-Naqi'a', pp. 264-86; Ben-Barak, 'Succession to the Throne', pp. 85-100.

3.   See C.J. Gadd, 'The Harran Inscriptions of Nabonidus', *Anatolian Studies* 8 (1958), pp. 35-92; A.L. Oppenheim, 'The Family of Nabonidus', *ANET*, pp. 311-12; D.B. Weisberg, 'Royal Women of the Neo-Babylonian Period', in P. Garelli (ed.), *Le Palais et la Royauté, XIXe RAI* (Paris: Geuthner, 1974), pp. 447-54; D.J. Wiseman, *Nebuchadrezzar and Babylon* (Oxford: Oxford University Press, 1985), pp. 7-12.

4.   See R.G. Kent, *Old Persian: Grammar, Texts, Lexicon* (New Haven: American Oriental Series, 1950), pp. 150 §§3-4; H. Tadmor, 'Autobiographical Apology in the Royal Assyrian Literature', in H. Tadmor and M. Weinfeld (eds.), *History, Historiography and Interpretation: Studies in Biblical and Cuneiform Literatures* (Jerusalem: Magnes, 1983), pp. 56-57; Herodotus, *Hist.* 7.2-3.

IV

The examples set out in the preceding account are evidence of the phenomenon of queen mothers who, by force of their personality and command of power and influence in the kingdom, were able to achieve significant authority and power during the reign of their sons. However, cases such as these were extremely rare, and few women of this station (from among the vast number of queen mothers in the history of ancient Israel and other monarchies of the ancient Near East) ever rose to such heights. No general rule can therefore be inferred from so miniscule a sample. Quite the contrary: these few examples tend rather to demonstrate that the phenomenon was very much out of the ordinary and in no way indicative of the conventional course of events. Additionally, we find that it is only in these isolated instances that two criteria were met: (1) the accession of a younger son who was not by right in line for the throne; and (2) this occurring through the exertions of his mother on his behalf. These circumstances lead us to conclude that, as a rule, the *gᵉbîrâ* or queen mother had no official political status in the kingdom, and the mere fact of her being a queen mother did not bestow upon her any official political status beyond the honor due to her by virtue of her position as a mother. On the other hand, in those cases in which the *gᵉbîrâ* did rise to a position of power in her son's domain, we confront a purely individual occurrence which is the direct consequence of the woman's character, ambition and personal abilities. This highly circumscribed evidence can hardly be taken as testimony of the status and prerogatives of the *gᵉbîrâ*. It points out the historical circumstances in which exceptional women were able to secure the royal succession for their sons, thereby themselves laying claim to a position of power in the realm.

THE QUEEN MOTHER IN THE JUDAEAN ROYAL COURT: MAACAH—A CASE STUDY

Ktziah Spanier

An examination of the biblical records indicates that the queen mother was the most important female in the Judaean royal court.[1] The succession formulae of the kings provide a manifestation of this status. They include the king's age, the duration of his reign, and the name, patronym and/or place of birth of his mother.[2] The queen mother sometimes appears as an important personage within the inner circle of the king's entourage.[3]

Royal marriages often reflected the political, economic and strategic interests of the reigning monarch. The primary wives in the polygamous royal household usually belonged to one of two general groups. They were either natives of Judah, or foreign women. The Judaean women either belonged to the Davidic family or were members of families who represented important political or economic interests within the kingdom.[4] The foreign women usually arrived at the court as a result of diplomatic marriages which involved economic or strategic agreements.[5]

---

1. The term *gᵉbîrâ* is most often used to describe the mother of the king rather than his wife. The office of queen is not acknowledged in the biblical text except in the cases of women who functioned in a foreign sphere. The Queen of Sheba and Esther were the only women to receive the appellation 'queen'.

2. The two notable exceptions are the succession formulae for Jehoram and Ahaz.

3. As in the cases of Bathsheba, Hamutal and Nehushtha, among others.

4. Rehoboam's wife Mahalath was a granddaughter of David. Nehushtha's father, Achbor, was an important personage in the Judaean court in the reign of Jehoiachin.

5. The foreign-born chief wife must have brought with her an entourage which constituted a partisan faction within the court.

The source of each woman's authority was her ancestry, and the extent of her power was determined by the initial terms of her marriage contract and, ultimately, by the agreements which the marriage ratified. The woman whose familial associations provided the most favorable terms for the Judaean king was the one who received the title of chief wife. This designation obviously afforded her a superior position in the court,[1] but, more importantly, it brought about the appointment of her son as the successor to the throne, regardless of his chronological position among the king's progeny.[2] This woman came into her full authority only after the death of her husband and following her son's coronation. As a rule, she retained this position and the privileges commensurate with it for her lifetime, or, if her son predeceased her, for the duration of his reign.[3]

A particularly vivid example of this phenomenon is provided in the textual treatment of Maacah. Two royal wives in the Davidic court are identified by that name.[4] The first is the daughter of Talmai, king of Geshur, who is the wife of David and the mother of Absalom. This woman's namesake, described as the daughter of Absalom, was the wife of Rehoboam (2 Chron. 11.21) and, somehow, the mother of both Abijah and

1. Jezebel provides a good example of this phenomenon. She is the only wife of Ahab to be mentioned in the text. This is despite the fact that Ahab is reported to have fathered as many as seventy sons. Her sphere of influence included the hundreds of prophets who were under her direct supervision, as well as her authority to order the elders of Israel to follow her instructions (1 Kgs 16.31-32; 18.19; 19.1-3; 21.7-16).

2. Note that this was despite the prevalence of the custom and law which required that, in matters of inheritance, the firstborn takes precedence over all his siblings.

3. The office of queen mother or $g^e b\hat{\imath} r\hat{a}$ as it appears in the biblical text, and its equivalent in ancient Near Eastern sources, has received considerable scholarly attention. See G.W. Ahlström, *Aspects of Syncretism in Israelite Religion* (Lund: Gleerup, 1963), pp. 57-88; N.-E. Andreasen, 'The Role of the Queen Mother in Israelite Society', *CBQ* 45 (1983), pp. 179-94; Z. Ben-Barak in this volume; S.R. Bin-Nun, *The Tawananna in the Hittite Kingdom* (Heidelberg: Carl Winter, 1975), pp. 185-97; G. Molin, 'Die Stellung der Gebira im Staate Juda', *TZ* 10 (1954), p. 164.

4. It also appears several times as a place name, as well as male and female personal names. See for example Gen. 22.24; Josh. 13.13; 2 Sam. 10.6; 1 Kgs 2.39; Jer. 40.8; 1 Chron. 2.48; 7.16 among others.

his son, Asa (1 Kgs 15.2, 10; and see below).

Each of the six sons born to David at Hebron is given a different matronym (2 Sam. 3.2-5).[1] Only the first three mothers receive appellatives which indicate their place of origin, and only Maacah has foreign royal ancestry.[2] Ahinoam the Jezreelite was the mother of Amnon, who received the title of David's firstborn.[3] Her place of origin indicates that she was a native of the district of Jezreel. This fertile plain was situated on a juncture of several important primary routes including the Via Maris.[4] The city of Jezreel was an Israelite stronghold, and was evidently one of Saul's principal royal residences. It was there that the Israelite forces were assembled for Saul's last battle against the Philistines (1 Sam. 29.2, 11; 31.1). The strategic importance of Ahinoam's place of origin was, no doubt, a determining factor in David's association with this woman, and the designation of her son as his heir apparent.

Abigail, whose appellative is 'the wife of Nabal', was the mother of Kileab, who was second on the list. She was a native of Carmel, which was within the Calebite area of the Judaean territory south of Hebron. Saul had erected a victory stela there to commemorate his victory over the Amalekites (1 Sam. 15.12). This earned him the respect and loyalty of the local Judahite population.[5] David's marriage to this woman must have brought

1. Since it is highly unlikely that each of the six wives had only one son, the account may be hierarchical rather than chronological.

2. Kileab is never mentioned again in the text, and was therefore not in the subsequent horizontal line of succession, which went from Amnon directly to Absalom and then to Adonijah, who was the fourth in this list. Each of these sons may have been his mother's firstborn, but the order in which they appear does not necessarily follow the rules of primogeniture.

3. See J.D. Levenson and B. Halpern, 'The Political Import of David's Marriages', *JBL* 99.4 (1980), pp. 507-18. This article suggested that David actually possessed Ahinoam, who was the only wife of Saul to be mentioned by name. It is also possible that David took another woman from that district or family, and gave her that name, in order to legitimate his rule.

4. Y. Aharoni, *The Land of the Bible* (London: Burns & Oates, 1967), pp. 21-22, 258.

5. See Nabal's response to David, in which he acknowledges loyalty to Saul, the reigning monarch (1 Sam. 25.10).

with it the pacification and support of the local population in the southern Judaean district which had been loyal to Saul.

David's union with these two women evidently took place in the course of his struggle against Saul. His effort to legitimate his claim to the throne through his union with Saul's daughter, Michal, had failed. His marriages to the namesake of Saul's wife and to the independent Abigail afforded him close associations with powerful elements in economically and strategically import- ant regions at the center of Saul's kingdom, and in the southern Judaean territory which had been controlled by him.

David's marriage to Maacah must have been arranged after he began his rule at Hebron. Having secured control over much of the area which had been under Saul's control, he sought to consolidate his power and to insure the goodwill of Israel's neighbors to the east and north. Maacah is the only one of his wives to receive a foreign royal appellative. In addition to being the daughter of the king of Geshur, her name recalls an ances- tral, probably matriarchal, connection with the district of Maacah. This territory was located to the north and west of the Geshurite kingdom.[1] This marriage looks like part of a compre- hensive treaty agreement between David and Maacah's father, Talmai.

The kingdom of Geshur and the district of Maacah appear together in the territorial description at the time of the con- quest, and were part of the area which is reported unconquered by the Israelites (Josh. 12.5; 13.11). It is situated on the western slopes of the fertile Bashan, its territory extending along the eastern shore of the Sea of Galilee and continuing north following the Jordan River to the Hulah valley. It controlled the eastern sources of the Jordan river and the inland sea of Galilee. The district of Maacah extended to the north and west of Geshur. The climate, soil conditions and geographical position of this area facilitated the development of a flourishing agricultural system, and the establishment of cities which were on the vital

---

1. Cf. the association of Geshur and Maacah in Deut. 3.14 and Josh. 13.11, among others. See also B. Mazar, 'Geshur and Maacah', *JBL* 80 (1961), pp. 16-28, and M. Kochavi, 'The Land of Geshur Project', *IEJ* 39.1 (1989), pp. 1-15.

international trade routes.[1] The cities of Abel-beth-Maacah, Iyyon and Dan were within this territory. They were located along the water sources of the Jordan river, and were later mentioned as storage centers (2 Chron. 17.4). They were also along the principal route to Damascus and points north, and to the coastal cities of Tyre, Sidon and Byblos.

Therefore, David's marriage to Maacah was consistent with the practice of consolidating territorial alliances through familial ties. It provided him with a measure of protection from attacks by his Aramaean neighbors, and also opened up trade routes with the Phoenicians.[2] It was probably at this time that the principal cities in the district of Maacah became part of the Davidic kingdom.[3] Maacah's position in David's court must have been commensurate with these advantages. This may have been an important factor in Absalom's later claim to the throne.

The assassination of Amnon placed Absalom in the primary position as heir apparent to David's throne. The king refused to acknowledge this and, perhaps, threatened to have him killed. Absalom fled to his maternal grandfather's territory, and remained in Geshur for three years (2 Sam. 13.38), before being summoned back to Jerusalem (2 Sam. 14.24). It is likely that Absalom was given a member of the Geshurite royal family as a wife during his sojourn in Geshur. Rehoboam's wife Maacah was probably a descendant of that marriage. Soon after his return, Absalom began to plan his insurrection against his father. It was at Hebron that he obtained the allegiance of all the Israelite tribes with the exception of the Judaeans (2 Sam. 15.10-14).[4] Absalom's death finally put a halt to the bitter civil war which had ensued.[5] This rift foreshadows the later division

1. Aharoni, *Land of the Bible*, pp. 216, 264.

2. Aharoni, *Land of the Bible*, pp. 133, map no. 8.

3. Several years later, the Wise Woman of Abel-beth-Maacah points out to Joab that her city is part of the Israelite territory (2 Sam. 20.18-19).

4. The significance of Hebron should not be overlooked, since it was there that David began his rule and from there that he proceeded to become ruler over all of Israel (2 Sam. 5.1-4).

5. David's lament reflects his need to distance himself from the killing (2 Sam. 15.1-8). It suggests that many of Absalom's supporters later harbored a resentment against David and against his chosen successor, Solomon.

of the united kingdom under Rehoboam.

Only two of Rehoboam's eighteen wives are mentioned by name. His first primary wife was Mahalath, who had several sons. This woman's genealogy indicates that she was a member of the Davidic family. Rehoboam subsequently married Maacah, who is listed as the daughter of Absalom.[1] The Chronicler reports that the king 'loved' Maacah better than all his wives and concubines and, as a consequence, elevated her son Abijah to the throne (2 Chron. 11.18-22). It would seem that Maacah's ancestral connection with Absalom and nominally with his Geshurite mother brought about her elevation to the position of chief wife. Her genealogical association made Abijah an ideal successor, since he was the scion of two important branches within the Davidic family.

Rehoboam, who succeeded to the throne of Judah at a rather late age, was confronted with a rebellion at the inception of his reign. Solomon had expanded Israelite territory and established a commercial empire. His reign marked a long period of relative peace and prosperity. These developments, however, were not without consequence. Textual evidence suggests that in the last years of Solomon's rule there was a considerable amount of unrest within the kingdom. This discontent culminated in a failed assassination attempt which was led by Jeroboam, who had gathered popular support as the leader of the 'House of Joseph'.[2] He is said to have fled to Egypt, where he remained until he received news of Solomon's death (1 Kgs 11.26-40).

Rehoboam, in his position as heir apparent to the throne, had assembled around him a partisan faction of courtiers. A conflict developed between this faction and Solomon's veteran advisors immediately following his accession to the throne (1 Kgs 12.6-8). Solomon's advisors urged Rehoboam to abate some of his father's burdensome decrees. In an effort to assert his indepen-

---

1. It may be assumed that Absalom was Maacah's significant ancestor rather than her biological father. The terms 'daughter' and 'son' were often used in this fashion. Thus, for example, both Abijah and Asa are referred to as the sons of David (1 Kgs 15.3, 11).

2. Jeroboam achieved this position by royal appointment. The 'House of Joseph' evidently included the territories of the Ephraimites and Manassehites.

dence from his father's advisors, Rehoboam refused to heed their counsel. This increased the alienation among the people, who rebelled against his rule under the leadership of Jeroboam. The ensuing struggle ended with the secession of most of the tribes, and the loss of the northern Israelite territory, reducing the area under Judaean control to the traditional tribal boundaries of the Judahites and Benjaminites (1 Kgs 12.12-20). Rehoboam then fortified, armed and equipped cities within his new borders, and sought the support of Yahwistic cultic personnel who came to Jerusalem from their cities in the north (2 Chron. 11.1, 5-17).

It was probably at this juncture that Rehoboam elevated Maacah to the position of chief wife, and declared her son Abijah the heir apparent to the throne, disregarding his chronological placement in the horizontal line of succession to the throne (2 Chron. 11.18-22).[1] Rehoboam's decision to elevate her must have been part of his plan to regain the territory he had lost, and to try to unify the country under his own rule. Maacah's ancestry and familial connections made her a particularly desirable wife. Her association with the kingdom of Geshur and the district of Maacah provided the Judaean king with protection on Judah's eastern border and provided a staging area for pre-emptive attacks along the northern reaches of the expanding Israelite kingdom.[2] In addition, a perceived advantage existed in

---

1. The preference of the firstborn in matters of inheritance and succession is well attested in the Hebrew Bible and in other ancient Near Eastern literatures. Exceptions, however, abound. In Akkadian the term *maru rabu*, 'chief son', is used in reference to the firstborn. In many documents, however, this term took on a legal meaning which was not necessarily synonymous with primogeniture. See RS 14.166, and discussion by Thureau-Dangin, 'Six textes de Ras Shamra', *Syria* 28 (1951), p. 174. Similarly, when Jacob adopts Joseph's two elder sons as his own, he gives Ephraim, who is the younger, the status of firstborn (Gen. 48.18-19). A marriage document from Nuzi includes a clause which provides for the bride's firstborn to become his father's chief heir. The context of this document makes it clear that this marriage was not the husband's first, and that he had already fathered several sons by other women. Cf. HSS, vol. IX, #24.

2. Jereboam's revival of Dan as a cultic center in the traditional district of Maacah may have been motivated by his effort to overcome Maacah's influence in that area (1 Kgs 12.26-30).

her ancestry. Her son Abijah's paternal familial connection was with Solomon, while his maternal association was with Maacah's significant ancestor, Absalom. This was an important element in the king's effort to retain the support of different partisan factions within Judah, and to convince the Israelite tribes to return to Davidic rule.

Abijah died three years after his accession to the throne, and was succeeded by his son Asa. The textual rendering of the familial relationships of Maacah, Abijah and Asa is unclear. Abijah is listed as the father of Asa, and Maacah appears as the mother of both (1 Kgs 15.2, 10; 2 Chron. 11.20; 15.16).[1] The most plausible explanation is that Maacah was the mother of Abijah and upon her son's early death did not yield her official position to Asa's mother, but rather remained in her post during the first years of her grandson's reign. The appellative 'mother of the king' or $g^e b\hat{\imath}r\hat{a}$ was evidently used to describe her official position in the court rather than her actual maternal status in relation to Asa (2 Chron. 15.10-16).[2]

Maacah's position in the Judaean court may be compared to that of the Hittite *tawananna*. The title, derived from the name of the chief wife of King Labarnas, was that of queen mother. She assumed her official position when her son inherited the throne. She held the office of high priestess to the sun goddess of Arinna.[3] Her son died after a short reign and was replaced at the throne by his agnatic brother. The *tawananna* did not yield her position for a period during the following reign. Her stepson finally had her removed from her position after accusing her of abusing her ritual position.[4] Like the *tawananna*, Maacah, in her role as queen mother, was actively involved in

1. It should be noted that the Chronicler's succession formula for Abijah mentions Micaiah, daughter of Uriah of Gibeah, as the king's mother (2 Chron. 13.2). Note that through her patronymic, this woman is associated with Bathsheba's first husband, and that her place of birth connects her to the Saulide capital at Gibeah.

2. J. Bright, *A History of Israel* (Philadelphia: Westminster Press, 1981), p. 240, and Ben-Barak in this volume.

3. Bin-Nun, *The Tawananna*, pp. 185-97.

4. According to the Bible Ahab's wife, Jezebel, also sponsored the cult of the Ashera. The text indicates that she provided maintenance for over 400 priests of that cult (1 Kgs 18.19).

the promulgation of the cult—in her case, the Ashera cult at the Judaean court.[1]

Rehoboam and Abijah had spent most of their rules battling against the northern Israelite kingdom. While supporting the worship of YHWH in Jerusalem, they remained tolerant of other cults. Judaean society continued the pluralistic pattern which had been established in the Solomonic era. At the same time it was steadily losing ground to the larger and more powerful northern kingdom. Asa apparently determined that it was no longer possible for him to maintain his power over the Judaean kingdom, let alone take over more Israelite territory under these conditions. He needed to consolidate his rule and eliminate the pluralistic attitudes which were most evident in the various cult practices. He therefore initiated a series of reforms which were aimed at strengthening the exclusive worship of YHWH in Jerusalem.

Maacah's removal from her position as queen mother, and the ritual destruction of the cult object which she had sponsored, were the climactic events of the promulgation of these reforms (1 Kgs 15.13; 2 Chron. 15.8-19). They served a dual purpose for the young king. He asserted his authority and consolidated his own rule under the banner of the Yahwistic cult. He was thus able to sever his connection with the foreign cult sponsored by the queen mother. Thus he also unseated the political faction which had been in power during the reigns of his predecessors, and which was under the protection of the queen mother.

It was at this point, when Asa was no longer able to rely on Maacah's familial connections in Geshur and the district of Maacah, that he engaged the Aramaean king Ben-Hadad to attack the cities of Abel-beth-Maacah, Iyyon and Dan, which were the northernmost bastions of the Israelite kingdom. Facing the Aramaean threat, the Israelite king Baasha was forced to abandon his fortification work at Ramah, which had effectively placed the border of the Judaean territory under siege (1 Kgs 15.16-21; 2 Chron. 16.1-5). In addition, Asa captured and fortified several Ephraimite strongholds. According to the Chronicler,

1.   S. Ackerman, 'The Queen Mother and the Cult in Ancient Israel', *JBL* 112.3 (1993), pp. 385-401.

he also gained the allegiance of members of the Manassehite and Simeonite tribes (2 Chron. 15.8-9).

It may be concluded that Maacah was a powerful queen mother who wielded a great deal of influence in the Judaean royal court. Her authority probably derived from her ancestry and the contractual arrangements which brought her into the Judaean royal household. Her marriage was part of a comprehensive diplomatic treaty, and included a clause which required that her son become the heir to the throne. The extent of her authority was manifested by the elevation of her cult to official status within the court.

Maacah did not yield her official position following Abijah's death. She accomplished this by redefining her familial relationships, perhaps adopting her grandson, Asa, as her son. In the fifteenth year of his reign, Asa ousted her from office. She was confronted on a ritual occasion and her cult was ceremoniously destroyed: '[Asa] removed Maacah, the mother of Asa the king, from being queen mother, because she had made an obscene image of the Ashera; and Asa cut down her obscene image, crushed it, and burnt it by the Brook Kidron' (2 Chron. 15.16).[1] Her removal was followed by large-scale political and cultic reforms, and by an upsurge in the power and prosperity of Judah.

The power of the queen mother derived from her ancestry as well as from the territorial, commercial and diplomatic connections she represented. Maacah was unique among the queen mothers in that she not only represented the lines of David and Absalom, but had strong foreign connections as well. She wielded considerable authority, as evidenced by the fact that she was able to retain her position as chief wife and queen mother for over thirty years, during the reigns of three Judaean kings. The cult in which she officiated was that of the Ashera, the mother goddess, the divine parallel of her own position as the premier female member in the courts of Abijah and Asa.

1. Translation according to the New King James version.

JEZEBEL RE-VAMPED

Tina Pippin

Southern women in the United States define Jezebel in the following ways:[1] everything negative; wicked; scheming; whore; cheap harlot; either promiscuous or a complete whore; female form of gigolo; the name has seductive connotations; biblical queen; wife of Ahab; gave her husband bad advice; evil and treacherous; two-faced; one who seduces men and leads them to destruction; a woman who gets around; not ashamed; bimbo; I didn't know what it meant until my roommate called me this; someone who is wild, free, and comfortable with her sexuality; uninhibited, some might say slutty; a beautiful name; a Southern belle with a mind and will and sex drive who is damned for not fitting the stereotype of a helpless, frigid woman; Scarlett O'Hara; Bette Davis in the red hoop dress in the 1938 film; condescending term used for African American women in the time of slavery; Gene loves Jezebel; you're a jezebel, a flirty girl, light, flighty, aloof or dirty slut; free spirit, happy, cute, very feminine; always a lady (but not always nice); slinky; powerful; ambitious; calculating; ruthless; eaten by dogs; taking pleasure from material things; self-centered; decorated woman; painted face; Cosmo clothes; sensual; she has been given a 'bad rep' by many scholars and people; she is famous for her badness; vamp, vampire, temptress, femme fatale, siren, witch—a woman who takes or ruins the life of another.

The complex and ambiguous character of Jezebel in the Bible serves as the archetypal bitch–witch–queen in misogynist representations of women. Beginning in 1 Kings 16 through 2 Kings 9

---

1. I conducted an informal survey of college students (ages 18 to 50), Atlanta area artists, and members of both Episcopal and Southern Baptist congregations.

and reappearing again in Rev. 2.20, Jezebel is the contradictory, controlling, carnal foreign woman. The common pronouncement (still widely used in the Southern United States), 'She is a regular Jezebel', underlies the imagining of Jezebel beginning with the Rev. 2.20 passage and has referred to countless women, from political queens—including Mary Tudor, Mary Stuart and Isabella I—to movie queens, such as Bette Davis, Vivien Leigh and Elizabeth Taylor.

A sampling from different biblical commentaries, both older and more recent, corroborates this view of Jezebel as sexually evil and a demon woman: Ahab's 'evils...are laid at her door... she came near to bringing the house of David to extinction'.[1] She totally disregarded Israelite law and custom. To these more common reactions add: 'She was a woman of masculine temperament and swayed her husband at will'... 'Jezebel is the foreign influence that is dangerous and brings destruction'.[2] In

---

1. R.D. Culver, 'Jezebel', in M.C. Tenney (ed.), *The Zondervan Pictorial Encyclopedia* (Grand Rapids: Zondervan, 1975), III, pp. 589-90.

2. H.S. Gehman (ed.), *The New Westminster Dictionary of the Bible* (Philadelphia: Westminster Press, 1970), p. 492. On the masculinity of the Jezebel figure, see P. Morton, *Disfigured Images: The Historical Assault on Afro-American Women* (New York: Greenwood, 1991), p. 153: Black women's history 'has been shaped in the image of Jezebel who deserved what she got because she was other than womanly. And the image of black womanhood as other than womanly has served to confirm black manhood as other than manly, and thus to confirm that the Negro was other and less than fully deserving of racial equality'.

In an early twentieth-century drama (H.M. McDowall, *Jezebel: A Tragedy* [Oxford: Basil Blackwell, 1924]) Jezebel speaks twice her desire to be male: 'Oh, would I were a man that I might go myself with them and face Elijah too' (p. 12); and 'Oh! God! If only I had been a man!' (p. 21). In film representations the jezebel is termed a 'superfemale' as opposed to the more masculine 'superwoman'. The superfemale is 'a woman who, while exceedingly "feminine" and flirtatious, is too ambitious and intelligent for the docile role society has decreed she play. She is uncomfortable, but not uncomfortable enough to rebel completely; her circumstances are too pleasurable' (M. Haskell, *From Reverence to Rape: The Treatment of Women in the Movies* [Chicago: University of Chicago Press, 1987], p. 214). The film image that comes to mind is Bette Davis in her Academy Award-winning role in the 1932 *Jezebel*, in which she plays a Southern woman who schemes and destroys those around her and eventually almost destroys herself. In considering Jezebel, her reputation precedes her, regardless of how narrowly or misogynistically the reputation is presented.

The Woman's Bible of 1895 turns to another dimension of Jezebel: 'Jezebel was a brave, fearless, generous woman, so wholly devoted to her own husband that even wrong seemed justifiable to her, if she could thereby make him happy'.[1] In that respect she seems to have fitted completely the Southern Methodist's ideal of the pattern wife entirely fulfilled in her husband! Jezebel is the equal rival of Elijah; both their deeds of genocide are seen as 'savage'.[2] Cheryl Exum states that Jezebel 'met her death with characteristic audacity: she painted her eyes, adorned her head, and greeted Jehu from her window with a caustic insult'.[3]

the final scene she rides off toward possible vindication. The *Publisher's Weekly* (March 30, 1992) describes this jezebel image of Bette Davis from a recent book on the actress, Elizabeth Fuller's *Me and Jezebel: When Bette Davis Came to Dinner and Stayed*: 'Fuller tells us little more about Jezebel herself than that she eats Carnation Instant Breakfast, reads the *Daily News* and smokes Vantage cigarettes by the carton. Davis's fans won't be surprised by her abrasive and distant manner. But they may tire of hearing the star shrieking, "Kee-ryst!" while smashing out cigarettes wherever she pleases, over and over again' (p. 101; reviewer's name not stated).

Teresa de Lauretis expresses a parallel notion in her feminist critique of Derrida: 'Were I to do so, however, I would earn Derrida's contempt for "those women feminists so derided by Nietzsche", I would put myself in the position of one "who aspires to be like a man", who "seeks to castrate" and "wants a castrated woman"...I shall not do so, therefore. Decency and shame prevent me, though nothing more' (*Technologies of Gender: Essays on Theory, Film and Fiction* [Bloomington: Indiana University Press, 1987], p. 47).

1.   E.B. Dietrick, in E. Cady Stanton (ed.), *The Woman's Bible* (New York: European Publishing Co., 1895), p. 75.

2.   Elijah is 'that much-overestimated "man of God"' (Cady Stanton [ed.], *The Woman's Bible*, p. 75). Ellen Battelle Dietrick adds a contemporary note, calling on the reader 'to imagine why Jezebel is now [1895] dragged forth to "shake her gory locks" as a frightful example to the American women who ask for recognized right to self-government' (p. 75). Are these 'gory locks' also an allusion to Medusa: dread/dreaded/dreadful/dreadlocks?

3.   J.C. Exum, 'Jezebel', in P.J. Achtemeier (ed.), *Harper's Bible Dictionary* (San Francisco: Harper & Row, 1985), p. 489.

I am 're-vamping' the generally accepted view of Jezebel as an evil woman from the biblical to the modern representations of her. Using theories on intertextuality from Bakhtin to Thibault and contemporary film theory, I want to trace the relations between the biblical text and other texts (drama, poetry, film and art). The codes and 'signifying practices' of the presence of Jezebel in a variety of texts have implications for the hermeneutics of gender and sexuality. In other words, the 'trace' of Jezebel is in her adorned face peering through the lattice (representing the face of the goddess Asherah), with the image of her corpse as a vivid reminder of the defeat of the goddess-centered cultures: 'they found no more of her than the skull and the feet and the palms of her hands' (2 Kgs 9.35). The text of the goddess is distorted and placed in only negative terms.

I do not intend to uncover or recover a heroic woman figure from the biblical narrative or to redeem a 'bad' woman of the Bible. I want to deal with the cultural representations and the interactions of readers with the image of Jezebel. A rereading of different texts of Jezebel reveals the complexities of 'that cursed woman' who fought to retain her indigenous culture, and the continuation of the 'curse' for all women who claim autonomy—sexual, religious or political.

Jezebel

The term 'jezebel' has ambiguous definitions: from 'unexalted, unhusbanded; or the brother is prince',[1] or 'where is the prince?',[2] to meaning '*chaste* as does the common European name Agnes—quite inappropriate'.[3] The term 'jezebel' means the monstrous female—loose and let loose, the loose woman.[4] Why

1. Gehman, *New Westminster Dictionary*, p. 492.
2. Exum, 'Jezebel', p. 489. E.B. Johnston ('Jezebel', in G.W. Bromiley [ed.], *The International Standard Bible Encyclopedia* [Grand Rapids: Eerdmans, 1982], p. 1057) finds a wordplay in Jezebel's name: *zebel* is made a pun in 2 Kgs 9.37 with the word 'dung' (*dōmen*).
3. Culver, 'Jezebel', p. 589.
4. On the double monster in the mother and daughter relationship see J. Gallop, 'The Monster in the Mirror: The Feminist Critic's Psychoanalysis', in R. Feldstein and J. Root (eds.), *Feminism and Psychoanalysis* (Ithaca, NY: Cornell University Press, 1989), pp. 13-24. She finds the mother–daughter

is the monster, here the jezebel, so fascinating? What is the 'seduction', the draw into the dangerous darkness where the 'monster' lurks?

As the 'curse on Ham' was used as a justification for slavery of Africans, so 'jezebel' was the designation of the sexually dangerous African American slave woman. The juxtaposition of the images of the mammy and the jezebel served as an apologetic for the exploitation of the female slave. Deborah White[1] describes these divisions in terms of the madonna–whore: the mammy is asexual, loving, warm, maternal, dark-skinned, big, older; she wears formless clothes and covers her hair with a kerchief; she is loyal, religious and pious. The jezebel is sexual, provocative, young, with changing skin color; she is comely,

relationship reflected in groups of women: 'One monster cannot be separated from the other'. I think this idea has interesting implications for the Jezebel–Athaliah connection; is the narrator of 1–2 Kings presenting us with a pair of monsters?

1.　D.G. White, *Ar'n't I a Woman? Female Slaves in the Plantation South* (New York: Norton, 1985). See ch. 1, 'Jezebel and Mammy: The Mythology of Female Slavery'. On p. 46 White states: 'Southerners, therefore, were hardly of one mind concerning African-American women. Jezebel was an image as troubling as it was convenient and utilitarian... On the one hand there was the woman obsessed with matters of the flesh, on the other was the asexual woman. One was carnal, the other maternal. One was at heart a slut, the other was deeply religious'.

Patricia Morton (*Disfigured Images*, p. 10) follows White's argument: 'by labeling the female slave as a Jezebel, the master's sexual abuse was justified by presenting her as a woman who deserved what she got...by labeling the slave woman as a sexual animal—not a real woman at all'. Morton adds (p. 33) that the jezebel was scapegoated: 'still cast as Jezebel, the black woman was assigned responsibility for the supposed sins of black as well as white men'. See also V. Bynum, *Unruly Women: The Politics of Social and Sexual Control in the Old South* (Chapel Hill: University of North Carolina Press, 1992), pp. 35-39. In discussing the Jezebel in Rev. 2, Elisabeth Schüssler Fiorenza rightly draws on the Southern tradition: 'Like the historical queen Jezebel, she has served in Western thought as the archetype of the sexually dangerous woman. During the time of slavery, for instance, the image of Jezebel, the whore, became the controlling image of black womanhood in white, elite, male propaganda' (*Revelation: Vision of a Just World* [Proclamation Commentaries; Minneapolis: Fortress Press, 1991], p. 135). There is no solid evidence of the extent to which the jezebel title was used to describe these women.

promiscuous, provocatively dressed; a breeder, rebellious, a whore.

The white masters created these images to control and dominate the female slave. The mammy represents the desire for a positive image for African Americans. The jezebel was an excuse for masters to justify their own adolescent and later adulterous behavior. White women blamed the jezebels in order to deny the rape and oppression of slave women. The jezebel acted out of the constraints of race and gender. The African cultural norms of women having children before marriage and of exposing more of their bodies in the field as they work were misunderstood by whites. The whole system was based on the white male, which left white women finding ways to discredit the slave women.

So jezebel is not an abstract sign but a real physical presence, for antebellum culture and also in popular culture in the United States. Can one get outside the popular culture meaning of Jezebel?

Re-Vamped

Recent biblical scholarship reveals the ambiguity of the character Jezebel and the religious or political rather than sexual intention of her painted face in the murder scene. But the term 'jezebel' has a distinct social meaning that is biblical (in Hosea; Ezek. 16; the 'strange woman' of Proverbs; the false prophetess of Rev. 2). Whoring and fornication is associated with strange religion and strange culture. Claudia Camp remarks that in the story of Naboth's vineyard, the Deuteronomic Historian may have blamed Jezebel for Ahab's deed: 'shifting of the blame to the foreign woman forms part of that era's polemic on the dangers of intermarriage'.[1] The jezebel schemes with both her mind and

---

1. C.V. Camp, '1 and 2 Kings', in C.A. Newsom and S.H. Ringe (eds.), *The Women's Bible Commentary* (Louisville, KY: Westminster Press/John Knox, 1992), p. 104. Camp is following Alexander Rofé on this point. Peter Ackroyd states that 'Jezebel becomes a type; into her figure is projected in detail the hostility to what is believed to be alien practice' (P.R. Ackroyd, 'Goddesses, Women and Jezebel', in A. Cameron and A. Kuhrt [eds.], *Images of Women in Antiquity* [Detroit: Wayne State University Press, 1983], p. 256). E. Boulding (*The Underside of History: A View of Women through Time*

body. She has 'been around'—in foreign territory (Tyre; Africa), and she brings danger with her. Therefore, her body must be destroyed. Look closely at the remains: skull; feet; palms of her hands (2 Kgs 9.35).

Tom Robbins recreates a modern Jezebel/Salome in his book *Skinny Legs and All* and questions the tradition handed down in Western culture. The main character, Ellen Cherry, thinks to herself:

> What had Queen Jezebel done to earn the distinction as our all-time treacherous slut: In the Bitch Hall of Fame, Jezebel had a room of her own; nay, an entire wing. For fixing her hair and applying makeup? Was it implied that she went to the window to *flirt* with the rebel warrior? And if so, was that so wicked that it should wreck her reputation for three thousand years? The trimillennial lash bat?
>
> As Ellen Cherry walked the rain-rippled pavement of Seattle, bumpershooting from restaurant to restaurant in search of a job, she bore upon her back the weight of a skull, a pair of feet, and the palms of two hands. The nails of the feet were lacquered vermilion, a pretty ribbon fluttered from a lacuna in the skull. And she would wonder as she walked, 'What is the Bible trying to tell us?'
>
> That Satan is a hairdresser?
>
> That Elizabeth Arden ought to be fed to the poodles?[1]

Mieke Bal points to the Jezebel narrative as an 'ideo-story'; that is, a story taken out of context. Bal gives the example of a

[Newbury Park: SAGE Publications, rev. edn, 1992], p. 209) adds: 'Foreign women were dangerous role models for Israelite women, with their political ways and priestess notions. We shall see the same scenario played out again 1,000 years later, in the Christian church fathers' distrust of pagan women and their priestess tradition. The sexual seduction aspect of this struggle is, I suspect, a male rationalization'.

1.   T. Robbins, *Skinny Legs and All* (New York: Bantam Press, 1990), p. 33. Robbins's protagonist Ellen Cherry considers Jezebel her 'doppelgänger'. He describes her search for the biblical Jezebel: 'she had procured a Bible and gone searching for the lurid details of Jezebel's debauchery. From Sunday school, she had a hazy picture of a thoroughly immoral harlot who costumed herself like a rock 'n' roll vamp, but she couldn't recall a single biographical fact. Imagine her surprise when the Old Testament Book of Kings informed her that Jezebel was a royal—and faithful—wife' (*Skinny Legs*, p. 32).

tabloid story, 'Devilish Ladies who Everybody Loves to Hate', which includes 'Lilith, Jezebel, Delilah, and...Sappho... The combination of the four figures is a function of the principle of coherent reading... Both within and between the four stories, contradictions and problems are repressed'.[1] That Delilah is not a liar or that Jezebel is not an adulteress gets lost in the ideo-story. The reproduction of popular mythology is a priority in the reading process.

This reading of Jezebel in predominantly sexual terms is socially grounded, a social semiotics which draws on Bakhtin's heteroglossia. The textual voices on Jezebel are many; they overlap, origins unknown (except the general patriarchal culture which is women's context). Paul Thibault promotes a 'neomaterialist social semiotic', uniting theory and practice into the study of semiotics.[2] Thibault is involved in asking ethical questions of theory, asking to what extent intertextual theorizing challenges existing hegemonic relations. In other words, intertextuality is grounded in a social context or community with certain dominant assumptions about how the world operates. The sign 'jezebel' is imbedded in social relationships and in a range of 'texts'. As John Frow states,

1. M. Bal, *Death and Dissymmetry: The Politics of Coherence in the Book of Judges* (Chicago: Chicago University Press, 1988), p. 11.

2. P. Thibault (*Social Semiotics as Praxis* [Minneapolis: University of Minnesota Press, 1991]) defines social semiotics as a theory that moves semiotics 'beyond its self-identification with many of the foundational ideological assumptions of Western culture' (p. 3). Social semiotics is connected with social heteroglossia as follows: 'The systems of voices in the social semiotic, including potentially unvoiced meanings and practices, comprise the relations of social heteroglossia through which relations of alliance, consensus, opposition, conflict, and co-optation among voices are positioned and articulated in specific texts and intertextual formations' (p. 25). T.E. Morgan ('Is there an Intertext in this Text? Literary and Interdisciplinary Approaches to Intertextuality', *American Journal of Semiotics* 3.4 [1985], p. 8) relates this point: 'Indeed, *culture* itself, or the collection of signifying practices in a society, *is radically intertextual*'. On the materiality of language see J. Kristeva, *Revolution in Poetic Language* (trans. M. Waller; New York: Columbia University Press, 1975).

> Texts are therefore not structures of presence by traces and trac-
> ings of otherness. They are shaped by the repetition and the
> transformation of other textual structures.[1]

Jezebel is not an image but *images*, a plural form.

The whoring Jezebel is of course the most seductive image. In discussing seduction and prostitution in Flaubert, Ross Chambers writes:

> In the homosocial world, literature must pose, in order to gain
> acceptance, as a figure of powerlessness, helpless or charming: a
> child or a woman...Literature, in short, must camp it up.[2]

Thus, the passage in Revelation 2 stands out: Jezebel refuses to repent and continues to beguile and fornicate. 'Beware, I am throwing her on a bed, and those who commit adultery with her I am throwing into great distress, unless they repent of her doings; and I will strike her children dead' (Rev. 2.22-23). And the Jezebel in 2 Kings 9 paints her face and fixes her hair boldly to face death and fulfillment of the prophecy of the enemy. What would the apocalyptic Jezebel say to the narrator John in reply? What would Queen Jezebel say to the narrator of her life story? Are there only traces, skull and feet and palms of the hands and dead children?

An outside Jezebel has invaded the text, a Jezebel who would proclaim (as did Ellen Cherry's cynical mother Patsy in *Skinny Legs and All*), 'Of the Seven Deadly Sins, lust is definitely the pick of the litter'.[3] But the biblical Jezebel does not seek or find sexual pleasure. Looking out from the lattice, Jezebel is framed. She is also imprisoned. In the biblical text, as well as in early twentieth-century 'devotional fiction', Jezebel is a prisoner in her own palace; she never leaves or confronts men (like Elijah) on the outside. Jezebel remains inside; acting behind the lattice. All attempts to colonize her fail.

The colonial nature of the jezebel text and the oppression of the jezebel voice is apparent in the sadistic retelling of her death.

1. J. Frow, 'Intertextuality and Ontology', in M. Worton and J. Still (eds.), *Intertextuality: Theories and Practices* (Manchester: Manchester University Press, 1990), p. 45.
2. R. Chambers, 'Alter Ego: Intertextuality, Irony and the Politics of Reading', in Worton and Still (eds.), *Intertextuality*, p. 155.
3. Robbins, *Skinny Legs and All*, p. 106.

In her book on the effects of imperialism on the reading process, Laura Donaldson calls for a 'materialist-feminist semiotics' that 'requires that we not only recognize how micrologies of power keep certain information systems in place while simultaneously suppressing others but also resist the temptation of an unmediated politics of meaning'.[1] The discourse on Jezebel is guided through the colonial mind. The image of the Other, the foreign, the dangerous and thereby seductive woman is used against medieval women and slave women and Southern women who break with tradition. Tom Robbins attempt to decolonize Jezebel:

> Jezebel. Jezebel. Painted Queen of Israel. I am praising thee, O Queen of Israel. Whore of the Golden Calf. Strumpet of Baal. Jezebel. Slut of Samaria. Our queen whom the dogs are eating. The watercourse of the Jews is flowing through thee. Jezebel. My Queen. Whose daughter is ruling in Jerusalem. From whose womb is pouring the House of David. Mmm. Jezebel. Priestess of Fornication. Mmm. Queen of Spades. Queen of Tarts. O Jezebel, you are my queen, I exalt thee and praise thy sandals.[2]

The image of Jezebel is difficult to identify iconographically; her portrait and scenes of her life are rare.[3] Still, she is imaged as the temptress. Both men and women are drawn to her. Even though 2 Kgs 9.37 pronounces that 'no one can say, This is Jezebel', the irony is that 'This is Jezebel' is exactly what people have said ever since this Deuteronomic proverb. Even though in popular Western culture to be called a jezebel is not a compliment, there is a strange connection to/disconnection from Jezebel. Women read themselves as Jezebel, as having the 'jezebel spirit'.[4] Are we happy or satisfied when Jezebel is splattered and trampled by horses and eaten by dogs? Are we

---

1. L.E. Donaldson, *Decolonizing Feminism: Race, Gender and Empire Building* (Chapel Hill: University of North Carolina Press, 1992), pp. 120-21.

2. Robbins, *Skinny Legs and All*, p. 348.

3. The Index of Christian Art at Princeton University lists about twenty representations of Jezebel up to 1400 CE. Of these there are approximately ten portraits; the rest are from three scenes of her life.

4. An older woman student of mine recently commented that Jezebel is that (or any!) evil woman who steals husbands. Then she added with a wink, 'There's a part of Jezebel in me'.

happy when Rhett Butler walks away?[1] What have we done with the story of Jezebel? Is her story continually recolonized, reopened, the brief scenes of her life re-enacted and reinscribed?

---

1.   The obsession with this *Gone with the Wind* figure of Scarlett prompted a second novel and a made-for-TV movie. At the tryouts for the role of Scarlett in Atlanta recently, after much deliberation, the part was not filled.

Part V
FEMALE, FEMALENESS/PROPHETS, PROPHECY

Toward a 'Female' Reading of the Elijah Cycle: Ideology and Gender in the Interpretation of 1 Kings 17-19, 21 and 2 Kings 1-2.18

Jan Tarlin

From the perspectives of orthodox Jewish and Christian theologies, the entire corpus of Elijah texts in the books of Kings (1 Kgs 17–19, 21 and 2 Kgs 1–2.18) can, quite convincingly, be read as a manifesto of patriarchal Yahwism, with the theophany at Horeb constituting a high point of male bonding between the prophet and his God. Yet, read from another vantage point, the text suggests a way of contesting that patriarchal interpretation. To show how I have arrived at this alternative reading, and to clarify the conflict it enters into with more standard readings of these texts, I must begin with a discussion of the way ideology and gender converge in the act of reading.

The French Marxist philosopher Louis Althusser has written that 'all ideology has the function (which defines it) of constituting concrete individuals as subjects'.[1] Ideology is thus the set of processes by which a social order attempts to shape the identities of individuals and groups in ways accommodated to the smooth functioning of that order. Ideological forces are at work both within the texts we read and within our activity as readers.

According to the semiotician and film theorist Kaja Silverman, texts act as verbal mirrors[2] in which readers perceive a subjectivity, a structure of identity, formed and promoted by a specific social ideology. That ideology seeks to persuade the

1. L. Althusser, *Lenin and Philosophy* (London: Monthly Review Press, 1971), p. 171.
2. K. Silverman, *The Subject of Semiotics* (New York: Oxford University Press, 1983); *The Acoustic Mirror: The Female Voice in Psychoanalysis and Cinema* (Bloomington: Indiana University Press, 1988).

reader that identity, acceptability and, indeed, existence as a self
are dependent upon identifying with the image in the mirror.
The ideology of our own society shapes the conventions we
have been taught to read with. These conventions tell us what
to look for in the mirror and how to respond to what we see
there; they tell us what features of subjectivity are most
important, which qualities of those features should be
accentuated and which should be disguised or altered.

Both the ideology that has structured the image presented by
the textual mirror and the ideology that has taught a given
reader how to look at and respond to that image contain, like all
human artifacts, some degree of internal contradiction. Similarly
the relation between these two ideologies may contain greater
or lesser degrees of conflict, but it is never entirely conflict-free.
Thus, what the textual mirror can make of us—the reconstitu-
tion of our subjectivity in the process of reading—is bound up
with what we make of the flaws that emerge as we contemplate
its surface.

The subjectivity that emerges from this intricately negotiated
encounter is, I suggest, the foundation upon which are built the
form and meaning that the reader ultimately attributes to the
text. In the work of interpretation, the human subject is constructed by ideological systems even as it serves as the locus in
which those systems are elaborated and restructured. But what
draws our gaze into the textual mirror in the first place? What is
the hook on which ideology attempts to hang the subjectivity in
which it would clothe us?

That hook is actually a gap. Following the theories of the late
French psychoanalyst Jacques Lacan, Kaja Silverman writes:

> [L]ack of being is the irreducible condition of [human] subjec-
> tivity. In acceding to language, the subject forfeits all existential
> reality, and forgoes any future possibility of 'wholeness'. If we
> were in possession of an instrument that would permit us to
> penetrate deep into the innermost recesses of the human psyche,
> we would find not identity, but a void.[1]

The defining characteristic of our humanity—the fact that our
perception of ourselves and our world is mediated, indeed

---

1. K. Silverman, *Male Subjectivity at the Margins* (New York: Routledge,
1992), p. 4.

structured, by language—cuts us off absolutely and permanently from any sort of direct experience of pure being. This separation we perceive as a lack or void at our very core.

We go to the textual mirror, then, in hopes of seeing something to identify with that will fill or at least clothe the void that enculturation has left where our being should be. Gender is one of the primary discourses by which the subjectivities that ideologies offer us for this purpose are positioned in relation to that void. Silverman defines 'male' discourse as a strategy for denying the central lack around which human subjectivity is built by claiming for the 'male' subject a delusionary wholeness, coherence, power and solidity. This delusion is shored up by projecting lack, inconsistency, vulnerability and instability onto an other constructed by that process of projection: the 'female'.[1]

I have placed the words 'male' and 'female' in quotation marks throughout this essay to emphasize their status as constructs of discourse rather than biological realities. Silverman argues that although Western culture encourages the identification of 'male' discourse with biological masculinity and privileges individuals in whom that identification is embodied, both the link between discursive gender and biological sex and the privileging of 'male'-gendered masculine individuals over all others are highly unstable ideological formations and can be radically restructured. The Elijah texts from the books of Kings can be read so as to stimulate just such a restructuring. To do so, however, is to read against the weight of scholarly tradition.

In fact, simply to read the full corpus of Elijah texts as a meaningfully related ensemble is to make a major break with previous scholarship. Virtually all previous scholarly treatments of 1 Kings 17–19, 21 and 2 Kings 1–2.18 either break these texts down into a plethora of originally unrelated raw materials or focus on very narrow slices of the Masoretic Text, thought to exhibit the quality of literary unity in exemplary fashion. There is no study that elaborates a consecutive reading of the texts as they stand in the books of Kings.[2] I suggest that these

---

1. Silverman, *Mirror*, pp. 1-41.
2. A possible exception is M. Buber, *The Prophetic Faith* (New York: Macmillan, 1949), p. 77 and *passim*. Buber's comments, however, are scattered hints that do not add up to a fully articulated reading.

strategies of atomization and concentration have been applied to the Elijah texts in the service of critical methodologies whose fundamental aim is to locate a 'male' subjectivity in the textual mirror for the critic to identify with.

Source, historical, form, canonical and rhetorical criticism can each be seen as a means of focusing on the reflection of a particular kind of 'male' figure in the text. These figures are, respectively: the redactor who embodies the social authority of tradition, the solid body of history on which the text is founded, the historical consciousness that produces ordered knowledge from texts of diverse date and genre, the Holy Spirit whose inspiration gives the canon its coherence, and the author whose consummate artistry gives the text aesthetic unity. The construction of these authoritative interpretations, then, takes place in accord with the same ideological principles that govern the establishment of authority and privilege in our culture at large: identification with a 'male' subjectivity and the repression of the 'female'. The Elijah texts must be dismembered or excerpted for critical examination in order that the discernment of the 'male' figure which is the goal of that examination may proceed unimpeded by any obstructive or distracting 'female' material.[1]

It is impossible, therefore, for all the Elijah texts in 1 and 2 Kings to be read in meaningful relation to each other by scholars whose reading practice is determined by identification with male subjectivity because, taken together, these texts do not yield easily to masculinization. When read consecutively, these texts refuse to play by the rules of orderly 'male' development of

---

1.   Examples of these strategies may be found in E. Sellin and G. Fohrer, *Introduction to the Old Testament* (Nashville: Abingdon Press, 1968), pp. 232-37, and O. Eissfeldt, *The Old Testament: An Introduction* (New York: Harper & Row, 1965), pp. 290-93, representing source criticism; J.M. Miller and J.H. Hayes, *A History of Ancient Israel and Judah* (Philadelphia: Westminster Press, 1986), pp. 252-55, representing historical reconstruction; B.O. Long, *1 Kings—With an Introduction to Historical Literature* (FOTL, 9; Grand Rapids: Eerdmans, 1984), especially pp. 174-77 and 223-30, representing form criticism; B.S. Childs, 'On Reading the Elijah Narratives', *Int* 34 (1980), pp. 128-37, representing canonical criticism; and A.J. Hauser and R. Gregory, *From Carmel to Horeb: Elijah in Crisis* (JSOTSup, 85; Sheffield: Almond Press, 1990) representing rhetorical criticism.

narrative, character and style: time is fluid, character unstable, discourse ambiguous. No 'male' figure appears in the textual mirror capable of taming this mass of 'female' unruliness. The only way of reading the full corpus of Elijah texts as a meaningful entity would be to evoke and identify with a 'female' figure in the textual mirror: not a common scholarly practice in a culture where truth, power and respectability are 'male' attributes.

As I noted at the outset, my reading of the Elijah texts does not just run counter to the centrifugal treatment of these texts by modern biblical scholarship; it also differs from the centripetal reading of these materials put forward by the Jewish and Christian theological traditions. Jewish and Christian exegesis links 1 Kings 17–19, 21 and 2 Kings 1–2.18 with each other through the encompassing medium of the narrative of the books of Kings. Within that narrative, the Elijah texts are read as a cycle of legends about the temporary triumph of Yahweh and Elijah over the forces of foreign idolatry and Israelite apostasy. My reading treats these Elijah texts as a book of fragments within the larger corpus of 1 and 2 Kings: fragments related to each other both by a common subject matter and by common literary strategies of contradiction and ambiguity that undermine any possibility of literary or theological closure. My reading, then, by concentrating on 'female' aspects of the Elijah texts—fragmentation, contradiction, ambiguity, lack of closure—subverts not only the theological and scholarly tradition, but my own subjectivity to the degree that it has been shaped by ideological pressures to assume a 'male' form suitable to my masculine anatomy. I have developed a close reading of 1 Kings 17–19, 21 and 2 Kings 1–2.18 focused on three issues: first, narrative structure; secondly, the texts' explicit concern with the power of language; and thirdly, the specific functioning of the texts' own language in an exemplary passage, 1 Kgs 19.1-18, the narrative of Elijah's flight to Horeb and the theophany on the mountain. In the space of a short essay, it will be necessary to present the results of my intricate engagement with this textual mirror in summary form. Even in summary form, however, these results can further illumine the convergence of ideology and gender in my reading of the Elijah texts.

I will begin the condensed presentation of my reading by

summarizing my view of the narrative structure of the Elijah texts. Martin Buber has observed that the whole Elijah cycle has 'to do with going, wandering'.[1] If one breaks with the 'male' assumption that narrative is a linear movement to a definitive culmination, this wandering can be read as the manifestation of a narrative structure that resists any movement toward closure, centering or stability. This inconsistent, unstable, nonlinear 'female' narrative makes no pretensions to unity, wholeness or completion, but rather exposes itself as a tissue of ambiguities and conflicts.

The circuitous paths of the narrative and its hero are shaped by the struggles between the discourses of the characters (among whom I include both Yahweh and the narrator) for the definition of power relationships, the assertion of individual identity and the control of the flow of events. None of these discourses is capable of coercing the others into subordination or synthesis. Meaning emerges from this narrative not at the culmination of a linear drive toward totalization but in the gaps and fissures opened up by unresolved conflict.

Elijah appears out of nowhere and disappears into the sky; between his appearance and his disappearance both Elijah and the narrative that surrounds him are in constant motion. Elijah moves through a series of geographical and social locations which may be characterized as marginal, liminal or both; yet his influence is felt at the very centers of spiritual and political power in the northern kingdom. Nor is Elijah's identity any more fixed than his location in geographical and social space. Burke O. Long observes that 'as Elijah's lineage is only suggested mysteriously, so his power is only hinted at darkly'.[2] Long's remark refers specifically to Elijah's first appearance in 1 Kgs 17.1, but the impression it describes continues throughout the Elijah cycle. The narrative of the Elijah cycle is structured as the labyrinthine journey of a moving target.

Thus, Elijah is not only denied any fixed location, stable identity, clear mission or assured power: he is even denied the final closure of death. However, the twists and turns of the Elijah cycle's narrative structure destabilize more than just the

---

1. Buber, *Prophetic Faith*, p. 77.
2. Long, *1 Kings*, p. 179.

cycle's central character. The royal power and prerogatives of Ahab, Jezebel and Ahaziah are undermined. Baal's claim to deity and his prophets' authority and power are overturned. The power of the voice that narrates the Elijah cycle to shape the story it tells is challenged and shaken. Even the intentions of Yahweh are deflected and reoriented between enunciation and fulfillment. Read as a 'female' narrative, the Elijah cycle is structured precisely to undermine any emergent center of discursive authority within the text.

The next step in my reading is to examine what happens when the narrative structure I have described articulates an explicit meditation on the power of language: a meditation concentrated on the relationship of the word of Elijah to the word of Yahweh. In the texts leading up to 1 Kgs 19.9-18, Elijah speaks an unbending 'male' claim to authority and potency. Elijah's word is the penetrating fire which can dry up the rain and the dew (1 Kgs 17.1), the disempowering blow which can bring low his royal or religious rivals (1 Kgs 18.36), the sword which can kill those whom the prophet regards as Yahweh's enemies and his own (1 Kgs 18.40). Precisely because Elijah's word can drain fertility, power and life from others, it seems to absorb those qualities into itself, thereby becoming the embodiment of that which its victims lack. The word of Elijah signifies both the price that must be paid to establish the covenant of Yahweh as the prophet understands it and the power which enables and feeds off the exaction of that price. When Elijah speaks he is attempting to establish power relations in which he and his God occupy positions of patriarchal dominance.

At first, the word of Yahweh seems to constitute a 'female' discourse of gratuitous inconsistency. Yahweh does not initially speak as a patriarch, rewarding those who have paid the price of submission to him and punishing those who have not. Yahweh lets the spring which nourishes the zealous Yahwist Elijah dry up (1 Kgs 17.7), but performs life-giving miracles for people totally outside the Yahwistic covenant: the widow of Zarephath and her son (1 Kgs 17.10-24). The rain returns to the Northern Kingdom not because Ahab, Jezebel and their subjects have become obedient to Yahweh but simply because Yahweh has decided that it is time to send rain—even on a nation that is still in a state of rebellion against the covenant (1 Kgs 18.1).

Appearances are deceptive, however, for although the word of Yahweh is more than 'male', it is not 'female'. From the first of the Elijah texts on, there is an unspoken complicity between the discourse of Yahweh and the discourse of Elijah. Yahweh sustains the man who has spoken drought on the Northern Kingdom. Yahweh maintains an ambiguous silence as Elijah's word instigates the extermination of the prophets of Baal. During the encounter at Horeb, Yahweh's unspoken complicity in 'male' discourse is spoken for the first time.

The final step in my reading is a close look at the way language operates in the description of the theophany at Horeb and the events leading up to it (1 Kgs 19.1-18). Elijah arrives at Horeb having recently suffered two deeply unsettling challenges to the power and potency of his discourse. First, Jezebel, the Baal-worshipping Phoenician queen of Ahab, king of Israel, vows in the name of her gods to kill Elijah in revenge for his massacre of her prophets of Baal (1 Kgs 19.2); the oath is similar in kind to the oath in the name of Yahweh by which Elijah brought drought on Israel. Women are not supposed to wield 'male' discourse in this way! Elijah flees in fear before this uncanny phenomenon.

As a fugitive, alone in the desert, Elijah tries to reassert the power of his word. In a display of suicidal bravado, Elijah prays to Yahweh for his own death (1 Kgs 19.47). Yahweh thwarts Elijah's word by sending an angel to force the prophet to eat and drink, thereby renewing his life. It is at this point that Elijah decides to go to Mount Horeb.

Elijah's reasons for coming to Yahweh's most sacred ground are unclear at first. He certainly does not state his business like a supplicant. In response to Yahweh's מה לך פה ('What is here that concerns you?'), Elijah adopts a tone which, though self-pitying, is basically boastful (19.9-10). Elijah says that he 'has surely been zealous for Yahweh', behind which may be read a not-so-veiled suggestion that he has, indeed, been more zealous *than* Yahweh. After all, Yahweh's word of life looks like pretty weak stuff next to the prophet's word of destruction. Elijah further declares (by implication of course) that he is a very important person. Elijah is the only zealous spokesperson for

Yahweh left in Israel; yet his activities are so important that the Israelites (*en masse* it would seem) seek his life. The prophet begins to sound rather as if he has come to challenge Yahweh on the deity's home turf. Having had his word turned against him by Jezebel and thwarted by the angel, Elijah seems to have come to Horeb to undertake the final test of his word against the ultimate antagonist.

At this point the discourse of the text's narrator merges with the 'female' facet of Yahweh's discourse to oppose Elijah's 'male' challenge. In 19.11-12 Yahweh's self-manifestation is inscribed in a passage of exposition constructed around a series of participle verb forms that suspends any attempt on the part of the narrator at wholeness, completion, consistency or clarity:

> Yahweh passing by. And a great and strong wind breaking the mountains and shattering the cliffs before Yahweh—not in the wind is Yahweh. And after the wind, an earthquake—not in the earthquake is Yahweh. And after the earthquake, a fire—not in the fire is Yahweh.

This passage culminates in the most remarkable expression of 'female' discourse in any of the Elijah texts: 'and after the fire קול דממה דקה'. The phrase I have left in the Hebrew is untranslatable because it has no fixed meaning in its original language. Translations as various as the RSV's 'still small voice', 'roaring thunderous voice',[1] 'the sound of utmost silence'[2] and 'a thin petrifying sound'[3] are all equally plausible.

Elijah, however, stands his ground and refuses to be engulfed by this wave of 'female' indeterminacy. In 19.14 the prophet repeats his arrogant, self-pitying challenge from 19.10 verbatim. Elijah and Yahweh stand word to word in a stalemate.

The stalemate is broken from the side of the deity: Yahweh speaks the word of Elijah! Yahweh pronounces a death sentence against all Baal worshippers in Israel. In order to beat Elijah at his own game, Yahweh has swallowed and incorporated the 'male' word with which the deity had previously

---

1. J. Lust, 'A Gentle Breeze or a Roaring Thunderous Sound?', *VT* 25 (1975), p. 113.

2. S. Terrien, *The Elusive Presence: Toward a New Biblical Theology* (Religious Perspectives, 26; New York: Harper & Row, 1978), p. 232.

3. F.A.H. de Boer, cited in Long, *1 Kings*, p. 199.

maintained a silent, distanced complicity. From here on there is absolutely no question of Yahweh's word being 'female'. But if Yahweh's discourse is not 'female' neither is it 'male'. From here on in the Elijah texts, the divine word becomes an unsteady mix of doom and salvation, strength and weakness, 'male' and 'female'. What 1 Kgs 19.9-18 reveals when read in this way is the impossibility of maintaining a purely 'male' or purely 'female' subjectivity—even, or especially, for God.

My reading began as an exercise in what Silverman calls 'the feminization of the male subject':[1] focusing on a 'female' image in a textual mirror where previously only 'male' ones had been discerned, identifying my own male subjectivity, constructed at the behest of my culture, with the newly discovered image in the mirror. Yet such an exercise in 'female' reading pushes beyond the limits of the categories 'male' and 'female'. When a text that has traditionally been read as patriarchal propaganda reveals the impossibility of constructing its own 'male' subjectivity or the subjectivity of its 'female' other in pure form, when a 'male' scholar discovers that he can produce a 'female' reading, then the dualistic Western gender system collapses. At that point we can glimpse in the flawed textual mirror of the Elijah cycle forms of subjectivity that humanity has dreamt of since these texts were written but which ideological pressures on our scholarly language still deny us the words to name.

---

1. Silverman, *Mirror*, p. 149.

THE GREAT WOMAN OF SHUNEM AND THE MAN OF GOD: A DUAL INTERPRETATION OF 2 KINGS 4.8-37

Fokkelien van Dijk-Hemmes

In the summer of 1988 I attended the annual conference of the International Society of Biblical Literature in Sheffield. For the first time in such a conference, considerable attention was paid to the results of feminist research in biblical studies. The items discussed within this framework varied from 'Women, Gender Roles and the Household Economy of Early Israel' to 'the Implications of the Text of Esther for African Women's Struggle for Liberation in South Africa'. For the first time, and apart from being nervous about my own presentation, I felt at ease during an SBL conference. On the last evening I went, feeling in a festive mood, to the reception offered to us by the Lord Mayor of Sheffield. 'The Lord Mayor is a lady,' our colleagues from Sheffield told us proudly. 'On official occasions the Lord Mayor is always accompanied by "his" Lady Mayoress. In this case it is her daughter who acts as Lady Mayoress; our Lord Mayor is a widow'. Thus we were given a reception by the woman decorated with the chain of office and by the woman standing next to her with a bouquet of flowers in her hand.

The Lord Mayor spoke to us in a way a man could not have surpassed. It is true that she was shaking a little and, after she had finished her speech, her daughter pinched her arm encouragingly. The picture of this new little crack within the patriarchal bulwark moved and encouraged me. Later I got into a heated debate on this issue with Esther Fuchs, author of a number of sharp articles on the strategies deployed by biblical authors of stories about women. She was furious and at the same time sad about the course of things during the reception: example number one thousand and one of women's enforced adaptation to masculine rituals and traditions.

'Unmasking' or 'Liberating' Reading

The difference between Esther Fuchs's and my own views on the reception ritual in Sheffield is illustrative of the different modes feminists employ for reading the Bible. Phyllis Bird's pithy statement, 'The Old Testament is a collection of writings by males from a society dominated by males',[1] is indeed the starting point of all feminist exegetes but, from this point onwards, they might travel different roads and in different directions. Some of them keep looking for liberating threads within this collection of male-oriented, androcentric writings. In so doing they are no longer as optimistic as they were at the beginning of feminist biblical criticism, when one woman's story after another was excavated out of the biblical dust and their potentially 'liberating' contents considered. Rather, feminist criticism has evolved into methods of wrestling with the text, a wrestling that is comparable to Jacob's wrestling at the Jabbok. Jacob says to his divine opponent, 'I shall not let you go unless you bless me' (Gen. 32.26).[2] Other feminist critics demonstrate that such attempts to read for liberating threads are in fact attempts to throw dust in one's own and in others' eyes. Strangely, or so it may seem, the most 'woman-associated' biblical stories are precisely those whose thoroughly patriarchal content needs to be unmasked.

A clarifying example seems to be in order at this point. Since the rise of the women's movement and feminist interpretation of the Bible, the story of Tamar and Judah (Gen. 38) has attracted great interest in religious and theological circles. The 'I shall not let you go unless you bless me' approach recognizes that in this story the limits of patriarchy are not transcended. At most they are—for a short while—transgressed by Tamar's unorthodox activities. Her behaviour is characterized as prophetic and messianic. Tamar, a 'whore' in Judah's eyes, and a 'sacred

---

1. P. Bird, 'Images of Women in the Old Testament', in R. Radford Ruether (ed.), *Religion and Sexism: Images of Women in the Jewish and Christian Traditions* (New York: Simon & Schuster, 1974), p. 41.

2. This notion is taken from P. Trible, *Texts of Terror: Literary-Feminist Readings of Biblical Narratives* (Philadelphia: Fortress Press, 1984).

woman' (קְדֵשָׁה, Gen. 38.21) in the eyes of Hirah the Canaanite, holds the mirror up to Judah, a mirror in which his morality of double standards is shattered to pieces.[1]

Over and against the liberating mode of reading, the 'unmasking' reading mode reveals that powerful ideological strategies are deployed in texts concerning women. Tamar serves the patriarchal interests which, in the story, are presented as her own interests in an exemplary fashion:

> It should be ascribed to the imaginative and artistic ingenuity of the biblical narrator that one of the most vital patriarchal concerns [i.e. the birth of sons] is repeatedly presented not as an imposition on woman but as something she herself desires more than anything else.[2]

Does this second mode of interpretation invalidate the first? And, to come back to the story of the female Lord Mayor's reception at the 1988 SBL conference in Sheffield, is Esther Fuchs's critical vision more legitimate than my own vision? Is it better to avoid receptions given by female Lord Mayors as long as such rituals have not been reformed so that they conform to feminist sensibilities? When we look for stories that are inspiring and beneficial for women, should we not rather look for them *outside* the biblical canon? Feminist biblical scholars like Carol Christ and Jonneke Bekkenkamp have indeed decided to do so. In 'Diving Deep and Surfacing',[3] Christ shows how modern women's literature can guide women in their social and spiritual quest. Bekkenkamp[4] makes a passionate plea for regarding

1. F. van Dijk-Hemmes, 'Tamar and the Limits of Patriarchy: Between Rape and Seduction (2 Samuel 13 and Genesis 38)', in M. Bal (ed.), *Anti-Covenant: Counter-Reading Women's Lives in the Hebrew Bible* (JSOTSup, 81; Sheffield: JSOT Press, 1989), pp. 135-56.

2. E. Fuchs, 'The Literary Characterization of Mothers and Sexual Politics in the Hebrew Bible', in A. Yarbro Collins (ed.), *Feminist Perspectives on Biblical Scholarship* (SBL Centennial Publications; Atlanta: Scholars Press, 1985), p. 130.

3. C. Christ, 'Diving Deep and Surfacing', in *Women Writers on Spiritual Questions* (Boston: Beacon Press, 1980).

4. J. Bekkenkamp, *Canon en keuze: Het bejbelse Hooglied en de Twenty One Love Poems van Adrienne Rich als brannen van theologie* (Kampen: Kok, 1993).

modern women's literature, just as we consider the Bible, as a source for theology. By way of an example, she reads the Song of Songs together with Adrienne Rich's *Twenty-One Love Poems*.[1] I too endorse the necessity of shaping new canons in which women take possession of the Word. Still, I am not prepared to exchange the old canon for those new ones. In my experience, rereading the Bible from a feminist perspective remains an exciting and challenging enterprise. However, the dilemma of moving between the two modes of critical reading—the 'unmasking' mode and the 'liberating' mode—has not been successfully solved as yet.

A Dual Hermeneutic

Not only the biblical, but also the general literary canon suffers from the defect that women-authored writings hardly form part of it. Almost all the literary masterpieces recognized as such by the cultural world have indeed been written by masters in the gender-specific sense of the word, and often contain misogynistic ideology. Feminist literary criticism has by now borne impressive and striking witness to that. In the realm of general feminist literary criticism, too, voices are heard demanding that we should leave the recognized canon as it is and, instead, focus our attention exclusively on literature written by women. In an excellent article Patricinio Schweickart has recently argued that she does not feel happy with this proposal. 'Why,' she asks, 'do some (not all) demonstrably sexist texts remain appealing even after they have been subjected to thorough feminist critique?', and she goes on,

> The usual answer—that the power of male texts is the power of the false consciousness into which women as well as men have been socialized—oversimplifies the problem and prevents us from comprehending both the force of literature and the complexity of our responses to it.[2]

1. A. Rich, 'Twenty-One Love Poems', in *Dream of a Common Language* (New York: Horton, 1977).
2. P. Schweickart, 'Reading Ourselves: Toward a Feminist Theory of Reading', in E.A. Flynn and P. Schweickart (eds.), *Gender and Reading: Essays on Readers, Texts and Contexts* (Baltimore and London: Johns Hopkins

Good literature, according to Schweickart, is always utopian. Therefore,

> *certain* (not all) male texts merit a dual hermeneutic: a negative hermeneutic that discloses their complicity with patriarchal ideology, and a positive hermeneutic that recuperates the utopian moment—the authentic kernel—from which they draw a significant portion of their emotional power.[1]

Schweickart's plea for a dual hermeneutic is, I think, applicable to many (not all?) biblical texts. The 'unmasking' as well as the 'liberating' reading mode merits a place in any feminist critique. When using both modes, the risk of developing an exclusively one-sided negative interpretation or, conversely, a positive interpretation that is not critical enough and unwarranted by the text, may be avoided.

Schweickart's article has inspired me to a dual interpretation of 2 Kgs 4.8-37. The method I use derives from narratological theory. The questions narratology entails are: Who speaks? Who sees? Who acts? Which objects are pursued by the different characters in the text?[2] My first interpretation confines itself to the text of this specific narrative; in the second, references to various biblical intertexts are also drawn into the exegesis. The two interpretations are prefaced with a short description of the narrative's structure.

The Narrative

The story about the Shunammite forms part of the 'history' of the prophet Elisha, which is described in 2 Kgs 2–13.21. The inverted commas around the word 'history' were put in advisedly. In the so-called historical books of the Bible (Joshua to Kings) we do not deal with historiography in the modern sense of the term, but with *prophetic* historiography. Events from the past are narrated in order to achieve a certain effect on the audience, not in order to register the past as accurately as

University Press, 1986), p. 42.
    1.   Schweickart, 'Reading Ourselves', pp. 43-44.
    2.   For a survey of narratological principles see M. Bal, *Narratology: Introduction to the Theory of Narrative* (Toronto: University of Toronto Press, 1985).

possible. Hence in Jewish tradition—in contradistinction to Christian tradition—the books of Joshua, Judges, Samuel and Kings are considered prophetic literature.

The story of 2 Kgs 4.8-37 consists of three episodes, each of which can be divided into two scenes. In the first scene (vv. 8-10) of episode 1 (vv. 8-17) the two protagonists are presented: Elisha, who is on his way to Shunem, and 'the great woman'. In this scene the woman is the one who takes the initiative. She invites Elisha for dinner. After this has happened several times she says to her husband,

> Behold I know that he is a holy man of God this one who passes
> by us continually.
> Let us make a little roof-chamber surrounded with walls
> and let us set for him there a bed a table a stool and a lampstand
> so that it will come to pass that when he comes there
> he shall turn aside to the room and rest there
> (vv. 9-11).

In the second scene (vv. 11-17), Elisha responds to the woman's initiative. He wants to do something on her behalf out of gratitude for her hospitality. By means of his servant Gehazi he inquires,

> What to do for you
> Is there to speak on your behalf
> to the king or to the commander of the army
> (v. 13a).

This question remains unsuccessful. 'Among my own people I dwell', answers the woman proudly. Elisha now poses his question to Gehazi, who appears to know quite well what the woman needs:

> Alas she does not have a son and her husband is old (v. 14).

Now Elisha knows what he has to do. He promises a son to the woman. But, once again, he meets with a refusal:

> No my lord man of God
> Do not tell a lie with your handmaid (v. 16b).

However, she falls pregnant and gives birth to a son.

In the first scene (vv. 18-20) of episode 2 (vv. 18-28) the child, who has meanwhile grown up, goes to see his father in the field.

> He said to his father
> My head my head (v. 19a).

His father charges one of his servants with the task of bringing the child to his mother. There, on her knees, the boy dies. In the second scene (vv. 21-28) the woman immediately takes measures. She lays the child on the bed of the man of God; and calls upon her husband to provide her with a servant and a she-ass 'so that I may run to the man of God and come back again' (v. 22b). Amazingly, her husband asks at this point,

> Why are you going to him today
> It is neither new moon nor Sabbath (v. 23).

Her only answer is 'Shalom', which might be best translated here as 'God bless you too'. She hastens to the man of God, who is at Mount Carmel. When he sees her coming he sends Gehazi to her in order to ask,

> Shalom with you?
> Shalom with your husband?
> Shalom with your child? (v. 26).

Her answer is, once more, a curt 'Shalom'. And, with the same tenacity applied earlier in order to get hold of Elisha and press him to have dinner with her (v. 8), she now holds on to his feet. Gehazi wants to shove her away, but the man of God says,

> Let her alone
> Truly her soul is bitter
> YHWH has hid it from me
> and he has not told me (v. 27b).

In the first scene of the last episode (vv. 29-31) Elisha gives his staff to Gehazi and orders him to lay it 'upon the child's face'. While on his way, Gehazi is not to speak to anyone. The child's mother, however, swears that she will not leave Elisha in the meantime. She thus effects a situation whereby he has to follow her. Gehazi goes to meet them and lets them know that the child has not revived. In the last scene (vv. 31-37) Elisha himself goes to the child. He prays to God and stretches himself upon the child. 'The child's body waxed warm' (v. 34b). After walking in the house to and fro, Elisha stretches himself upon the child a second time. Then, the child sneezes seven times and opens his eyes. Elisha calls to Gehazi,

> Call for this Shunammite.

And Gehazi obeys:

> He called for her
> She came to him
> He said
> Take up your son
> She came fell at his feet and bowed herself to the ground
> She took up her son and went out (vv. 36-38).

A First Interpretation: Who is the Real Father?

The woman who at the beginning of the story is presented as a 'great woman', throws herself at the end at Elisha's feet. At his command, she silently carries her son away. She has reached her goal, her destiny. Thanks to the man of God she, again, has become a mother. But, after all, did she actually want to be a mother? The story is not unambiguously clear about that. Hence, let us first determine which objects the woman has been pursuing. In the first scene this is definitely clear. She wants Elisha to have dinner with her. Subsequently she wants him to take up residence in her house each time he comes to Shunem. In both instances the woman realizes her wishes, so that there is nothing left for her to desire. Elisha's repeated questions about what he can do for her in return are met with a refusal. Despite her refusal, the woman gets pregnant and gives birth to a son. When, after some years, the child dies she hastens to the man of God and says to him reproachfully:

> Did I ask my lord for a son
> Did I not say
>   Do not deceive me (v. 28).

The last words she says to Elisha are an oath formula:

> As YHWH lives and as your soul lives
> I will not leave you (v. 30).

Rather than a desire for a child, a desire for the man of God is thus revealed in the woman's words and behaviour.

How does Elisha react to this desire? His response is ambiguous. It is true that he gratefully takes advantage of the hospitality the woman offers to him but, for his part, the communication with her is rather uneasy. He speaks *about* the woman as 'this Shunammite' and he speaks *to* her through his servant Gehazi. He does not acquire the object he pursues in the second scene too easily. His offer to speak on her behalf to the king is proudly rejected by the woman. That she surely is in need of something has to be divulged to him by Gehazi. Elisha himself had apparently not noticed it. Thanks to Gehazi's tip, and despite the woman's renewed refusal, Elisha finally attains *his* object: he sees to it that the woman acquires a son. When the woman, after the child's death, arrives at Mount Carmel Elisha again addresses himself to her through Gehazi. The question Gehazi has to ask on his behalf is another demonstration of his master's ignorance. And from what follows we can deduce that Elisha's communication with YHWH is not perfect either: 'YHWH has hid it from me and he did not tell me' (v. 27). Elisha's attempt to turn over his responsibilities to Gehazi (in order to get rid of the woman?) fails. Gehazi does not succeed in reviving the dead child. The woman does not want to leave the man of God. Hence, perforce, he goes after her and eventually effects her becoming a mother again. Only twice does Elisha address himself directly to the woman: the first time in order to tell her that she will embrace a son; the second time in order to command her to take her son with her. Hence, only when there is occasion to speak to her in her capacity as mother does Elisha break through his distant behaviour towards the woman.

The woman longs for Elisha. Elisha merely views her as a mother. What is the position of the child between those two contradictory desires or aims? The boy acts as an autonomous character just for a short while. Having grown up a little, he goes to his father and screams 'my head, my head'. These words may perhaps indicate that he has suffered a sunstroke, as suggested in many commentaries. This is eisegesis, derived from circumstantial textual evidence. (It is summer. The child is in the field. It is hot.) I think, though, that the child's words might also be understood literally, and in a somewhat different sense. The boy wants to know who is his 'head', that is, his father. He want to know where he belongs and where he comes from (the Hebrew word ראש means 'head' also in the sense of, for instance, 'family head' as well as 'origin, beginning'). This question—if a question it is—signifies the child's death. The man who in this story is called the child's father, and who is marked by Gehazi as 'old', does not want to be held responsible for his own presumed paternity. He sends the child off to his mother. And when she, a little later, lets her husband know that she wants to visit the man of God, he asks what the reason for so doing might be. Gehazi, the child's 'spiritual father' (it was Gehazi who suggested to Elisha that the woman lacked a son), is denied the honour of paternity too. He is unable to beget the child anew with the help of the man of God's staff, which he needs to handle as if it were a holy phallus (v. 29).[1] It is Elisha himself who, with God's assistance, brings the child back to life by both giving birth to and siring him. If we read the child's words, ראשי ראשי, as a question ('My head? My head?'), then his question has now been answered. Acting as a father and mother combined, the man of God has now granted life to the child.

Our story can, it seems, be interpreted as an extraordinary feast of patriarchal propaganda. According to patriarchal ideology, women have to become mothers whether they want to or not. However, woman's contribution to procreation, which is giving birth to a child and a male child at that, is in this case exceeded by a man in a much more impressive way. Thanks to him, the child is reborn. (In our story, *he* is a man of God. In more contemporary patriarchal relations *he* may be a pastor or priest—and those roles are more commonly filled by males than by females—who baptizes a child; or a physician—and, again, in our society most physicians are still males—who will save a child's life.) It is therefore highly appropriate that the mother throws herself at the man's feet, gratefully accepts the child, and continues to take care of him. Father, naturally, has to tend to matters that are much more important.

---

1.   My depiction of Elisha's staff as a (holy) phallus is admittedly impressionistic. However, this depiction is informed by the widely recognized functionality of staffs and similar objects, as formulated in psychoanalytic theory.

A Second Interpretation: 'I Shall Not Let You Go Unless You Bless Me' (Genesis 32.26)

The fact that the patriarchal order has to be promoted so emphatically and that it needs to be reaffirmed time and again, indicates that this order is not a matter of course and that it requires ideo-literary support. For women, the confrontation with such reiterated reaffirmation often implies a painful encounter. Nevertheless, it is exactly this painful encounter that enables women to see through the comical packagings which sometimes encase the patriarchal message.

We have already seen that the way Elisha is presented in our story is coloured by irony. The talents of this man of God for making contact leave much to be desired. Beyond that, we find that God withholds information from Elisha, and this contrasts him to other men of God. For instance, God says about Abraham (Gen. 18.17).

> Shall I hide from Abraham that thing that I do;

and God reveals the coming of Jeroboam's wife to the blind prophet Ahijah (1 Kgs 14.4-6). Also, Elisha's portrait provides a stark contrast to his great predecessor Elijah. The stories about Elisha seem to be parodic offshoots of stories about Elijah. The same narrated events are recounted in a grotesque way; the narration becomes more fanciful when it concerns Elisha. For example, while Elijah's resuscitation of the widow's son in Zarephath (1 Kgs 17.21-22) is soberly depicted, the resuscitation of the Shunammite's son by Elisha appears to be a much more complex and laborious process.

That Elisha ultimately proves to be a man of God is due to the Shunammite woman. Already in the first scene she testifies to her insight:

> And she said to her husband
> Behold I know that he is a holy
> man of God this one (2 Kgs 4.9).

That is why she is so keen to take Elisha into her home. Sacred persons or things surely generate divine blessings (see, for instance, 2 Sam. 6.11); and a blessing entails prosperity and fruitfulness. Was fruitfulness indeed what the woman was hoping for from the outset? Elisha's wording when he promises her a son (4.16) is almost identical to YHWH's wording to Abraham about Sarah (Gen. 18.14). Elisha says to the woman,

> In this time next year you shall embrace a son,

and God says to Abraham,

> I shall return to you at the time (appointed) about next year and Sarah will have a son.[1]

In Genesis 18 Abraham extends hospitality to the men of God who come to him; in 2 Kings 4 the 'Great Woman' does the same. Just like Sarah's husband, hers is old. Just like Sarah, she responds sceptically to the promise of a son. After all, she knows full well—as exemplified by the story—that her husband cannot manage the responsibility of fatherhood. When her child dies, the woman does not want to accept the event for a fact; instead she hurries to the man of God. In spite of the abundant use of the word 'shalom' (שׁלום, literally 'peace') in this scene (vv. 22-28), there is no longer a question of שׁלום. The words sound bitter in her mouth, as Elisha rightly states (v. 27). However, her bitter reproach to him (v. 28) does not stimulate Elisha to become active. Only after the woman says to him (v. 30) the words he himself has spoken three times to Elijah (2 Kgs 2.2, 4, 6),

> As YHWH lives, and as your soul lives, I will not leave you,

does Elisha recall his vocation, recognize that he cannot shake off his responsibilities any longer, and follow her. God's help is withheld from him no longer. His prayer is granted. Thanks to the persistence and actions of the 'Great Woman', Elisha proves to be a man of God and the child is brought back to life.

---

1.   The Hebrew expression translated 'next year' in both passages is the rare כעת חיה.

'In Memory of Her'[1]

My first interpretation illuminated the strategies with which the patriarchal order attempts to prove itself, and the position women occupy within it: they are victims. When one remains satisfied with this interpretation, one does injustice to the woman-in-the-text, and to one's readerly self. Therefore, the second interpretation was also necessary. The struggle the woman-in-the-text has to undertake in order to acquire a blessing, or שלום, becomes visible through it. Perhaps this might inspire contemporary women to continue their struggle after their own fashion. The first interpretation protects women from rash optimism and provides them, albeit for short interludes, with a smile: the need for patriarchal self-affirmation is too conspicuous to be overlooked.

The memory of the 'Great Woman' deserves to be kept alive. Moreover, the present woman(ly) reader can pay her the homage that the author and narrator of the biblical text withheld from her. The woman can be named. And what name is more appropriate than the adjective with which she is introduced? Her name is therefore here designated *Gedolah* (Hebrew: גדולה, 'great'), the 'Great One'.[2]

---

1. E. Schüssler Fiorenza, *In Memory of Her: A Feminist Theological Reconstruction of Christian Origins* (New York: Crossroad, 1983).
2. Editor's note: Fokkelien van Dijk-Hemmes died on February 6, 1994, shortly after completing the expansion and translation of this article (the original version of which was published in Dutch).

HULDAH THE PROPHET—OF YAHWEH OR ASHERAH?*

Diana Edelman

The portrayal of Huldah in 2 Kgs 22.14-20 and 2 Chron. 34.22-28 raises several fundamental questions: how much of vv. 16-20 reflects a genuine prophecy delivered by her in response to the purported finding of the scroll of the law and how much is put into her mouth by a later biblical writer or writers? Is the literary Huldah presented as a true prophet whose utterances are fulfilled or as a false prophet whose words are contradicted? Was the historical Huldah a prophet of Yahweh, the male divine head of state, or a prophet of his wife, Asherah, the female divine head of state? Much of the phrasing and thought in 2 Kgs 22.15-20 echoes that in the book of Jeremiah, raising the possibility that most, if not all, of the prophecy is not derived from court records but was created by someone who wrote in the style of Jeremiah during or after the exile. With this understanding, I will propose that Huldah's casting as a prophet of Yahweh could also be secondary and that, historically, she might well have been a prophet of Asherah. Asherah's probable role as divine intercessor would have made her a logical deity to consult under the circumstances depicted in 2 Kings 22, rather than running the risk of angering Yahweh by asking him directly about his connection with the purported document. When Asherah was written out of the former Judahite national pantheon, Huldah would have been made a spokesperson for Yahweh instead of for the former 'first lady' of heaven.

*   I want to thank Professors Stuart Lasine and Pauline Viviano for their comments on the final draft of this article. The finished product is smoother and clearer as a result.

*The Language of the Oracle and Huldah's Status as a True or False
Prophet*

According to 2 Kgs 22.3-20, during repairs to the temple in
Jerusalem made in the eighteenth year of King Josiah's reign
Hilkiah the high priest found 'the book of the law' (vv. 3-8). He
gave the book to Shaphan, Josiah's secretary, who read it himself
and then read it before the king (vv. 8-10). In response
to hearing the words of the book, the king tore his clothes and
sent five officials to inquire of Yahweh on his behalf and on
behalf of the people, for all of Judah, about the words in the
book, 'for great is the wrath of Yahweh that is kindled against
us because our fathers have not obeyed the words of this book'
(vv. 11-13). The five officials then went to Huldah the prophet,
the wife of Shallum the son of Tikvah ben Harhas, keeper of the
wardrobe, who 'dwelt' in the Mishneh, and talked with her
(v. 14). She then delivered a two-part oracle of Yahweh. The
first part proclaimed that the divine wrath was to be kindled
against Jerusalem and its inhabitants because of their idolatry
(vv. 15-17). The second part declared that Josiah's acts of peni-
tence and humility in response to hearing the divine words spoken against Jerusalem and its inhabitants were to lead to his
being gathered to his fathers in peace so that his eyes would
not see all the evil that Yahweh would cause to enter Jerusalem
(vv. 18-20).

Huldah's status as a prophet in general is confirmed by the
king's order that Hilkiah, Ahikam, Achbor and Shaphan 'seek
Yahweh' on his behalf and on behalf of the people and all Judah
concerning the words of the scroll (v. 13). The idiom *dāraš 'et-
yhwh* means to seek a divine oracle that will be spoken through
a human agent. In all but one instance, the agent is a prophet
(see for instance 1 Sam. 9.9; 1 Kgs 14.5; 22.8, 18); in 1 Sam. 28.7
the agent is a (female) medium. The phrase excludes the priestly
use of Urim and Thummim to determine the divine will; this
form of divine consultation is associated with the idiom *šā'al bᵉ*
(cf. 1 Sam. 14.37; 23.2; 2 Sam. 2.1). Thus, to fulfill the king's
command, Hilkiah needed to seek the services of a prophet.
Whether Huldah is to be judged a true or false prophet remains

to be determined after an analysis of the content of her prophecy.

Huldah's prophecy in 2 Kgs 22. 16-20 is replete with phrasing and ideology that is found especially in the book of Jeremiah. The prophetic announcement is framed by the idea of Yahweh 'bringing evil' upon Jerusalem and its inhabitants. In v. 16, the idea is expressed by the statement, 'I will cause evil to enter this place and its inhabitants', while in v. 20 it appears in the variant formulation, 'all the evil that I shall cause to enter this place'. The phrase '[Yahweh] is causing evil to enter (*mēbî' rā'â*) Jerusalem' is found elsewhere in the Hebrew Bible only in Jer. 19.3, 15 and 44.2 (in the past tense), and in a variant formulation in 39.16. In Jer. 35.17 evil is to enter all of Judah. Yahweh's 'causing evil to befall the inhabitants of the city' appears in Jer. 6.19; 32.42; 35.17; 36.31. In Jer. 42.17 the expression is applied to Jerusalemites who flee to Egypt in the face of the neo-Babylonian attacks on Jerusalem, while in 23.12 it is used in connection with Judahite prophets and in 45.5 with all flesh.[1] Otherwise, the references to Yahweh doing or causing evil in the prophetic literature are phrased as *qr' hr'h* (Jer. 32.23) and *zmm lhr' l'* (Zech. 8.14). The expression *qr' hr'h* also appears in Deut. 31.29.

The phrase 'because they have forsaken me and have sacrificed to other gods, that they might provoke me to anger with all the work of their hands' in v. 17 is similar to the wording of Jer. 1.16. Both include the ideas of forsaking Yahweh, sacrificing to other gods, and 'the work of their hands', a reference to the

---

1. A. Šanda has cited Jer. 6.19, 11.11 and 19.3 as parallels to v. 16a (*Die Bücher der Könige* [EHAT, 9.2; Münster: Aschendorff, 1912], p. 334). A.D.H. Mayes has also noted that the expression 'I will cause evil to enter' is found in Jeremiah, in what he considers to be 'late layers'. He cites 19.3, 15 and 32.42 only (*The Story of Israel between Settlement and Exile* [London: SCM Press, 1983], p. 129). M. Rose notes its appearance especially in Jer. 19, yet cites it as 'a familiar deuteronomistic phrase' ('Bemerkungen zum historischen Fundament des Josias-Bildes in II Reg 22f.', *ZAW* 89 [1977], p. 55 n. 23). H.D. Hoffmann cites Jer. 19.12 as a parallel to the phrase 'upon this place and upon its inhabitants' and claims it is Deuteronomistic (*Reform und Reformen: Untersuchungen zu einem Grundthema der deuteronomistischen Geschichtsschreibung* [ATANT, 66; Zürich: Theologischer Verlag, 1980], p. 180 n. 42).

making of idols. The ideas of serving other gods and idolatrous handiwork occur also in Jer. 25.6. The expression 'the work of their hands', *ma'ⁿseh yᵉdêhem*, appears also in Jer. 32.30 and 44.8. In addition to the four occurrences in Jeremiah the idiom for idolatry is found once in Hos. 14.4, three times in Isaiah (2.8; 17.8; 37.19), twice in Deuteronomy (27.15 and 31.29), three times in Kings (1 Kgs 16.7; 2 Kgs 19.18 and the present passage, with its quotation in 2 Chron. 32.19), and twice in the Psalms (115.4 and 135.15). It is not clear whether it was a common idiom through time, an idiom created by Hosea and imitated subsequently by other prophets and writers, or a late idea that was written back into selected texts.[1]

By contrast, the two favorite designations of an idol in Ezekiel, who lived in the same period as Jeremiah, are 'abomination' (*tô'ēbâ*) and 'idol' (*gillûl*). The first term is also used with some frequency in Jeremiah as well as Leviticus, Deuteronomy and Proverbs, while the second occurs only once in Jeremiah (50.2) but a few times in Kings and other books. Ezekiel also uses the common euphemism 'detestable thing' (*šiqqûṣ*) to designate idolatry, which occurs in Jeremiah (4.1; 13.27; 7.30; 16.18; 32.34) as well as other prophetic and non-prophetic writings.

In v. 19 the phrase 'I have spoken against this place and its inhabitants, that they should become a desolation and a curse' resonates with expressions in Deuteronomy, Isaiah and Jeremiah, but is especially close to Jer. 25.18; 42.18; 44.12, 22 in their combination of the terms 'desolation' (*šammâ*) and 'curse' (*qᵉlālâ*) to describe the fate of Jerusalem or its inhabitants.[2]

---

1. Mayes argues that the expression 'that they might provoke me to anger' also belongs to the later layers of Jeremiah, citing 7.18, 25.7 and 32.29 as examples (*Story of Israel*, p. 129), while M.A. O'Brien points out that the statement that Yahweh's wrath will be kindled and not quenched is similar to statements in Jer. 4.4 and 7.20 (*The Deuteronomistic History Hypothesis: A Reassessment* [OBO, 92; Freiburg: Universitätsverlag; Göttingen: Vandenhoeck & Ruprecht, 1989], p. 247 n. 73). H. Spieckermann notes that v. 17aα has parallels in 2 Chron. 34.25; Jer. 1.16; 19.4 (*Juda unter Assur in der Sargonidenzeit* [FRLANT, 129; Göttingen: Vandenhoeck & Ruprecht, 1982], p. 63 n. 69), while Šanda cites as parallels to v. 17a Jer. 19.4; 25.6b, 7b (after Deut. 31.29); and as a parallel to v. 17b, Jer. 7.20 (*Bücher der Könige*, p. 335).

2. M. Weinfeld claims that the use of the expressions *hyh lšmmh* and *hyh qllh* as part of a series is typically Deuteronomistic (*Deuteronomy and the*

Elsewhere, each individual term is used to describe the fate of Jerusalem or its inhabitants. The term *šammâ* is frequently used in Jeremiah to describe the condition or fate of the state of Judah, its capital, or its citizens (Jer. 2.15; 4.7; 5.30; 18.16; 19.8; 25.9, 11, 38; 29.18), as well as the fate awaiting other nations (46.19; 48.9; 50.3, 23; 51.29, 37, 41, 43). Of its 38 uses in the Bible, 24 are in Jeremiah; the only occurrence in Kings is in 2 Kgs 22.19, and there is one use in Deuteronomy (28.37), with other scattered uses in Isaiah (24.12), Ezekiel (23.33), Hosea (5.9), Joel (1.7), Micah (6.16), Zephaniah (2.15), Zechariah (7.14), Psalms (73.19) and 2 Chronicles (29.8; 30.7). The term *qᵉlālâ* is applied to the state or fate of Jerusalem or its inhabitants in Jer. 24.8, 9; 26.6; 44.8 and to Bozrah in 49.13. Otherwise, the term is frequently used in Deuteronomy (11.26, 28, 29; 23.6; 27.13; 29.26; 30.1, 19) and appears in other scattered passages (Gen. 27.12; Josh. 8.34; 1 Kgs 2.8; Zech. 8.13; Ps. 109.17, 18; Prov. 27.14; Neh. 13.2).

Although none of the language in Huldah's prophecy in 2 Kgs 22.16-20 is otherwise found only in the book of Jeremiah, the data above suggest that the combination of phrasing and ideas in the five verses closely resembles and echoes the style and thought in that book. The cumulative evidence points to a reflection or imitation of sections of that book more than to a reflection or imitation of Deuteronomistic style and thought, with which it is commonly associated.[1] The Deuteronomistic

Deuteronomistic School [Oxford: Clarendon Press, 1972], pp. 348-49). He is followed by Hoffmann (*Reform und Reformen*, p. 180 n. 42). Rose notes the occurrence of the two together in post-587 BCE passages in Jeremiah, and singly in Deuteronomy ('Bemerkungen', p. 55 n. 19), while Šanda cites Jer. 42.18 and 44.22 as parallels to *hyh lšmmh* (*Bücher der Könige*, p. 335). O'Brien (*Deuteronomistic History Hypothesis*, p. 247 n. 73) has cited Jer. 25.18, 42.18, 44.22 and 49.13 as the closest parallels. I have omitted the latter since it does not apply to Jerusalem or its inhabitants.

1.   Huldah's prophecy has been seen to have an old, genuine core in vv. 18-20 that has been heavily reworked and expanded to include vv. 16-17 by a later, exilic Deuteronomistic editor by for example J. Gray, *I & II Kings: A Commentary* (OTL; Philadelphia: Westminster Press; London: SCM Press, 2nd rev. edn, 1970), p. 727; F.M. Cross, *Canaanite Myth and Hebrew Epic* (Cambridge, MA: Harvard University Press, 1973), p. 286 n. 46; Rose, 'Bemerkungen', pp. 50-62; R.E. Friedman, *The Exile and Biblical Narrative*

History constitutes the second closest body of literature to the language and ideas expressed in 2 Kgs 22.16-20, but the closer parallels to the book of Jeremiah need to be acknowledged and weighed accordingly.[1]

(HSM, 22; Chico, CA: Scholars Press, 1981), pp. 41-42; Spieckermann, *Juda unter Assur*, pp. 69-71; B. Long, *2 Kings* (FOTL, 10; Grand Rapids: Eerdmans, 1991), pp. 263, 265. On the other hand, those who favor an old core in vv. 15-17 also include W. Dietrich, *Prophetie und Geschichte* (FRLANT, 108; Göttingen: Vandenhoeck & Ruprecht, 1972), p. 58 and R.D. Nelson, *The Double Redaction of the Deuteronomistic History* (JSOTSup, 18; Sheffield: JSOT Press, 1981), p. 79. S.L. McKenzie, on the other hand, argues that most of the oracle is the work of a pre-exilic Dtr 1 (*The Chronicler's Use of the Deuteronomistic History* [HSM, 33; Atlanta: Scholars Press, 1984], p. 199). Dissenters who argue for no pre-Deuteronomistic core include E. Würthwein, 'Die Josianische Reform und das Deuteronium', *ZTK* 73 (1976), pp. 404-406; Hoffmann, *Reform und Reformen*, pp. 170-81; Mayes, *Story of Israel*, p. 129; C. Levin, 'Joschija im deuteronomistischen Geschichtswerk', *ZAW* 96 (1984), pp. 364-68; apparently, B. Peckham, *The Composition of the Deuteronomistic History* (HSM, 35; Atlanta: Scholars Press, 1985), p. 92 n. 165; I.W. Provan, *Hezekiah and the Books of Kings* (BZAW, 172; Berlin: de Gruyter, 1988), p. 149. O'Brien identifies a core in vv. 15aαb, 18b and 20aα that he assigns to the Dtr rather than to a pre-Dtr source, yet argues that the Dtr drew on 'reliable information to compose the prophecy' and sees much exilic reworking (*Deuteronomistic History Hypothesis*, p. 247). A. Jepsen assigns vv. 15-18, 20b to R II and vv. 19 and 20a to a later Chronistic editor, but argues that R II did not compose the material from scratch but probably had a written report produced by the family of Shaphan, which had already included revisions in vv. 15aα, 17a and 18 (*Die Quellen des Königsbuches* [Halle: Niemeyer, 2nd edn, 1956], pp. 28-29, 102-104).

    1.   The close connection with Jeremiah was pointed out already by F. Horst ('Die Kultusreform des Königs Josia [II. Rg. 22-23]', *ZDPV* 77 [1923], pp. 224-38). He thought he could isolate two levels within the prophecy, as well as within 2 Kgs 22–23 at large, that corresponded to two layers within the book of Jeremiah. He assigned vv. 15, 16, 17b, 19aβ-γ and 20aβ to a Jeremianic Source A, which he dated to the period before the prophetical activity of Haggai and Zechariah and before the composition of the book of Deuteronomy; while he assigned vv. 18a, 17a, 18b, 19 and 20aα to a Jeremianic Source B, which he dated to c. 500 BCE, by which time Deuteronomy was composed. He tended to use single words and a number of prepositions as stylistic indicators, many of which seem too limited in scope to produce reliable results (see esp. p. 229 n. 3). His basic argument is followed by Levin, who concludes that vv. 16-17 are an

It is true that most of the passages cited from the book of Jeremiah belong to the prose narratives and prose sections that are commonly perceived to reflect expansions of an older prophetic core by someone who was well versed in Deuteronomistic thought and language. Excluding the citations for the use of the single terms *šammâ* and *qᵉlālâ* that are too limited to serve as significant parallels, the only exceptions that would be assigned to the older prophetic core are Jer. 6.19; 23.12; and 19.15.[1] Nevertheless, slight differences in linguistic patterns and usage exist between the Deuteronomistic History and these sections of Jeremiah.[2] They tend to indicate that the expanded sections of Jeremiah are not merely Deuteronomistic but, rather, the work of one or more representatives of a Jeremianic tradition who shared many idioms and concerns with the Deuteronomistic tradition. The person who created Huldah's prophecy appears to have known both the older prophetic core and the expanded sections of the tradition.

In addition to the stylistic similarities to the book of Jeremiah, a number of ideas in 2 Kings 22 have been associated with what are commonly considered to be Priestly materials. H.D. Hoffmann has argued that the system of collecting funds, the

interweaving of citations from Jer. 19.3, 1.16, 25.7 and 7.20, with influence also from Deut. 28, while vv. 19-20 also show Jeremianic-Deuteronomistic diction ('Joschija', pp. 366-67). Others who have emphasized the primacy of the Jeremianic connections over the Deuteronomistic include Jepsen, *Quellen des Königsbuches*, p. 28; Dietrich, *Prophetie und Geschichte*, pp. 68-78 and M. Rehm, *Das zweite Buch der Könige: Ein Kommentar* (Würzburg: Echter Verlag, 1982), p. 219.

1. I am using the delineation of 'Deuteronomistic' sections in Jeremiah made by J.P. Hyatt ('The Deuteronomic Edition of Jeremiah', in R.C. Beatty, J.P. Hyatt and M.K. Spears [eds.], *Vanderbilt Studies in the Humanities I* [Nashville: Vanderbilt University Press, 1951], pp. 71-95).

2. For extensive, detailed analyses of the relationship between the prose sections of Jeremiah and other Deuteronomistic texts, see esp. H. Weippert, *Die Prosareden des Jeremiabuches* (BZAW, 132; Berlin and New York: de Gruyter, 1973), and W. Thiel, *Die deuteronomistische Redaktion von Jeremia 26–45* (WMANT, 52; Neukirchen–Vluyn: Neukirchener Verlag, 1981). For a comparison of the poetic sections of Jeremiah and other Deuteronomistic texts, see esp. Thiel's earlier volume, *Die deuteronomistische Redaktion von Jeremia 1–25* (WMANT, 41; Neukirchen–Vluyn: Neukirchener Verlag, 1973).

designation of Hilkiah as 'high priest', and the mention of other temple personnel reflect the language and concerns found elsewhere in passages assigned to the Priestly tradition.[1] His understanding has been challenged, however,[2] and there is a widespread recognition only that the modifier 'high' that is now attached to some references to Hilkiah the priest is a secondary addition to the text. J. Van Seters has noted the weak connection in the present form of the chapter between the discovery of the law scroll and the repairing of the temple and has concluded that the latter section is a secondary addition.[3] A.D.H. Mayes and M.A. O'Brien, on the other hand, noting the same weak connection, have argued that the account of the temple repairs is the earlier material and the finding of the law scroll a secondary addition.[4]

A non-Deuteronomistic, perhaps Priestly idiom occurs in v. 20, in what many consider to be the authentic ancient core of Huldah's prophecy. The expression *'sp 'l 'btyw* is unique in the books of Kings; the normative, Deuteronomistic expression is *škb 'm 'btyw*, with minor variations. The former phrase is found elsewhere only in Judg. 2.10. J. Priest has noted that the variant expression, *(n)'sp 'l 'm(y)w*, is found predominantly, if not exclusively, in what are typically designated P passages.[5] However, it might be more accurate to describe such passages as examples of the use of late biblical Hebrew rather than expressive of a

---

1. Hoffmann, *Reform und Reformen*, pp. 124, 192-96.

2. See for instance O'Brien, *Deuteronomistic History Hypothesis*, pp. 241-43.

3. J. Van Seters, *In Search of History* (New Haven: Yale University Press, 1983), p. 318. He points out that the Chronicler's drastic rewriting of the account in 2 Chron. 34.8-18 seems to have been motivated by a desire to overcome the loose connection (n. 92).

4. Mayes (*Story of Israel*, p. 130) concludes that the story of the temple repairs is an ahistorical creation of the Deuteronomistic Historian, based directly on 2 Kgs 12.9-16, and the finding of the law scroll is an addition by an exilic Deuteronomistic editor. He has not commented on the presence of so-called P materials. O'Brien (*Deuteronomistic History Hypothesis*, p. 239), noting that the temple repair verses 'are not essential for the conceptual plan and structure of DtrH', assigns them to the first edition of the DtrH, which he dates to the exile.

5. J. Priest, 'Huldah's Oracle', *VT* 30 (1980), p. 367.

particular theological outlook. Priest argues that the two expressions using *'sp* are interchangeable, and concludes that the phrase *'sp 'l 'btyw* is a genuine part of Huldah's prophecy. As a court prophet, she 'naturally would have used language emanating from "priestly" circles'; and the retention of the technical term that was contrary to his own usage indicates that the Deuteronomistic historian has preserved this authentic oracle intact.[1]

In light of the apparent imitation of 'Jeremianic' style, however, and the presence of the idioms 'high priest' and 'be gathered to one's fathers' that seem to reflect the idiom of late biblical Hebrew, an alternate possibility should be given serious consideration: the entire oracle is a late composition by someone who has imitated the style found in the book of Jeremiah in its expanded form that already included the prose sections.[2] In so doing, he has carefully crafted the oracle to respond to the two groups on whose behalf the king ordered the oracular

1.   Priest, 'Huldah's Oracle', pp. 367-68. Contrast the discussion by B. Alfrink, who suggests that the phrase *n'sp 'l 'btyw* has been used by Huldah because the standard Deuteronomistic redactional expression, *škb 'm'btyw*, could not be used since it connoted a non-violent death ('L'expression נֶאֱסַף אֶל־עַמָּיו', *OTS* 5 [1948], pp. 118-19). He asks rhetorically if the expression *wn'spt 'l qbrtyk* was not also used 'expressly to let show through, in a veiled manner, the death on the battlefield' (p. 120). He has failed to note that his proposed overtones of a violent death do not apply to the use of the phrase in Judg. 2.10. O'Brien suggests that the reference to 'fathers' rather than 'people' is 'required because the promise is directed to a member of the Davidic Dynasty' (*Deuteronomistic History Hypothesis*, p. 245 n. 64). This approach is more promising.

2.   Another late feature is the use of *kn'* in *niphal*, in v. 19, to describe Josiah's action before Yahweh; such usage is typical of the Chronicler's style and theology, as noted previously by, for example, Jepsen, *Quellen des Königsbuches*, pp. 102-104; Würthwein, 'Josianische Reform', p. 404; Rose, 'Bemerkungen', p. 54 n. 18; and Levin, 'Joschija', p. 368. Since v. 11 reports only that Josiah rent his clothes when he heard the words of the scroll, it is likely that the reference to his humbling himself before Yahweh and weeping in v. 19 are secondary expansions of the oracle after its already late composition to reflect Chronistic theology; *contra*, for example, Levin, who uses it to suggest that vv. 19-20, which he believes is the earlier section of the oracle, must be dated close to the Chronicler, around the third century BCE ('Joschija', p. 368 n. 61).

consultation in v. 13, the king and the people, who constitute all Judah,[1] beginning with the latter group first. Whether this individual should be identified with one of the later Deuteronomistic editors is not clear and would require analysis that would go well beyond the scope of the present article.

The exact meaning of the phrase *'ōsīp^{e}kā 'al '^{a}bōteykā* and the one that immediately follows it in v. 20, *w^{e}ne'^{e}saptā 'el qibrōteykā b^{e}šālôm*, need to be discussed to determine whether or not Huldah's prophecy was fulfilled. Although the former phrase is commonly thought to designate a non-violent death by natural causes, this may not be accurate.[2] The phrase is used regularly in contexts that detail the specific mode of death, the act of dying and the act of burial, so its precise import is not clear. It often seems to be superfluous. As an idiom, it appears to trace back to the practice of interment in family tombs, where the bones of the dead were intermingled in a pile as they were swept aside to make room for the latest body.[3] Burial would seem therefore to be a logical primary meaning, although, by extension, the idiom could have been broadened to include both death and burial. I am not convinced that it implies any

---

1. The latter phrase is best understood to be in apposition to the preceding phrase, *ûb^e'ad-hā'ām*, rather than the third element in a series. Its initial *waw* is thus to be understood as a *waw explicativum*, not a *waw copulativum* like the one that introduced the preceding phrase as the second element in a series of two.

2. The phrase's counterpart, 'he slept with his fathers', is similarly associated with peaceful death. See esp. B. Alfrink, 'L'expression שָׁכַב עִם אֲבוֹתָיו', *OTS* 2 (1943), pp. 106-18 and Rose, 'Bemerkung', p. 59. However, the use of the latter phrase in connection with Ahab, who was mortally wounded on the battlefield (1 Kgs 22.34, 40), indicates that it does not always import a non-violent death, and this example should not be dismissed from the body of data for the sake of convenience or consistency.

3. *Contra* Alfrink ('L'expression נֶאֱסַף אֶל־עַמָּיו', p. 129), who rejects this theory in favor of the sense that the individual experiences an ancestral reunion in Sheol. Alfrink points out that since neither Moses nor Aaron, both of whom were 'gathered to their people', were buried in ancestral tombs, the meaning does not apply. However, the phrase need not have a literal sense in all applications; it may well have developed from this physical practice, but become an idiom for proper ritual burial, whether in an individual or a multiple tomb.

particular mode of death, violent or non-violent; it seems rather
to be a phrase that summarizes the dying process and proper
ritual disposal of the body.[1]

The ensuing phrase, 'you shall be gathered to your grave in
peace', seems to build upon the former, repeating the root *'sp*
and specifying the conditions of burial. The precise sense of
bᵉšālôm as an adverbial qualifier is crucial to determine; it is the
key phrase upon which Huldah's status as a false or true
prophet hinges. In its present context, it means that Josiah will
not personally see all the evil that Yahweh will cause to enter
Jerusalem, as the final phrase of the sentence makes clear.[2] In
this sense, 'peace' contrasts with the implication of impending
'war' that will lead to the destruction of the city. The phrase
bᵉšālôm is used in a similar way in Gen. 15.15, where Yahweh
reassures Abram that, unlike his descendants who will be slaves
in a foreign land and suffer oppression, he will 'go to his fathers
in peace' and 'be buried at a ripe old age'. In the Genesis
passage, a contrast is made between 'peace' and 'oppression'.[3]

As suggested by Hoffmann,[4] the statement may also imply by
extension that Josiah will receive a proper, ritual burial in his
family tomb in Judah so that he can have peace in Sheol, unlike
his successors Jehoahaz, Jehoiachin and Zedekiah, who died
and were presumably buried on foreign soil. Such an implication
of burial in the family tomb may also be present in Gen. 15.15,
where the descendants who are oppressed slaves in Egypt will
be buried in that foreign land, rather than in their traditional
family grave.

In its present context, then, Josiah's burial 'in peace' seems to
mean that he will not personally experience oppression in the

1. The neutrality of the phrase concerning manner of death is also
suggested by Provan (*Hezekiah*, p. 149).

2. So noted already in the Talmud (*b. M. Qaṭ.* 28b), and properly
understood by a surprisingly small number of modern scholars.

3. *Contra* e.g. Nelson, who argues that the two phrases in v. 15 are
synonymous, so that to die 'in peace' means to reach a ripe old age (*Double
Redaction*, p. 77).

4. *Reform und Reformen*, pp. 183-85. Hoffmann's argument is also
adopted by, for example, Rehm, *Zweite Buch der Könige*, pp. 217-18; Van
Seters, *In Search of History*, p. 318, and Long, *2 Kings*, p. 255.

form of a besieging of the capital by enemy troops. Accordingly, Huldah's prophecy is accurate and she is portrayed as a true prophet. The common perception that Josiah's death at the hands of Pharaoh Necho at Megiddo contradicts the statements in v. 20, making Huldah a false prophet by the definitions in Jeremiah 28 and Deut. 18.20-22, rests on a misunderstanding of the import of one or both of the phrases analyzed above.[1] Early Jewish tradition, which evaluates Huldah positively, suggesting she was consulted because, as a woman, she would be more compassionate and more likely to intercede with God on Josiah's behalf,[2] and making her the head of a school of learning and a person after whom the southern gates to the temple were named, has correctly understood her presentation in the text as a true prophet.[3]

1.   The Chronicler's changes to the prophecy are minor and do not affect the main lines of theological thought. His omission of the reference to Yahweh's making Jerusalem a desolation and a curse reflects his living in the rebuilt city of the post-exilic period, and his aversion to applying such labels to God's holy city. His addition of a second reference to Josiah's 'humbling himself' before God, the report that he rent his clothes, emphasizes his own theological agenda, where Yahweh forgives those who truly repent and humble themselves before him. It is worth noting that the Chronicler's changes in the account of Josiah's death in 36.20-24 appear to have been motivated by a desire to clarify the fact that Huldah's prophecy was indeed fulfilled. The announcement by Necho that he was not at war with Josiah and was not planning to attack him sets up a situation in which Josiah's death at his hand will allow him to die 'in peace'. In addition, instead of having Josiah die on the battlefield at Megiddo in the course of battle, he reports that he was wounded there, but that he died only subsequently back home under 'peaceful' conditions, i.e. not conditions of war. The Chronicler appears to have tried to prevent his readers from mistakenly focusing on Josiah's death at the hand of Pharaoh Necho as relevant to the sense of the phrase *bᵉšālôm*, whose true meaning is connected instead with the pending fate decreed against monarchic Jerusalem.

2.   Cf. *b. Meg.* 14b.

3.   For the suggestion that Huldah conducted an academy in Jerusalem, see the Targumic rendering of 2 Kgs 22.14, where *mišneh* is construed in its later sense of 'study'. See *b. Mid.* 1.3 for the gates of Huldah in the temple complex, and Rashi's comments on 2 Kgs 22.14 for the idea that the gate led to Huldah's schoolhouse. While none of these traditions is probably grounded on historical fact, each derives from a sense that Huldah was a positive rather than negative prophetic figure.

Which God did Huldah Serve?

It is strange that in choosing Huldah for the oracular consultation, the writer reports that Hilkiah and the others had to leave
the palace and temple complex to meet with her. The situation
implies that she was not necessarily a regular court prophet
attached to the main temple of Yahweh. This anomaly disappears if the parenthetical aside in v. 14, 'now she dwelt in
Jerusalem in the Mishneh', is eliminated as a later gloss.
However, the use of disjunctive syntax to give background
information in a sentence is a regular writing technique that can
be used by an original author or a later redactor, so there is no
a priori reason to reject the phrase as secondary. Zeph. 1.10
confirms that the Mishneh existed during Josiah's reign. Why
did the author feel it necessary to include this item as a further
means of understanding Huldah?

The import of the phrase is no longer clear to a modern
reader, who cannot know what associations were attached to
the expanded section of Jerusalem known as the Mishneh. For
an ancient audience, the information provides further localiza-
tion that could have borne positive or negative connotations. It
can be noted that Huldah's description as the spouse of Shallum
ben Tikvah ben Harhas, keeper of the wardrobe, provides all
the identification commonly required when a character is introduced, making the specific reference to her place of 'dwelling'
unnecessary and, therefore, probably significant information.

Was Huldah consulted in her private home, or in her work-
place, perhaps at another temple or sanctuary located in the
new section of the city? The verb *yāšab* could be construed as a
reference either to her abode or to the place where she 'sat' to
perform her prophetic duties. The lack of temporal indicators
throughout ch. 22 creates ambiguity about whether Huldah was
a court prophet who was consulted at home in the evening or
whether she was consulted during the day at her place of
work.[1] Their absence prevents further understanding of the

---

1. Since we do not know if court prophets served in monthly rotations
as the priests and Levites may have done during the monarchy, or even
whether they were expected to be at court during the day when they were

exact import of the reference to Huldah's 'dwelling' or 'sitting' in the Mishneh. At the same time, it prevents the elimination of a possible negative connotation in the reference to Huldah's activity in the Mishneh and a lurking suspicion, reinforced by the apparent lack of any portion of a genuine prophecy uttered by Huldah on the occasion of the purported finding of the law scroll during Josiah's reign, that she may have regularly prophesied in the name of a deity other than Yahweh.

At the time Huldah lived, the national Yahwism of the state of Judah appears to have shared with the official religions of the other states in Syria-Palestine belief in a couple at the head of the divine realm. In Judah, this couple consisted of Yahweh and Asherah.[1] Although Yahweh was made a widower in subsequent Judaism, and his status as formerly 'married' was well concealed by the alteration of texts that mentioned Asherah by name, there are clear traces of the former spouse in extant biblical texts. Of the 40 uses of *'ašērâ* in the Bible only two can possibly be construed grammatically as the proper name of the deity (Deut. 16.21; 2 Kgs 17.16); and both may well be indefinite singular forms of a common noun designating her cultic object instead. The 38 remaining occurrences appear to use the term as a common noun.

It is clear that many of the uses as a common noun designating a cultic representation of the deity who shared the same proper name are ancient and genuine. On closer inspection, however, it becomes obvious that there has been some deliberate tampering with the grammatical construction in five instances where Asherah has been made into a mere asherah, thereby removing an objectionable female deity from the texts and replacing her with a neutralized cultic object. These references are 1 Kgs 15.13; 2 Kgs 18.4; 21.7; 23.4, 7. In each case a definite article has been placed before the feminine term to make it a common noun instead of a proper name. It is possible that other

working or merely available to be summoned to court if necessary, we are unable to pick up on any nuances that might have been apparent to the intended and actual ancient audiences in the situation depicted.

1.   For a discussion of the pre-exilic pantheon of national Yahwism, see L. Handy, 'Dissenting Deities or Obedient Angels: Divine Hierarchies in Ugarit and the Bible', *BR* 35 (1990), pp. 18-35.

occurrences of *hā'ăšērâ* may likewise have originally read *'ăšērâ*; there is no way to prove or disprove the presence of tampering where the sense would allow either meaning. It is also possible that the proper name originally lay behind some of the current uses of definite and indefinite plural forms, even if it is likely that most of these reflect ancient usage of the common noun. Again, the presence of tampering cannot be established when the proper name of the deity or her cultic symbol makes equally good sense in a given context.

Asherah's official status within the national cult of both Judah and Israel is also demonstrated by her worship within the official temple cults of Jerusalem and Samaria, as well as by her royal patronage. Her reported expulsion from the Jerusalemite temple by Hezekiah and Josiah only reinforces her official status under the other Judahite kings, who permitted and presumably sponsored her worship in the central temple complex.

Her status as Yahweh's spouse is suggested by both biblical and extrabiblical texts. The prohibition in Deut. 16.21 against planting an asherah beside the altar of Yahweh indicates that the two deities were closely associated by some in Judah. Three inscriptions from Kuntillet 'Ajrud, a way-station in the northern Sinai dating somewhere between 850 and 750 BCE, specifically link the two in blessing formulae.[1] Two refer to Yahweh of Teman and his Asherah, and the third to Yahweh of Samaria and his Asherah. The third confirms Asherah's association with Yahweh in the cult of Israel, while the first and second associate her with a cult of Yahweh of Teman, whose national association is not clear. If the site is indeed Israelite, the label 'Teman', 'South', could conceivably be an oblique reference to the Judahite cult or could at least include this cult within its geographical confines, if it is not a reference to a more specific territory along the trade route which Kuntillet 'Ajrud serviced.

The attempt by some to deny the plain sense of the blessings at Kuntillet 'Ajrud by arguing that, in normal biblical Hebrew, proper names cannot have possessive suffixes, so that the expression 'his Asherah' must refer to some sort of cultic object

1. For the inscriptions, see conveniently G.I. Davies, *Ancient Hebrew Inscriptions: Corpus and Concordance* (Cambridge: Cambridge University Press, 1991), pp. 80-81.

used in the worship of Yahweh and not the goddess Asherah, is unconvincing.[1] This argument fails to explain why such a proposed object in Yahweh's worship just happens to bear the identical name of a well-known goddess who is named in texts as the wife or consort of the head male god in at least two other West Semitic pantheons, those of the Third Dynasty of Ur and Ugarit.[2] Since it is not known when normative Hebrew developed, there is no reason to deny the possibility that suffixes could have been used on a proper name in this period or by writers who may not have known all the formal rules.[3] In

---

1. So e.g. A. Lemaire, 'Who or What was Yahweh's Asherah?', *BARev* 10.6 (1984), pp. 47, 50; W.A. Maier III, *'Ašerah: Extrabiblical Evidence* (HSM, 37; Atlanta: Scholars Press, 1986), pp. 169-71; M. Smith, *The Early History of God* (New York: Harper & Row, 1987), pp. 85-88, 94; P.K. McCarter, Jr, 'Aspects of the Religion of the Israelite Monarchy', in P.D. Miller, Jr, P. Hanson and S.D. McBride (eds.), *Ancient Israelite Religion: Essays in Honor of Frank Moore Cross* (Philadelphia: Fortress Press, 1987), pp. 146-47. The grammatical abnormality has led to the alternative suggestions that the phrase should be read 'his consort' (so Z. Meshel, 'Did Yahweh have a Consort?', *BARev* 5.2 [1979], p. 31); 'his female deity' (so B. Halpern, 'The Baal [and the Asherah] in Seventh-Century Judah: Yhwh's Retainers Retired', in R. Barthelmus, T. Krüger and H. Utzschneider [eds.], *Konsequente Traditionsgeschichte: Festschrift für Klaus Baltzer zum 65. Geburtstag* [OBO, 126; Freiburg: Universitätsverlag; Göttingen: Vandenhoeck & Ruprecht, 1993], pp. 124-26); or 'his cultic object', representing the goddess Asherah (so J.A. Emerton, 'New Light on Israelite Religion: The Interpretation of the Inscriptions from Kuntillet 'Ajrud', *ZAW* 94 [1982], pp. 14-15, 18; S. Olyan, *Asherah and the Cult of Yahweh in Israel* [SBLMS, 34; Atlanta: Scholars Press, 1988], p. 34). M. Weinfeld sees it as an embodiment of the female element of divinity whether the phrase is translated as a reference to a goddess, a tree or a wooden pole ('Kuntillet 'Ajrud Inscriptions and their Significance', *SEL* 1 [1984], pp. 121-22). Others who accept the translation 'his Asherah' include M. Gilula, 'To Yahweh Shomron and his Asherah', *Shnaton* 3–4 (1978–79), pp. xv-xvi (Eng.), pp. 129-37 (Heb.); G.W. Ahlström, *An Archaeological Picture of Iron Age Religions in Ancient Palestine* (StudOr, 55.3; Helsinki: Painatusjaos, 1984), pp. 20-21; D.N. Freedman, 'Yahweh of Samaria and his Asherah', *BA* 50 (1987), pp. 246-49; W.G. Dever, *Recent Archaeological Discoveries and Biblical Research* (The Samuel and Althea Stroum Lectures in Jewish Studies; Seattle: University of Washington Press, 1990), pp. 144-48.

2. For the texts, see conveniently Maier, *'Ašerah*, pp. 3-55, 199-200.

3. See esp. E.A. Knauf, 'War Biblisch-Hebräisch eine Sprache?

addition, since the two inscriptions seem to refer to two different manifestations of Yahweh, the suffix may have been used to distinguish between the corresponding manifestations of Yahweh's partner, Asherah.

Unfortunately, Asherah's traits and tasks as co-head of the divine pantheon in Judah have been lost in the development of monotheism and many have probably been transferred to her former husband Yahweh, the new sole ruler of heaven. It is likely, nevertheless, that one of her prominent roles was that of intercessor, mediator, or go-between, a trait that seems to have been common to many female gods in the pantheons of ancient patriarchal societies. Three examples will be cited, but more undoubtedly could be added to them.

Asherah plays the role of intercessor or mediator in the mythic cycle from Ugarit, where she talks on Baal's behalf with her husband El to persuade him to allow a temple to be built for the young god (CTA 4.3.26-36; 4.4.1–4.5.63). Similarly, Anat, the sister and consort of Baal, intercedes on his behalf with El (CTA 3.4.51–3.5.52) and then, accompanying her brother, with Asherah (CTA 4.1.12-24; 4.3.23-36; 4.4.8-22) in order to get a temple built for him. In the Gudea cylinder, it is not surprising to learn that the oracle-priestess of the gods is a female, Nina, who interprets and confirms the will of fellow gods for humans. This is arguably a mediatory role as well (Cylinder A. 1.1–VII.10). Nina is the sister but not the consort of Ningirsu, the warrior storm-god. I am confident such examples could be multiplied by anyone so inclined. It should be noted, however, that the monumental nature of so many of the inscriptions that have been preserved limits the number of clear examples, since kings rarely explain why they consult a given deity or the attributes of that god.

Without judging the historicity of the finding of the law scroll during temple repairs in the time of Josiah and his consultation of a prophet to confirm the nation's status in light of the divine words contained in the scroll, the situation as it is depicted in 2 Kings 22–23 would have been very conducive to the consultation of a divine intercessor rather than Yahweh himself. The

Empirische Gesichtspunkte zur Annäherung an die Sprache der althebräischen Literatur', *ZAH* 3 (1990), pp. 11-23.

time in question is one in which the cult of Asherah would still
have been in place as part of the national Yahwism. There
should have been officially appointed and sponsored priests and
prophets of Asherah. Had a scroll containing the words of
Yahweh been found in this era, and had it been discovered that
Yahweh's words had not been observed for a long time, it is
quite likely that the king would have sent a delegation to
consult a prophet of Asherah to determine Yahweh's frame of
mind, rather than consulting Yahweh directly through one of his
own prophets, thereby calling attention to the infractions and
raising the deity's wrath. An intercessor, in this case Yahweh's
consort, would have been able to diffuse the potentially
disastrous situation by underplaying the need for retribution or
persuading the other deity to be lenient in his punishment or
response.[1]

Synthesis

I would suggest the following tentative history for the development of the Huldah tradition. A late, post-exilic editor found a
reference to Huldah already in the text of 2 Kings 22 as the
person who was consulted in connection with the finding of a
law scroll, but no specific text of the prophecy she was to have
spoken. He wrote the prophecy, either presuming that she had
been a prophet of Yahweh or making her one now, but
knowing her actual ancient status. He imitated the prophetic
style of the book of Jeremiah, making Huldah a female alter ego
for the latter prophet whose importance seems to have grown
over time and whose ministry tradition was eventually also
associated with Josiah's reign. The writer betrayed his post-exilic

1.   Spieckermann has made an important observation about Huldah in
his comment that a female prophet with such important authority leads
one to think about the prophet of Ishtar of Arbela, with whom Judaean
vassals like Manasseh and Josiah became thoroughly acquainted in
Nineveh and in imitation of whose institution they may have been stimu-
lated to appoint a female prophet (*Juda unter Assur*, p. 303). He seems to
presume, however, that the imitation led to Huldah's appointment to the
cult of Yahweh, rather than drawing the more logical conclusion that she
was the head prophet of Asherah, the female member of the head divine
couple and Ishtar's counterpart in the native Judahite cult.

background, however, by using the late idiom '*sp 'l 'btyw* to describe Josiah's death and burial and by adding the modifier *haggādôl* to references to Hilkiah in vv. 4 and 8. At an even later time, the oracle seems to have been expanded in v. 19 by someone who shared the theological outlook of the Chronicler.

Either the first Dtr (writing in the exile or the late monarchy) or a later Deuteronomistic editor needed the name of a prophet from the period of Josiah for his story about the finding of the law scroll. It is possible that the earliest form of the chapter mentioned only the temple repairs undertaken by Josiah, written to recall to mind the repairs done by Jehoash in 2 Kings 12, and that the section dealing with the finding of the law scroll and the related consultation of Huldah was added secondarily. It is not clear whether the latter story is based on a historical event or was fabricated, perhaps in order to provide an acceptable pedigree for a law code being urged for adoption within the province of Yehud. I find no compelling reason to accept the historicity of the incident as portrayed, but see the use of Huldah and other historical personages from the reign of Josiah as an attempt to give an air of verisimilitude to a fictitious incident. The writer found Huldah's name in archival materials as a prophet who had lived during the reign of Josiah, but not necessarily one who had uttered an oracle in response to the finding of a law scroll. Presumably, the source would have mentioned the name of the deity she served.

Whether or not a law scroll was found in the temple under Josiah, the person responsible for creating the story about its discovery would have known the proper ritual procedure that would have been used under such circumstances to verify that it indeed expressed the will of the god with whom it was associated. In the late monarchic era, before Asherah's ousting from Yahweh's side, it is possible, if not likely, that an inquiry about the status of a long-neglected divine directive of the head male deity would have been made 'indirectly' through his female partner, to soften his anticipated negative reaction and perhaps diffuse his wrath and punishment. The circumstances being depicted in the story might well have prompted the writer to search the court records for the name of a prophet of Asherah on the presumption that such a prophet would have been consulted under the circumstances. He might have chosen not to present her original prophecy for the sake of brevity but, more likely, did not have it, perhaps because his source did not record its details but probably because it was never uttered. There was no need to specify which deity Huldah served in the original form of the story because the ancient audience would have been able to surmise her status from the circumstances, although such information may well be conveyed in the reference to Huldah's 'sitting' in the Mishneh, an expression whose significance is no longer understandable to the modern audience.

In contrast to the former writer, the later post-exilic writer who appears to have composed the two-part oracle, making Huldah essentially a female Jeremiah, seems to have lived in an age when Asherah's status as Yahweh's spouse and co-ruler of the heavenly court was no longer accepted in many Judaean circles. Not surprisingly, he made Huldah a spokesperson for the sole ruler of heaven, Yahweh, when he gave voice to her disturbing former textual silence, thereby reflecting and projecting his own theology. Unfortunately, we will never know if he simply presumed that she must have represented Yahweh because this god was now accepted by him and his peers as the sole ruler of the divine realm; if he also found confirmation of Huldah's historical status as a prophet of Yahweh in the text or other records; or if he knowingly removed Huldah from her historical status as a prophet of Asherah and made her instead a spokesperson of Yahweh in order to make her 'kosher' for his own contemporaries.

Epilogue
WOMEN IN LATER HISTORIOGRAPHY AND HISTORY

OUT FROM THE SHADOWS:
BIBLICAL WOMEN IN THE POST-EXILIC ERA*

Tamara C. Eskenazi

This paper has three related goals: first and foremost, to recover material concerning women for the purpose of shared communal inquiry; secondly, to begin to challenge the claim that the post-exilic era marks a decline in women's status; and, thirdly, to suggest a context for understanding the opposition to foreign women in Ezra 9–10 and to draw from it implications concerning women's roles and rights.[1] The paper confines itself to only one of the different tasks of a feminist historiography of religion: the recovery of women's stories and traditions.[2] As the title indicates, my purpose is to bring biblical women of the post-exilic era out from the shadows.

The post-exilic or Persian period (sixth to fourth century BCE) was a pivotal era, a time of restructuring Jewish life in the aftermath of military, economic and religious devastation. Recognizing the importance of the era we ask: where are the women? At first glance they seem absent. The long list of

---

*   This article is reprinted from *JSOT* 54 (1992), pp. 25-43.

1.   An abbreviated version of this paper was presented at the Annual Meeting of the Society of Biblical Literature (New Orleans, November 1990). The paper is in indirect conversation with H.C. Washington, 'The "Strange Woman" of Proverbs 1–9 and Post-Exilic Judean Society', also presented at that meeting. I thank Professor Washington for making a copy of his paper available to me. My own study supports some of his conclusions by approaching the issues from another set of concerns and texts.

2.   See, e.g., J. Plaskow, *Standing again at Sinai* (San Francisco: Harper & Row, 1990), esp. pp. 25-60. Plaskow identifies three necessary tasks: recovery, analysis and reconstruction (or reshaping of memory).

returnees often identifies the groups by referring to them as 'sons' (e.g. בני פרעש, lit. 'sons of Parosh', Ezra 2.3). The term אבות (lit. 'fathers', 'patriarchs') is a prominent word for community, replacing משפחה (lit. 'family') or שבט (lit. 'tribe/clan') of the pre-exilic era. It is perhaps such terminology that has encouraged some scholars to suggest that this era is responsible for an entrenchment of patriarchy, after a presumably more egalitarian pre-exilic period. Thus, S. Terrien concludes that 'the religious functions of men and women differed markedly before and after the exile in Babylon (sixth century BC). Ancient Israel ascribed to women a religious status that was displaced and lowered in nascent Judaism.'[1] By 'nascent Judaism' Terrien refers to the community and literature developed during the Babylonian exile in the sixth century BCE and shortly after (p. 71). He concludes, 'In the old days, woman worshipped on a footing of equality with man. After the exile, woman was relegated to the status of second-class religionist. It was only through man that she had access to the holy' (pp. 85-86).[2]

Terrien's conclusion echoes the opinions of others who have considered ancient Israel superior to early Judaism, only this time superiority is claimed on the basis of gender issues. But Bernadette Brooten[3] and Carol Meyers[4] have taught us to look more closely at available sources and ask new questions. Brooten identifies the presence of women in leadership roles in Judaism during the Graeco-Roman period. She shows how inscriptions contrast with and contest the evidence of the

1. *Till the Heart Sings: A Biblical Theology of Manhood and Womanhood* (Philadelphia: Fortress Press, 1985), esp. p. 4. See also E. Gerstenberger, *Jahwe—ein patriarchaler Gott? Traditionelles Gottesbild und feministische Theologie* (Stuttgart: Kohlhammer, 1988).

2. For a critique of several of Terrien's conclusions, see M.I. Gruber, 'Women in the Cult according to the Priestly Code', in J. Neusner, B.A. Levine and E.S. Frerichs (eds.), *Judaic Perspectives on Ancient Israel* (Philadelphia: Fortress Press, 1987), pp. 35-48.

3. See her book, *Women Leaders in the Ancient Jewish Synagogue: Inscriptional Evidence and Background Issues* (BJS, 36; Chico, CA: Scholars Press, 1982).

4. *Discovering Eve: Ancient Israelite Women in Context* (Oxford: Oxford University Press, 1988).

Mishnah. Meyers, on the other hand, illustrates ways in which we can recover a more plausible understanding of the reality of ancient Israelite women's lives (as distinct from biblical representations of women) through a critical rereading of the text and by using insights from the social sciences. I draw upon their work as I examine an era chronologically situated between the two that they explore. Like them, I argue that much more can be said about the roles and powers of ancient Jewish women than has been acknowledged hitherto.

With these observations as background, let us look at some post-exilic texts and ask our question: 'Where are the women, and what are they doing?' When we look closely we discover that, hidden in the shadows, stand several interesting Jewish women of the post-exilic period, some even more visible at times than their pre-exilic sisters. This paper focuses on two sources for the recovery of these women: the archives from the Jewish community in Elephantine, Egypt, and the book of Ezra–Nehemiah.

The Evidence of Elephantine

The prominence of women in the Elephantine documents has been recognized long ago. Several critical editions of the material have been available to scholars for some time.[1] About 25 years ago B. Porten had already highlighted the roles and lives of women in his book, *Archives from Elephantine*. As we come to ask new questions about women, Porten's pioneering work and the clarity with which the documents themselves speak about women prove to be exciting sources for fresh inquiry. I will sum

---

1. A.E. Cowley, *Aramaic Papyri of the Fifth Century BC* (Oxford: Clarendon Press, 1923); G.R. Driver, *Aramaic Documents of the Fifth Century BC* (Oxford: Clarendon Press, rev. edn, 1965 [1954]); E.G. Kraeling, *The Brooklyn Museum Aramaic Papyri: New Documents of the Fifth Century BC from the Jewish Colony at Elephantine* (New Haven: Yale University Press, 1953); B. Porten, *Archives from Elephantine: The Life of an Ancient Jewish Military Colony* (Berkeley: University of California Press, 1968); B. Porten and A.L. Yardeni, *Textbook of Aramaic Documents from Ancient Egypt* (2 vols.; Winona Lake, IN: Eisenbrauns, 1986, 1989). In this essay, C refers to Cowley and K to Kraeling.

up and illustrate some of the things that such an inquiry discloses.

The Jewish community in Elephantine consisted of Jewish mercenaries and some merchants who had settled there before the Persian conquest of Egypt in 525 BCE. The Jewish colony survived until about 400 BCE, when Egypt revolted against the Persians. Dozens of original contracts, family archives, letters and ostraca written during this period have been discovered in Elephantine since the nineteenth century. The Elephantine documents include the oldest Jewish papyri in existence, many of them in good condition. Like the Qumran Scrolls, these primary documents are significant for reconstructing the reality of an otherwise scarcely known Jewish group, this time in the sixth–fourth century BCE. Like the Scrolls, these documents challenge common perceptions about the Judaism of that time and present an alternative. Much attention had been lavished on the religious practices of the community. In particular, Jewish worship in a temple to Yahu at Elephantine has been of interest, as have the references to goddesses such as Anath (C 22.125). This paper, however, is limited to sketching some important facts about the lives of three women: Mibtahiah, Tapmut and Yehoishma.

The archives of Mibtahiah daughter of Mahseiah are fascinating. They reveal a thrice married woman able to buy and sell property, inherit, divorce and lend money. Cowley refers to her as the 'notorious' Mibtahiah,[1] but we may think otherwise. Mibtahiah's story emerges from a series of contracts involving property that her father bequeathed to her. When Mibtahiah first marries a Jewish man, her father secures her rights to property. A contract grants a portion of a house to Mibtahiah (C 8, 460 BCE). The future husband has no entitlement to the house (C 9); he may dwell there with her, but the property is hers.[2] This husband, who bears a Jewish name, disappears from the

1. *Aramaic Papyri*, p. 177.
2. In case of divorce, the contract, given to the husband, specifies: 'half of the house *shall be* hers to take, and as to the *other* half you have power over it in return for the improvements which you have made in this house' (C 9.10-12).

records, presumably because he died. Next Mibtahiah apparently marries an Egyptian architect and later divorces him.[1] Their marriage and divorce documents have not survived, but C 14 preserves the record of their amicable division of property in which arrangements are made to everyone's satisfaction (it appears that Mibtahiah was also this husband's business partner).

Shortly after, Mibtahiah marries another Egyptian architect. The marriage contract for this union (C 15, 441 BCE) is virtually complete, and it is very interesting for several reasons. It indicates that Mibtahiah brings much property to the marriage. It carefully spells out in detail what this property is, and it stipulates what may happen to the property and goods in the future. The contract shows that Mibtahiah's belongings remain hers, regardless of marriage. It also contains stipulations to protect both partners, allowing either to initiate a divorce.[2] There are, in addition, provisions in case of abuse. In the course of time, two children are born to this couple; they receive Hebrew names and the husband's name changes from an Egyptian to a Hebrew one, suggesting that he has become a member of her community, i.e., he has been integrated into the Jewish community.[3]

A different story is that of Tamut or Tapmut, a woman, probably Egyptian, who is one man's slave but another (free) man's wife. While still a slave, Tamut marries a Jew named Anani son of Azariah. A series of documents and contracts help us trace the fortunes of this woman and her daughter.[4] Her marriage is

---

1.   A property settlement is agreed upon (C 14, about 441 BCE).

2.   Mibtahiah can divorce Ashor (C 15.22ff.) and he can divorce her (C 15.27). Stipulations are made also concerning abuse (C 15.29).

3.   See C 18 and Cowley's comments and interpretation (*Aramaic Papyri*, p. 84). It is noteworthy that such marriage was possible and unhindered by Persian authorities. K.G. Hoglund, in his dissertation, 'Achaemenid Imperial Administration in Syria–Palestine and the Missions of Ezra and Nehemiah' (PhD dissertation, Duke University, 1989), claims, among other things, that Persian authorities required or preferred ethnic purity. The Elephantine documents clearly challenge this part of Hoglund's otherwise compelling thesis.

4.   Most of these documents are included in Kraeling, *Brooklyn Museum Aramaic Papyri*.

recorded in a contract known as K 2 (449 BCE), which is note-worthy for several reasons. First, Anani ben Azariah is described as a 'לחן of Yahu the god who is in Yeb the fortress' (K 2.2). The term לחן occurs several times in Elephantine docu-ments, and, although its meaning is unclear, it has been under-stood to refer to some kind of official in the temple.[1] Secondly, like other Elephantine marriage contracts, this one indicates that either partner can divorce the other, with financial burden falling on the one who initiates divorce:

> If tomorrow or another day Anani rises up on account of her [?] and says, 'I divorce Tamut my wife' the divorce money is on his head. He shall give to Tamut in silver 7 shekels, 2 R., and all that she brought in in her hand she shall take out, from straw to thread. If tomorrow or another day, Tamut rises up and says, 'I divorce my husband Anani', a like sum shall be on her head. She shall give to Anani in silver 7 shekels, 2 R., and all which she brought in in her hand she shall take out, from straw to thread (K 2.7-10).

According to this agreement, the surviving spouse also gains control over the property when the other dies. This contract shows that although Tapmut is still a slave, she is also a lawful wife and as such has property and legal rights.

Another document (K 4, Oct. 30, 434 BCE) tells us that Anani, who had purchased a house (K 3, Sept. 14, 437 BCE), gives Tapmut half of it. After her death, her portion is to go to the children of Tapmut and Anani, a son named Pilti and a daughter Yehoishma. Anani's portion likewise goes to these children when he dies.[2] It is clear in this document that both son and daughter inherit.

Approximately 10 years later (K 5, June 12, 427 BCE), Tapmut

1. See Kraeling, *Brooklyn Museum Aramaic Papyri*, pp. 140, 144-45. But see also Dan. 5.23. For a discussion of the term, see S.A. Kaufman, *The Akkadian Influences on Aramaic* (The Oriental Institute of the University of Chicago, Assyriological Studies, 19; Chicago: University of Chicago Press, 1974), p. 66 n. 176. I thank Donald R. Vance for this reference.

2. All other relatives are excluded. Those excluded from claim to Tapmut's rights are: son, daughter, brother or sister of Anani (4.13); and those excluded from rights over the children's property at the death of Anani or Tapmut are: 'mother, father, brother, sister or another person' (4.19-20).

and her children are released from slave status by their master.[1] A few years later, Anani gives Tapmut's daughter Yehoishma, here identified as his daughter (whether biologically or legally is not specified), a house or part of a house (K 6, July 11, 420 BCE). Later that year Yehoishma marries. Her very extensive marriage contract (K 7, Oct. 2, 420 BCE)[2] discloses a great deal about Yehoishma and her status.[3] From the list of items in the contract, we discover that Yehoishma, a former slave and the daughter of a former slave, is quite wealthy. Much property and many movable possessions are hers and will remain with her if either she or the groom divorces the other. As in K 2, either party may initiate divorce and pay the equivalent of 'divorce proceedings' costs. Other stipulations in the contract are also reciprocal. The recurrence of such features indicates that K 2 is not unique but rather typical for Elephantine.

One other document among the remaining contracts, K 12 (Dec. 12, 402 or 401 BCE), deserves our attention. This is a document given (i.e. dictated) by *both* Anani and his wife Tapmut to their son-in-law (husband of Yehoishma) in the course of the sale of yet another house. What is fascinating for our purpose is the fact that Tapmut, an ex-slave, now sells property with her husband. Moreover, Tapmut, whose husband had been identified as a לחן of the temple of Yahu, is herself now identified as a לחנה of the temple of Yahu. In other words, although born an Egyptian and raised as a slave, she now has an official temple role.[4]

---

1. Although she is expected to look after her master, as a daughter or son would (K 5.11).

2. This contract is 'the most elaborate of the known Aramaic marriage documents' (Kraeling, *Brooklyn Museum Aramaic Papyri*, p. 201). The contract has 44 lines.

3. Here Ananiah son of Haggai asks for the bride in marriage. The one who gives her away is her so-called brother, son of her former owner (not Pilti her brother and son of her mother, nor Anani son of Azariah, her probable biological father and husband of her mother).

4. For a discussion of the meaning of the term, see Kaufman, *Akkadian Influences on Aramaic*, p. 66, and Kraeling's comment on K 12.2 (Kraeling, *Brooklyn Museum Aramaic Papyri*, p. 274). One cannot claim that Tapmut is an official in her own right. More likely she receives the title because she is

These documents from Elephantine begin to sketch legal and social roles for women that we do not normally ascribe to biblical or post-exilic communities. They show women in the Jewish community who are able to rise from slavery to a position in the temple, to divorce their husbands, hold property, buy and sell. The documents also confirm the fact that daughters inherit even when there is a son. Consequently, these documents compel us to revise some typical assumptions about women's roles in the post-exilic era.

The Evidence of Ezra–Nehemiah

Since the Elephantine documents come from Egypt, it may be claimed that the practices they disclose are uniquely Egyptian, not Jewish, and therefore say little about Judaism at the time, if by Judaism we mean the traditions preserved in the Bible and its communities. One must therefore ask: are these roles and rights similar to those in Judah? I contend that there was continuity during this Persian period between the practices in one Jewish community and another when both were under the same Persian imperial government, and communication was relatively easy and contacts were frequent. Furthermore, there are reasons to suppose that the marriage documents from Elephantine reflect Mesopotamian rather than distinctly Egyptian customs, in which case similar influences could be supposed for Judah. E. Lipiński shows some important affinities between Elephantine marriage contracts and Mesopotamian ones. In particular, the provisions that enable a woman to initiate divorce appear in both Elephantine and Western Asiatic documents in contrast with earlier Egyptian marriage contracts. 'Thus the equal capacity of the spouses in Elephantine, at least as far as the dissolution of the marriage is concerned, is not due, in all likelihood, to the Egyptian environment, as some authors have surmised, but belongs to a genuine Semitic tradition.'[1]

the wife of an official. This, however, does not diminish the significance of the position and the title.

1. 'The Wife's Right to Divorce in the Light of an Ancient Near Eastern Tradition', *Jewish Law Annual* 4 (1981), pp. 9-27 (20, 21).

According to Lipiński, the fact that divorce on the wife's initiative first appears in Egypt in Persian times 'is best explained as the result of the Semitic influence'.[1] When we bear in mind that the decisive Jewish community in Judah had come from Babylonia, the influence of Mesopotamia upon its marriage practices becomes all the more probable. References to women in Ezra–Nehemiah indirectly support the view that wives in Judah had some similar rights.

As already noted, the use of the term אבות, 'fathers', sets a tone. It could be taken in at least two ways. The emphasis on 'fathers' could lead us to conclude that we are encountering 'patriarchy' and hence a system possibly inherently oppressive to women.[2] But we could instead understand 'fathers' to denote 'families', or 'ancestral houses' (as indeed many translators render the term),[3] signalling the resurgence of the family, or household, as the fundamental socioeconomic and political unit. Scholars have argued that the various social and economic conditions during the period of the monarchy will have undermined the authority and economic role of the family unit.[4] C.V. Camp, who sums up the evolving roles of the family, observes that the post-exilic family was reinvested with authority and meaning that it had lost during the monarchic period. In kingless Judah, the family once again 'not only functions as the primary unit of production of this period but also re-emerges as one locus of community-wide authority...'[5]

According to Meyers, socioeconomic realities in premonarchic Israel dictated a certain practical egalitarianism between women

1. 'The Wife's Right', p. 23. For a different view about the relation between marriage agreements from Babylonia and Egyptian practices, see M.T. Roth, *Babylonian Marriage Agreements 7th–6th Centuries BC* (AOAT, 222; Neukirchen–Vluyn: Neukirchener Verlag, 1989), esp. p. 14 n. 60.

2. But see Meyers, *Discovering Eve*, pp. 24-46.

3. See, e.g., J. Blenkinsopp, *Ezra–Nehemiah: A Commentary* (OTL; Philadelphia: Westminster Press, 1988), p. 76, translating Ezra 1.5.

4. See C.V. Camp, *Wisdom and the Feminine in the Book of Proverbs* (Bible and Literature Series, 11; Sheffield: Almond Press, 1985), pp. 244-46, for a convenient summary of pertinent changes during the monarchy.

5. *Wisdom and the Feminine*, p. 246. Camp devotes a whole chapter to 'The Ethos and World View of Post-Exilic Israel' (pp. 233-54).

and men in light of shared economic responsibilities. I suggest that conditions similar to premonarchic Israel recur in the post-exilic era. If, as Meyers holds, the emphasis on family in pre-monarchic Israel meant more equitable distribution of power for women, then the re-emergence of the family as the significant socioeconomic unit in the post-exilic era likewise leads to greater power for women than was available during the monarchy. Other important conditions that Meyers identifies as conducive to gender parity in premonarchic Israel also recur in the post-exilic era and can therefore be supposed to generate similar dynamics. Once again, pioneer-life conditions characterize Judahite reality, and once again, the population is primarily rural (note the need to settle Jerusalem by casting lots and seeking volunteers; Neh. 11.1-2). Once again, the community experiences an era when internal boundaries are in flux.[1] If Meyers's thesis correctly describes premonarchic Israel, I suggest that it also supports a measure of egalitarianism in post-exilic Judah.[2]

The particular importance of women's roles in the post-exilic period had already been recognized by A. Causse, writing in 1929 and 1937.[3] As R.J. Coggins points out, Causse's conclusions sharply contrast with works such as Terrien's in that Causse identifies 'an increasingly important role for women' in the post-exilic period.[4]

1. See D.L. Smith, *Religion of the Landless: The Social Context of the Babylonian Exile* (Bloomington, IN: Meyer Stone Books, 1988). See also R.R. Wilson, 'Family', in P. Achtemeier (ed.), *Harper's Bible Dictionary* (San Francisco: Harper & Row, 1985), pp. 302-303.

2. To some extent, the force of my assertions in this essay depends on the solidity of Meyers's findings for premonarchic Israel. In another sense, however, my assertions depend on hints in the biblical texts for this period combined with the evidence of Elephantine.

3. *Les disperses d'Israël: Les origines de la Diaspora et son rôle dans la formation de Judaïsme* (Paris: Alcan, 1929), and *Du groupe ethnique à la communauté religieuse: Le problème sociologique de la religion d'Israël* (Paris: Alcan, 1937).

4. R.J. Coggins, 'The Origins of Jewish Diaspora', in R.E. Clements (ed.), *The World of Ancient Israel* (Cambridge: Cambridge University Press, 1989), p. 170. Coggins says that, in *Du groupe ethnique à la communauté religieuse*, 'Causse explored such issues as the effect of the exile on the family and the particular roles of individual members of the family, with an increasingly important role for women (this is in sharp contrast to some other more

Let us turn to Ezra–Nehemiah in order to examine what roles
women have. As noted above, at first glance women seem all
but absent from Ezra–Nehemiah, except as a problem when
they are foreign. As such, their very presence is a problem for
which absence is a solution. The most important example of this
is Ezra 9–10. In these chapters Ezra is shocked by discovering
that religious and other leaders have married women from 'the
peoples of the lands' (Ezra 9.1-2).[1] He interprets this development as a dreadful violation of God's commandments, and he
inspires the community to take steps against these marriages
(Ezra 10).

The language of the opposition to these marriages is religious
and ethnic, claiming that such marriages encroach on the holiness of the community and compromise the separation thought
necessary for the maintenance of holiness. But recent studies
have suggested a more economic and political basis for the
opposition to mixed marriages. J.P. Weinberg, in particular,
depicts the post-exilic community as a 'civic temple community'

recent studies which have seen this as a time of increased patriarchalisation:
Terrien, 1986, pp. 71-86)' ('Origins', p. 170).

1.   The text states: 'After these things had been done, the officials
approached me and said, "The people of Israel and the priests and the
Levites have not separated themselves from the peoples of the lands whose
abominations are like those of the Canaanites, the Hittites, the Perizzites,
the Jebusites, the Ammonites, the Moabites, the Egyptians, and the
Amorites. For they have taken some of their daughters to be wives for
themselves and for their sons; so that the seed of holiness has mixed itself
with the peoples of the lands. And in this faithlessness the hand of the
officials and chief men has been foremost"' (Ezra 9.1-2). It is important to
realize that the prohibitions against mixed marriages pertain to both men
and women, according to Ezra's 'confession' (Ezra 10.12). The fact that the
problem here is confined to foreign wives, not husbands, suggests that it is
the men, thus far, who are the culprits. The patterns of intermarriage and
the differences in such patterns between women and men are worth
pursuing through the use of sociological models for analogous situations.
See Smith, *Religion of the Landless*, for a helpful use of contemporary sociological models for an analysis of the post-exilic era. See also T.C. Eskenazi
and E.P. Judd, 'Marriage to a Stranger in Ezra 9–10', in T.C. Eskenazi and
K.H. Richards (eds.), *Second Temple Studies*. II. *Temple and Community*
(Sheffield: JSOT Press, forthcoming).

(*Bürger-Tempel-Gemeinde*),[1] and K.G. Hoglund uses such an understanding of the post-exilic community to explain the specific economic and political grounds for opposition to mixed marriages.[2] These and other scholars suggest that concern with ethnic purity and objections to intermarriage are the products of the socioeconomic issues of the era. Thus Hoglund writes concerning Ezra 9–10,

> One dimension of marriage is as a means of transferring property and social status from one group to another. By circumscribing the options available in marriage through prohibition of marriage outside the group, all property, kinship-related rights and status remain within a closed group.[3]

Accordingly, ethnic purity may be an excuse for a more pragmatic economic and social concern about loss of inherited land. This explanation for the opposition to mixed marriages is appealing. Its strongest support comes, in my opinion, not from the sociological or linguistic analyses, but from Elephantine documents such as the ones we have discussed. *The fear of mixed marriages with their concomitant loss of property to the community makes most sense when women can, in fact, inherit.* Such loss would not be possible when women did not have legal rights to their husbands' or fathers' land. The Elephantine contracts thus help us understand the danger to the land and to the socioeconomic life of the Judean community. The perceived socioeconomic danger from foreign wives in Judah thereby implies that these women had similar rights to those held by women in Elephantine.

In reflecting on the subject of foreign wives, it is important to remember that an opposition to foreign women, so easy to criticize from a distance, is at the same time an affirmation of women who belong to the group. Although foreign women in Ezra 9–10 do not seem to have been given an opportunity to fight against

1. See, e.g., 'Die Agrarverhältnisse in der Bürger-Tempel-Gemeinde der Achämenidenzeit', *Acta Antiqua Academiae Scientiarum Hungaricae* 22 (1974), pp. 473-85.

2. See Hoglund, 'Achaemenid Imperial Administration', esp. pp. 380-453. See also Washington, 'The "Strange Woman" of Proverbs 1–9 and Post-Exilic Judean Society'.

3. Hoglund, 'Achaemenid Imperial Administration', pp. 436-37.

divorce, it is the case that Ezra–Nehemiah considers foreign husbands as abhorrent as foreign wives. Consequently, the Judahites solemnly pledge not only to keep their sons from marrying outside the group but likewise to prevent their daughters from doing so. The intermarriage prohibitions of Ezra–Nehemiah are consistently symmetrical.[1] Rather than being simply a misogynous act, this dismissal of foreign wives is an opposition to some women in favor of others.

Let us now look at some women who are hidden in Ezra–Nehemiah. We turn first to the lists of returnees in Ezra 2 and its parallel in Nehemiah 7. The returnees are listed according to ancestors' names, place of origin or, occasionally, occupation; the names of family 'heads' are generally masculine. One group in particular is of special interest. Ezra 2.55 mentions the descendants of *hassōperet* (*sôperet* in Neh. 7.57; cf. 1 Esdr. 5.33). The word literally means 'the female scribe'. Translators or commentators, however, tend to say that this name denotes either a profession that had become a proper name,[2] or 'the guild or office of scribes'.[3]

Unfortunately, scholars regularly ignore some of the implications of this feminine form. They do not read here a reference to a female. The rationale for bypassing a reference to a woman is derived from the one example in Eccl. 1.1 where a seemingly feminine noun (*qōhelet*) refers to a masculine subject; it overlooks, alas, the numerous other occurrences of such feminine nouns that are recognized as references to females (for example, the word 'herald', *mᵉbaśśeret*, in Isa. 40.9, referring to a female herald, not simply to any professional announcer who is a member of a guild). Overruling the obvious meaning of the word seems to depend on the prior assumption that the term in Ezra–Nehemiah could not refer to a female scribe because such guilds were not likely to have existed in ancient Judah.

---

1. E.g. 'We will not give our daughters to the peoples of the land or take their daughters for our sons' (Neh. 10.30).

2. H.G.M. Williamson, *Ezra, Nehemiah* (WBC, 16; Waco, TX: Word Books, 1985), p. 27.

3. F.C. Fensham, *The Books of Ezra and Nehemiah* (NICOT; Grand Rapids: Eerdmans, 1982), p. 55.

Recognizing that conclusions from names are always tenuous, I nevertheless propose that we indeed consider the possibility that this family owes its origin to a female scribe. The presence of female scribes in the ancient Near East has been documented.[1] Furthermore, Ezra–Nehemiah itself indicates that a clan may take the name of its matriarch (see below). Similar developments, I suggest, may account for this reference to a female scribe.[2]

When commentators ignore or dismiss the feminine aspect of the term, not so much on linguistic grounds as on the basis of presuppositions that mandate exclusion of women, they— translators and commentators, not the biblical text—efface women's presence. I have found only one who entertains the possibility of an actual female scribe: the Jewish mediaeval commentator who appears in *Miqra'ot Gedolot* for Ezra– Nehemiah as Abraham Ibn Ezra[3] proposes that the term could be translated as 'female scribe' (he writes concerning *hassōperet*, יתכן שהוא שם תואר לאשה או פועלה, 'It is possible that this is a title for a woman or a female worker').

Equally intriguing is the episode alluded to above, concerning a clan clearly named after the matriarch's family. According to

1. S. Meier, 'Women and Communication in the Ancient Near East' (unpublished paper, presented at the 1988 International Meeting of SBL, Sheffield), illustrates the presence and functions of female scribes.

2. Admittedly, one could argue that even if my assumption is correct that the reference is to a female scribe, the clan head would have been pre-exilic and therefore the text says little about post-exilic Judah (I am indebted to Donald R. Vance for this critique). The term, however, appears in two post-exilic lists (Ezra 2.55 and Neh. 7.57). Of the two, Ezra 2 is generally considered the later (see, e.g., H.G.M. Williamson, 'The Composition of Ezra i–vi', *JTS* NS 34 [1983], pp. 1-30). It is therefore noteworthy and significant that whereas Neh. 7.57 has *sôperet*, which could be either a name or a title, the later list in Ezra 2.55 has *hassōperet*, using the definite article and thereby eliminating the option of reading the word as a name. The fact that post-exilic scribes or transcribers apparently read *sôperet* as a title, not a name, indicates that the notion of a female scribe was a meaningful one in the post-exilic community.

3. Although the commentary on Ezra–Nehemiah in *Miqra'ot Gedolot* is attributed to Ibn Ezra, the actual commentator may be Moses Kimḥi (I thank Sara Japhet for this information).

Ezra 2.61 (Neh. 7.63 and 1 Esdr. 5.38), the Barzillai clan is named after the wife's family because the man has taken her name. Thus we read, 'the descendants of Barzillai (who had taken a wife from the daughters of Barzillai the Gileadite, and was called by their name)' (Ezra 2.61). Such appropriating of a wife's family name, which most likely indicates that the person also received a share of the wife's inheritance,[1] is rarely attested in the Bible. It therefore provides an important example of a deviation from the more common pattern where the woman is incorporated into her husband's family by taking his name.

It is interesting to note another reference to women in the list. Having stated that 42,360 people had returned, the list mentions that there were, in addition, male and female servants and male and female singers (Ezra 2.65 // Neh. 7.67). It is tempting to link the female singers with the Temple cult, but their place in the list (between servants and animals) suggests that they more likely held a position of entertainers without much status.

Another interesting name appears in yet another list. According to Ezra 8.10, the descendants of Shelomith go up with Ezra. Like some other post-exilic names, Shelomith can be masculine or feminine.[2] The Greek versions of Ezra add a name (Bani) here, rendering the sentence in a way that excludes reading Shelomith as a woman's name: 'from the descendants of Bani, Shelomith son of Josiphiah...' The Hebrew text, however, leaves the sex of the person unspecified. This sentence in the MT states: 'From the descendants of Shelomith: the son of Josiphiah, and with him one hundred sixty men'. According to 1 Chron. 3.19, Shelomith is a daughter of Zerubbabel, the last-known descendant of David to possess any political power (see his role in the return in Ezra 1–6). A seal bearing an inscription 'to

---

1.   Williamson writes, 'The difficulty in Barzillai's case was presumably that he had taken the name of his wife, who was not of a priestly family. He may have done this in order to become the family's heir. Kidner suggests that this "could have been regarded as a renunciation of his priesthood since priests were forbidden an inheritance in the land (Num 18.20)"' (*Ezra, Nehemiah*, p. 37).

2.   See J.J. Slotki: 'Only here is it used as a man's name; elsewhere it is borne by a woman (Salome)' (*Daniel, Ezra and Nehemiah* [London: Soncino, 1951], p. 157).

Shelomith, the maidservant of Elnathan' was discovered in 1975. E. Meyers identifies the seal with Shelomith, daughter of Zerubbabel, and argues that the seal offers a significant post-script to the fate of the Davidic house. He suggests that Elnathan, a governor of Judah (approximately 510–490 BCE), may have attached himself to the Davidic line by marrying Shelomith.[1] It is possible that Ezra 8.10 refers to descendants of the famed princess.

No one links Shelomith of the seal—or the one in 1 Chron. 3.19—with the Shelomith in Ezra 8.10. Instead, translations and commentaries typically erase Shelomith's presence by revocal-izing the name and following the LXX, usually citing M. Noth as a source of authority. The reasons for choosing the LXX for Ezra 8.10 go back to Noth who considers שלמית a man's name and a corruption of שלמות.[2] The implicit rationale is clear. A clan's head is masculine, but this biblical text has a woman's name; it must be a mistake, hence the name must be changed. The logic is of course circular, though perfectly understandable in light of the presuppositions that have governed our reading of the post-exilic era.[3] Unfortunately, most recent commentaries reiterate Noth's view without exploring further the implications of the given MT text.[4]

Another interesting reference to women occurs in a list of those who built Jerusalem's walls. Neh. 3.12 reads:...ועל ידו החזיק שלום הוא ובנותיו, 'Next to him...Shallum repaired—he and his daughters' (JPSV). The translations and commentaries are at

1. 'The Shelomith Seal and Aspects of the Judean Restoration: Some Additional Reconsiderations', *EI* 17 (1985), pp. 33-38.

2. *Die israelitischen Personennamen im Rahmen der gemeinsemitischen Namengebung* (Stuttgart, 1928), p. 165 n. 6. See also A.H.J. Gunneweg: 'Since this can only be a man's name, it is to be corrected' (*Esra* [KAT; Gütersloh: Gerd Mohn, 1985], p. 145 n. 10b).

3. It is the case that Shelomith can be both masculine and feminine. It is masculine in 1 Chron. 26.28 and possibly in 2 Chron. 11.20. Shelomoth appears in the *kethib* of 1 Chron. 23.9, 26.25 and 26, but is altered to Shelomith in the *qere*. Nevertheless, the fact that Ezra 8.10 refers to a clan name that elsewhere in this era refers to a woman has not been brought to the attention of the readers, let alone argued one way or the other.

4. See, e.g., Blenkinsopp, *Ezra–Nehemiah*, p. 159.

times amusing, often irritating. The Jerusalem Bible emends the text, saying that the building was done by 'Shallum...by him and his sons'.[1] Batten is particularly amusing. He writes,

> 'Daughter' is a regular term for the hamlets which grow up about a city and which are dependent upon it, 11[25-31]. Ryle prefers a literal interpretation that Shallum's daughters aided him in the work. But as women in the East were quite sure to have a large share in such work as this, their special mention here is unnecessary. Against the other view it may be urged that a solitary mention of hamlets is inexplicable. Berth[olet] says it would be easiest to reject the words but that such a course is arbitrary. *The meaning is really unknown.*[2]

Suddenly the meaning of 'he and his daughters' is unknown. It is most intriguing that a fairly clear statement should create such confusion, a confusion bred solely by a refusal to recognize the role of women in the building of the city walls. Fortunately, modern commentators fare better, both as translators and interpreters. Williamson and Brockington resist emendation and suppose a reference to women. They conclude, on the basis of Num. 36.8, that, if Shallum had no sons, 'it would be natural for the daughters to help on an occasion like this, since they would inherit his name and property'.[3] On the basis of the Elephantine documents, we may add that daughters could inherit even when there were sons.[4]

The lists that have been examined thus far are among the

---

1.   Shallum is 'ruler of half the district of Jerusalem' (Neh. 3.12), which suggests that he belongs to a prominent family.

2.   L.W. Batten, *A Critical and Exegetical Commentary on the Books of Ezra and Nehemiah* (ICC; New York: Charles Scribner's Sons, 1913), pp. 213-14 (emphasis added).

3.   Brockington, cited by Williamson, *Ezra, Nehemiah*, p. 207. Williamson writes, 'The reference to participation by Shallum's daughters is interesting. The temptation to emend to "sons" should be resisted... Nor can we interpret this as a reference to the (daughter) villages of Jerusalem, since the suffix, "his" is masculine. If Shallum had no sons, "it would be natural for the daughters to help on an occasion like this, since they would inherit his name and property" (Brockington, with reference to Num 36.8)' (*Ezra, Nehemiah*, p. 207).

4.   Thus Yehoishma daughter of Anani inherits even though she has a brother Pilti.

most important ones in Ezra–Nehemiah,[1] referring to key
events: the return from exile, and the building of the city's
walls. If my readings are correct, then a woman makes an
appearance in each of these events. These appearances are
significant even if mere tokens.[2] Obviously, they do not establish gender balance but they nevertheless reflect women's
presence in symbolic and practical ways.

Women have other roles in Ezra–Nehemiah. The prophetess
Noadiah (Neh. 6.14)[3] is an example. She appears as an opponent
of Nehemiah. Since Nehemiah attacks many a leader who dis-
agrees with his policies, little can be concluded about Noadiah's
message. All we can determine is her prominence. After a confrontation with another prophet, Nehemiah calls for vengeance:
'Remember Tobiah and Sanballat, O my God, according to the
things that they did, and also the prophetess Noadiah and the
rest of the prophets who wanted to make me afraid' (Neh.
6.14). We have no further information about Noadiah. The other
named opponents are well known: Tobiah was an Ammonite
official who has hampered Nehemiah all along; Sanballat was the
governor of Samaria. The mention of this otherwise mysterious
prophetess together with them suggests that her status may be
comparable, and that she, like them, was a prominent person.
The reference to Noadiah the prophetess further indicates that
the prophetic office was open to a woman in the post-exilic
period.[4]

Let me close with attention to women's presence at the climax
of the restoration, namely at the public reading of the Torah.
The climactic scene begins as follows:

> And Ezra the priest brought the Torah before the assembly (קהל),
> both men *and women* and all who could hear with understanding,
> on the first day of the seventh month. And he read from it facing

---

1. On the significance of lists, see T.C. Eskenazi, 'The Lists of Ezra–
Nehemiah and the Integrity of the Book', *JBL* 107 (1988), pp. 641-56.

2. Much as it is significant that one of the judges in the Book of Judges
is a woman.

3. Like Shelomith, the name Noadiah can be masculine and feminine. It
is masculine in Ezra 8.33.

4. Only four named women are called 'prophetess' in the Hebrew
Bible. The other three, Miriam, Deborah and Huldah, are pre-exilic.

> the square before the Water Gate from early morning until
> midday, in the presence of the men *and the women* and those who
> could understand; and the ears of all the people were attentive to
> the book of the Torah (Neh. 8.2-4, emphasis added).

Later generations considered this gathering as a second giving
of Torah, analogous to the Sinai event. *qāhāl*, after all, refers not
to a mere aggregate of people, but to a congregation constituted for official holy purposes.[1] But whereas there are doubts
about the role and presence of women at Sinai, given the androcentric message 'do not go near a woman' (Exod. 19.15), which
implies that only men were addressed, no such doubt belongs
to this event. Here women's presence is explicitly and emphatically recognized (note the repetition), indicating religious
egalitarianism, at least on this level of participation.

Conclusions

We have begun with two pictures, each one drawn from a separate community, and each based on different types of sources. I
suggest that we link them. I have tried to bring the women of
Elephantine to the fore as persons who have rights and roles
that our biblical texts do not explicitly describe. I have also
examined the overlooked presences of women in Ezra–
Nehemiah. Without more documents from Judah, it is impossible
to know for sure whether the Jewish women of Judah had
privileges and obligations similar to those of their sisters in
Elephantine. The evidence suggests that they probably did. The
tension concerning foreign women is one such indication; the
mention of women in key passages is another.[2] The pioneer
conditions of the return and the new emphasis on the family
add yet another piece of evidence. But even if one does not
wholly accept an analogy between Jerusalem and Elephantine,
one conclusion is nevertheless inevitable: whatever their precise
role, the Jewish women in the post-exilic era have not been
effaced from history. Their importance is attested in extant

---

1. See Deut. 31.9-13.
2. E.g. the reference to *hassōperet/sôperet* and the Barzillai clan likewise
contribute to this view.

literature, some of their names and also some evidence about their significance have been preserved. It has been my intention to make them more visible. Recognized, these women can help us reconstruct the world of our mothers with greater precision and enhance our understanding of the roots of our cultural and religious traditions.[1]

1.   Versions of this paper had been discussed in two settings: the Joint PhD Colloquium at Iliff School of Theology/Denver University in Denver, and the Jewish Feminist Critique Group in Los Angeles. I thank the participants for their rigorous critique and helpful suggestions. In particular, I thank Donald R. Vance (Iliff/Denver University), Miriyam Glazer (University of Judaism) and William Cutter (Hebrew Union College), who, as respondents, contributed stimulating insights to the work in progress.

BIBLIOGRAPHY

Abel, E., '[E]merging Identities: The Dynamics of Female Friendship in Contemporary Fiction by Women', *Signs* 6 (1981), pp. 413-35.

Abernik, M., *The Book of Samuel A, B* (Hebrew; Presburg, 1872).

Abrabanel, D.I., *A Commentary on the Former Prophets* (Hebrew; Jerusalem: Torah VeDa'at Publishing House, 1955).

Ackerman, S., 'The Queen Mother and the Cult in Ancient Israel', *JBL* 112.3 (1993), pp. 385-401.

Ackroyd, P.R., 'Goddesses, Women and Jezebel', in A. Cameron and A. Kuhrt (eds.), *Images of Women in Antiquity* (Detroit: Wayne State University Press, 1983), pp. 245-59.

—'The Succession Narrative (so-called)', *Int* 33 (1981), pp. 388-92.

Adar, Z., *The Biblical Narrative* (Hebrew; Jerusalem: Education Department of the World Jewish Agency, 2nd edn, 1963).

Aharoni, Y., *The Land of the Bible* (London: Burns & Oates, 1967).

Ahlström, G.W., *An Archaeological Picture of Iron Age Religions in Ancient Palestine* (StudOr, 55.3; Helsinki: Painatusjaos, 1984).

—*Aspects of Syncretism in Israelite Religion* (Lund: Gleerup, 1963).

Albright, W.F., 'The Seal of Eliakim, and the Latest Preexilic History of Judah, with some Observations on Ezekiel', *JBL* 51 (1932).

Alcoff, L., 'Cultural Feminism versus Post-Structuralism: The Identity Crisis in Feminist Theory', in E. Minnich, J. O'Barr and R. Rosenfeld (eds.), *Reconstructing the Academy: Women's Education and Women's Studies* (Chicago: University of Chicago Press, 1988), pp. 257-88.

Alter, R., 'How Convention Helps us Read: The Case of the Bible's Annunciation Type-Scene', *Prooftexts* 3 (1983), pp. 115-30.

—*The Art of Biblical Narrative* (New York: Basic Books, 1981).

Althusser, L., *Lenin and Philosophy* (London: Monthly Review Press, 1971).

Andersen, F.I., 'The Socio-Juridical Background of the Naboth Incident', *JBL* 85 (1966), pp. 46-57.

Andreasen, N.-E., 'The Role of the Queen Mother in Israelite Society', *CBQ* 45 (1983), pp. 179-94.

Aschkenasy, N., *Eve's Journey: Feminine Images in Hebraic Literary Tradition* (Philadelphia: University of Pennsylvania Press, 1986).

Atwood, M., 'Circe/Mud Poems', in *Selected Poems* (New York: Simon & Schuster, 1976).

Bach, A. (ed.), *The Pleasure of Her Text: Feminist Readings of Biblical and Historical Texts* (Philadelphia: Trinity Press International, 1990).

Bal, M., 'Myth à *la Lettre*: Freud, Mann, Genesis and Rembrandt, and the Story of the Son', in S. Rimmon-Kenan (ed.), *Discourse in Psychoanalysis and Literature* (London: Methuen, 1987); repr. in A. Brenner (ed.), *A Feminist Companion to Genesis* (The Feminist Companion to the Bible, 2; Sheffield: Sheffield Academic Press, 1993).

—*Death and Dissymetry: The Politics of Coherence in the Book of Judges* (Chicago: Chicago University Press, 1988).

—*Lethal Love: Feminist Literary Readings of Biblical Love Stories* (Chicago: Chicago University Press, 1987).

—*Murder and Difference* (Bloomington: Indiana University Press, 1988).

—*Narratology: Introduction to the Theory of Narrative* (Toronto: University of Toronto Press, 1985).

Baldwin, J.G., *1 & 2 Samuel* (TOTC; Downers Grove, IL: Inter-Varsity Press, 1988).

Barthes, R., 'Introduction à l'analyse structurale des récits', *Communications* 8 (1966), pp. 1-27.

Bass, D.C., 'Women's Studies and Biblical Studies: An Historic Perspective', *JSOT* 22 (1982), pp. 6-12.

Batten, L.W., *A Critical and Exegetical Commentary on the Books of Ezra and Nehemiah* (ICC; New York: Charles Scribner's Sons, 1913).

Begrich, J., 'Atalja, die Tochter Omris', *ZAW* 53 (1935), pp. 78-79.

Bekkenkamp, J., *Canon en keuze: Het bejbelse Hooglied en de Twenty-One Love Poems van Adrienne Rich als brannen van theologie* (Kampen: Kok, 1993).

Ben-Barak, Z., 'Succession to the Throne in Israel and in Assyria', *OLP* 17 (1986), pp. 85-100.

—'The Religious-Prophetic Background of the "Law of the King" (Deuteronomy 17.14-20), in J. Greenfield and M. Weinfeld (eds.), *Shnaton: An Annual for Biblical and Ancient Near Eastern Studies* (Hebrew; Jerusalem: Newman, 1975).

Berlin, A., 'Characterization in Biblical Narrative: David's Wives', *JSOT* 23 (1982), pp. 69-85; incorporated in *Poetics and Interpretation of Biblical Narrative* (Bible and Literature Series, 9; Sheffield: Almond Press, 1983).

Beuken, W.A.M., 'No Wise King without a Wise Woman (I Kings III 16–28)', in A.S. Van der Woude (ed.), *New Avenues in the Study of the Old Testament* (Leiden: Brill, 1989), pp. 1-10.

Bin-Nun, S.R., *The Tawananna in the Hittite Kingdom* (Heidelberg: Carl Winter, 1975).

Bird, P., 'Images of Women in the Old Testament', in R. Radford Ruether (ed.), *Religion and Sexism: Images of Women in the Jewish and Christian Traditions* (New York: Simon & Schuster, 1974), pp. 41-88.

—'The Harlot as Heroine: Narrative Art and Social Presupposition in Three Old Testament Texts', in M. Amihai, G.W. Coats and A.M. Solomon (eds.), *Narrative Research on the Hebrew Bible* (*Semeia* 46; Atlanta: Society of Biblical Literature, 1989).

—'The Place of Women in the Israelite Cultus', in P.D. Miller, Jr, P.D. Hanson and S.D. McBride (eds.), *Ancient Israelite Religion* (Philadelphia: Fortress Press, 1987), pp. 397-420.

—'Women's Religion in Ancient Israel', in B.S. Lesko (ed.), *Women's Earliest Records from Ancient Egypt and Western Asia* (BJS, 166; Atlanta: Scholars Press, 1989), pp. 283-98.

Blaikie, W.G., *The First Book of Samuel* (Expositor's Bible; New York: Armstrong & Son, n.d.).

Blenkinsopp, J., 'Theme and Motif in the Succession History (2 Sam. xi 2ff) and the Yahwist Corpus', in J.A. Emerton *et al.* (eds.), *Volume du Congrès International pour l'Etude de l'Ancien Testament* (VTSup, 15; Leiden: Brill, 1965), pp. 44-57.

—*Ezra–Nehemiah: A Commentary* (OTL; Philadelphia: Westminster Press, 1988).

Boulding, E., *The Underside of History: A View of Women through Time* (Newbury Park: SAGE Publications, rev. edn, 1992).

Bremond, C., 'La logique des possibles narratifs', *Communications* 8 (1966), pp. 60-76; ET 'The Logic of Narrative Possibilities', *NLH* 11 (1980).

Brenner, A., *Ruth and Naomi: Literary, Stylistic and Linguistic Studies in the Book of Ruth* (Hebrew; Tel Aviv: Afik, Sifriyat Po'alim and HaKibbutz HaMe'uchad, 1988).

—*The Israelite Woman: Social Role and Literary Type in Biblical Narrative* (The Biblical Seminar, 2; Sheffield: JSOT Press, 1985).

Bright, J., *A History of Israel* (Philadelphia: Westminster Press, 1981).

—*Jeremiah* (AB, 21; Garden City, NY: Doubleday, 1965).

Brooten, B., *Women Leaders in the Ancient Jewish Synagogue: Inscriptional Evidence and Background Issues* (BJS, 36; Chico, CA: Scholars Press, 1982).

Brueggemann, W., *First and Second Samuel* (Interpretation;. Louisville, KY: John Knox, 1990).

—*Genesis: A Bible Commentary for Teaching and Preaching* (Interpretation; Atlanta: John Knox, 1982).

—*In Man We Trust* (Richmond, VA: John Knox, 1972).

Brunner, H., 'Das hörende Herz', *TLZ* 11 (1954), cols. 698-99.

—'Gerechtigkeit als Fundament des Thrones', *VT* 8 (1958), pp. 426-28.

Buber, M., *The Prophetic Faith* (New York: Macmillan, 1949).

Bynum, V., *Unruly Women: The Politics of Social and Sexual Control in the Old South* (Chapel Hill: University of North Carolina Press, 1992).

Cady Stanton, E. (ed.), *The Woman's Bible* (New York: European Publishing Co., 1895).

Caird, G.B., *The First and Second Books of Samuel* (*IB*, II; Nashville: Abingdon Press, 1953).

Camp, C.V., '1 and 2 Kings', in C.A. Newsom and S.H. Ringe (eds.), *The Women's Bible Commentary* (Louisville, KY: Westminster Press/John Knox, 1992), pp. 96-109.

—*Wisdom and the Feminine in the Book of Proverbs* (Bible and Literature Series, 11; Sheffield: Almond Press, 1985).

Carlson, R.A., *David, the Chosen King: A Traditio-Historical Approach to the Second Book of Samuel* (trans. E.J. Sharpe and S. Rudman; Stockholm: Almqvist & Wiksell, 1964).

Causse, A., *Du groupe ethnique à la communauté religieuse: Le problème sociologique de la religion d'Israël* (Paris: Alcan, 1937).

—*Les disperses d'Israël: Les origines de la Diaspora et son rôle dans la formation de Judaïsme* (Paris: Alcan, 1929).

Chafin, K.L., *1, 2 Samuel* (The Communicator's Commentary; Dallas: Word Books, 1989).

Chambers, R., 'Alter Ego: Intertextuality, Irony and the Politics of Reading', in M. Worton and J. Still (eds.), *Intertextuality: Theories and Practices* (Manchester: Manchester University Press, 1990), pp. 143-58.

Childs, B.S., 'On Reading the Elijah Narratives', *Int* 34 (1980), pp. 128-37.

Christ, C., 'Diving Deep and Surfacing', in *Women Writers on Spiritual Questions* (Boston: Beacon Press, 1980).

Clines, D.J.A., 'Michal Observed: An Introduction to Reading her Story', in Clines and Eskenazi (eds.), *Telling Queen Michal's Story*, pp. 24-63.

Clines, D.J.A., and T.C. Eskenazi (eds.), *Telling Queen Michal's Story: An Experiment in Comparative Interpretation* (JSOTSup, 119; Sheffield: JSOT Press, 1991).

Coats, G.W., *Genesis: With an Introduction to Narrative Literature* (FOTL, 1; Grand Rapids: Eerdmans, 1983).

—'Parable, Fable, and Anecdote: Storytelling in the Succession Narrative', *Int* 35 (1981), pp. 377-80.

Coggins, R., 'On Kings and Disguises', *JSOT* 50 (1991), pp. 55-62.

—'The Origins of Jewish Diaspora', in R.E. Clements (ed.), *The World of Ancient Israel* (Cambridge: Cambridge University Press, 1989).

Cohen, S.J.D., 'Solomon and the Daughter of Pharaoh: Intermarriage, Conversion, and the Impurity of Women', in *Ancient Studies in Memory of Elias Bickerman* (*JANESCU* 16–17 [1984–85]).

Cohn, R.L., 'Convention and Creativity in the Book of Kings: The Case of the Dying Monarch', *CBQ* 47 (1985), pp. 603-16.

Colesin, J., and V. Matthews (eds.), *Go to the Land I Will Show You: Studies in Honor of Dwight W. Young* (Winona Lake, IN: Eisenbrauns, 1994).

Cowley, A.E., *Aramaic Papyri of the Fifth Century BC* (Oxford: Clarendon Press, 1923).

Crenshaw, J., 'Method in Determining Wisdom Influence upon Historical Literature', *JBL* 88 (1969), pp. 129-42.

Cross, F.M., 'A New Qumran Biblical Fragment Related to the Original Hebrew Underlying the Septuagint', *BASOR* 132 (1953), pp. 15-26.

—*Canaanite Myth and Hebrew Epic* (Cambridge, MA: Harvard University Press, 1973).

Culley, R., 'Some Comments on Structural Analysis and Biblical Studies', in J.A. Emerton *et al.* (eds.), *Congress Volume Uppsala 1971* (VTSup, 22; Leiden: Brill, 1972).

Culver, R.D., 'Jezebel', in M.C. Tenney (ed.), *The Zondervan Pictorial Encyclopedia* (Grand Rapids: Zondervan, 1975), III, pp. 589-90.

Davies, G.I., *Ancient Hebrew Inscriptions: Corpus and Concordance* (Cambridge: Cambridge University Press, 1991).

Delekat, L., 'Tendenz und Theologie der David-Salomo-Erzählung', in F. Maass (ed.), *Das ferne und nahe Wort* (BZAW, 105; Berlin: Töpelmann, 1967).

Deurloo, K.A., 'The King's Wisdom in Judgment: Narration as Example (I Kings iii)', in A.S. van der Woude (ed.), *New Avenues in the Study of the Old Testament* (Leiden: Brill, 1989).

Dever, W.G., *Recent Archaeological Discoveries and Biblical Research* (The Samuel and Althea Stroum Lectures in Jewish Studies; Seattle: University of Washington, 1990).

Dhorme, L.P., *Les Livres de Samuel* (Paris: Gabalda, 1910).

Dietrich, M., O. Loretz and J. Sanmartin, *Die Keilalphabetischen Texte aus Ugarit* (Neukirchen–Vluyn: Neukirchener Verlag; Kevalaer: Butzon & Bercker, 1976).

Dietrich, W., *Prophetie und Geschichte* (FRLANT, 108; Göttingen: Vandenhoeck & Ruprecht, 1972).

Dijk-Hemmes, F. van, 'Tamar and the Limits of Patriarchy: Between Rape and Seduction (2 Samuel 13 and Genesis 38)', in M. Bal (ed.), *Anti-Covenant: Counter-Reading Women's Lives in the Hebrew Bible* (JSOTSup, 81; Sheffield: JSOT Press, 1989), pp. 135-56.

Dim, A., 'Ha-Isha ha-gedolah mishunam (2 Kings 4)' (Hebrew; 'The Great Woman of Shunam'), in *Proceedings of the Eighth World Congress of Jewish Studies A: The Period of the Bible* (Jerusalem: World Union of Jewish Studies, 1982), p. 21.

Donaldson, L.E., *Decolonizing Feminism: Race, Gender and Empire Building* (Chapel Hill: University of North Carolina Press, 1992).

Donner, H., 'Art und Herkunft des Amtes der Königinmutter im Alten Testament', in R. Kienle *et al.* (eds.), *Festschrift Johannes Friedrich zum 65. Geburtstag* (Heidelberg: Carl Winter, 1959).

Driver, G.R., *Aramaic Documents of the Fifth Century BC* (Oxford: Clarendon Press, rev. edn, 1965 [1954]).

Dundes, A., *The Morphology of North American Indian Folktales* (Folklore Fellows Communications, 195; Helsinki: Suomalainen Tiedeakatemia, 1964).

Eissfeldt, O., *The Old Testament: An Introduction* (New York: Harper & Row, 1965).

Emerton, J.A., 'New Light on Israelite Religion: The Interpretation of the Inscriptions from Kuntillet 'Ajrud', *ZAW* 94 (1982), pp. 2-20.

Eskenazi, T.C., 'The Lists of Ezra–Nehemiah and the Integrity of the Book', *JBL* (1988), pp. 641-56.

Eskenazi, T.C., and E.P. Judd, 'Marriage to a Stranger in Ezra 9-10', in T.C. Eskenazi and K.H. Richards (eds.), *Second Temple Studies. II. Temple and Community* (Sheffield: JSOT Press, forthcoming).

Eslinger, L.M., *Kingship of God in Crisis: A Close Reading of 1 Samuel 1–12* (Bible and Literature Series, 10; Sheffield: Almond Press, 1985).

Even-Shoshan, A., *A New Concordance of the Bible* (Hebrew; Jerusalem: Kiryat Sefer, 6th edn, 1977).

Exum, J.C., 'Jezebel', in P.J. Achtemeier (ed.), *Harper's Bible Dictionary* (San Francisco: Harper & Row, 1985).

—'Murder they Wrote: Ideology and the Manipulation of Female Presence in Biblical Narrative', *USQR* 43 (1989), pp. 19-39; repr. in Bach (ed.), *The Pleasure of Her Text*, pp. 45-67.

Fales, F.M., 'Kilamuwa and the Foreign Kings: Propaganda vs. Power', *WO* 10 (1979), pp. 6-22.

Fensham, F.C., 'Widow, Orphan and Poor in Ancient Near Eastern Legal and Wisdom Literature', *JNES* 21 (1962), pp. 129-39.

—*The Books of Ezra and Nehemiah* (NICOT; Grand Rapids: Eerdmans, 1982).

Flanagan, J.W., 'Court History or Succession Document: A Study of 2 Sam. 9–20 and 1 Kings 1–2', *JBL* 91 (1972), pp. 72-81.

—'Succession and Genealogy in the Davidic Dynasty', in H.B. Huffmon,

F.A. Spina and A.R.W. Green (eds.), *The Quest for the Kingdom of God: Studies in Honor of George E. Mendenhall* (Winona Lake, IN: Eisenbrauns, 1983), pp. 35-55.

Fohrer, G., *Ezechiel* (Tübingen: Mohr [Paul Siebeck], 1955).

Fontaine, C.R., *Traditional Sayings in the Old Testament: A Contextual Study* (The Bible and Literature Series, 5; Sheffield: Almond Press, 1982).

Fox, M.V., *The Song of Songs and Ancient Egyptian Love Songs* (Madison: University of Wisconsin Press, 1985).

Freedman, D.N., 'The Song of Hannah and Psalm 113', *EI* 14 (1978), pp. 56-69.

—'Yahweh of Samaria and his Asherah', *BA* 50 (1987), pp. 241-49.

Friedman, R.E., *The Exile and Biblical Narrative* (HSM, 22; Chico, CA: Scholars Press, 1981).

Frow, J., 'Intertextuality and Ontology', in M. Worton and J. Still (eds.), *Intertextuality: Theories and Practices* (Manchester: Manchester University Press, 1990), pp. 45-55.

Frymer-Kensky, T., 'Law and Philosophy: The Case of Sex in the Bible', *Semeia* 45 (1989), pp. 89-102.

Fuchs, E., '"For I Have the Way of Women": Deception, Gender, and Ideology in Biblical Narrative', *Semeia* 42 (1988), pp. 68-83.

—'The Literary Characterization of Mothers and Sexual Politics in the Hebrew Bible', in A. Yarbro Collins (ed.), *Feminist Perspectives on Biblical Scholarship* (SBL Centennial Publications, 10; Chico, CA: Scholars Press, 1985), pp. 117-36.

—'The Literary Characterization of Mothers and Sexual Politics', in A. Yarbro Collins (ed.), *Feminist Perspectives on Biblical Scholarship* (SBL Centennial Publications; Atlanta: Scholars Press, 1985), pp. 117-36; *Semeia* 46 (1989), pp. 151-65.

—'Who is Hiding the Truth? Deceptive Women and Biblical Androcentrism', in A. Yarbro Collins (ed.), *Feminist Perspectives on Biblical Scholarship* (SBL Centennial Publications; Atlanta: Scholars Press, 1985), pp. 137-44.

Gadd, C.J., 'The Harran Inscriptions of Nabonidus', *Anatolian Studies* 8 (1958), pp. 35-92.

Gallop, J., 'The Monster in the Mirror: The Feminist Critic's Psychoanalysis', in R. Feldstein and J. Root (eds.), *Feminism and Psychoanalysis* (Ithaca, NY: Cornell University Press, 1989), pp. 13-24.

Gehman, H.S. (ed.), *The New Westminster Dictionary of the Bible* (Philadelphia: Westminster Press, 1970).

Gerstenberger, E., *Jahwe—ein patriarchaler Gott? Traditionelles Gottesbild und feministische Theologie* (Stuttgart: Kohlhammer, 1988).

Gilligan, C., *In a Different Voice: Psychological Theory and Women's Development* (Cambridge, MA: Harvard University Press, 1982).

Gilula, M., 'To Yahweh Shomron and his Asherah', *Shnaton* 3–4 (1978–79), pp. xv-xvi (Eng.), 129-37 (Heb.).

Ginzberg, L., *The Legends of the Jews* (Philadelphia: Jewish Publication Society of America, 1968), VI.

Girard, R., *Things Hidden since the Foundation of the World* (Stanford: Stanford University Press, 1987).

—*To Double Business Bound* (Baltimore: Johns Hopkins University Press, 1978).

—*Violence and the Sacred* (Baltimore: Johns Hopkins University Press, 1977).

Gordon, C.H., *Ugaritic Textbook* (Rome: Pontificium Institutum Biblicum, 1965).

Gordon, R.P., *1 & 2 Samuel* (OTG; Sheffield: JSOT Press, 1984).

Görg, M., 'A Divine Oracle through a Dream', in *ANET*, p. 449.

—*Gott–König-Reden in Israel und Ägypten* (BWANT, 105; Stuttgart: Kohlhammer, 1975).

Gottwald, N.C., *The Tribes of Yahweh: A Sociology of Liberated Israel 1250–1050 BCE* (London: SCM Press, 1979).

Gravett, S.L., 'Subject in Genesis 34: A Literary Analysis' (unpublished paper, Duke University, 1990).

Gray, J., *I and II Kings: A Commentary* (OTL; repr.; Philadelphia: Westminster Press; London: SCM Press, 2nd rev. edn, 1975 [1970]).

Greenberg, M., *Ezekiel 1–20* (AB, 22; Garden City, NY: Doubleday, 1983).

Greimas, A.-J., *Structural Semantics: An Attempt at a Method* (trans. D. McDowell, R. Schleifer and A. Velie, with an introduction by R. Schleifer; Lincoln: University of Nebraska Press, 1983).

Gressmann, H., *Die älteste Geschichtsschreibung und Prophetie Israels* [Göttingen: Vandenhoeck & Ruprecht, 2nd edn, 1921].

Gruber, M.I., 'Women in the Cult according to the Priestly Code', in J. Neusner, B.A. Levine and E.S. Frerichs (eds.), *Judaic Perspectives on Ancient Israel* (Philadelphia: Fortress Press, 1987), pp. 35-48.

Gunn, D.M., *The Story of King David: Genre and Interpretation* (JSOTSup, 6; Sheffield: JSOT Press, 1978).

—*The Fate of King Saul: An Interpretation of a Biblical Story* (JSOTSup, 14; Sheffield: JSOT Press, 1980).

Gunneweg, A.H.J., *Esra* (KAT; Gütersloh: Gerd Mohn, 1985).

Gurney, O.R., *The Hittites* (Harmondsworth: Penguin, 1954).

Hackett, J.A., 'Women's Studies and the Hebrew Bible', in R.E. Friedman and H.G.M. Williamson (eds.), *The Future of Biblical Studies: The Hebrew Scriptures* (SBL Semeia Studies; Atlanta: Scholars Press, 1987), pp. 141-64.

Hallo, W.W., 'From Qarqar to Carchemish: Assyria and Israel in the Light of New Discoveries', *BA* 23 (1960), pp. 34-61.

Halpern, B., 'The Baal (and the Asherah) in Seventh-Century Judah: Yhwh's Retainers Retired', in R. Barthelmus, T. Krüger and H. Utzschneider (eds.), *Konsequente Traditionsgeschichte: Festschrift für Klaus Baltzer zum 65. Geburtstag* (OBO, 126; Freiburg: Universitätsverlag; Göttingen: Vandenhoeck & Ruprecht, 1993), pp. 115-54.

Handy, L., 'Dissenting Deities or Obedient Angels: Divine Hierarchies in Ugarit and the Bible', *BR* 35 (1990), pp. 18-35.

Haran, M., *Temple and Sacrifice in Ancient Israel* (Oxford: Clarendon Press, 1978).

Haskell, M., *From Reverence to Rape: The Treatment of Women in the Movies* (Chicago: University of Chicago Press, 1987).

Hauser, A.J., and R. Gregory, *From Carmel to Horeb: Elijah in Crisis* (JSOTSup, 85; Sheffield: Almond Press, 1990).

Heltzer, M., *The Internal Organization of the Kingdom of Ugarit* (Wiesbaden: Reichert, 1982).

Hermisson, H.-J., 'Weisheit und Geschichte', in H.W. Wolff (ed.), *Probleme biblischer Theologie: Gerhard von Rad zum 70. Geburtstag* (Munich: Chr. Kaiser Verlag, 1971).

Herner, S., 'Athalja: Ein Beitrag zur Frage nach dem Alte des Jahwisten und des Elohisten', in *Vom alten Testament: Festschrift Karl Marti* (BZAW, 41; Berlin: de Gruyter, 1925).

Herrmann, S., 'Die Königsnovelle in Ägypten und Israel', in *Wissenschaftliche Zeitschrift der Karl-Marx Universität, Leipzig* (Gesellschafts- und Sprachwissenschaftliche Reihe, 3; Leipzig: Karl-Marx Universität, 1953–54, Part 1).

Hertzberg, N.H.W., *I & II Samuel* (trans. J.S. Bowden; OTL; London: SCM Press, 1964 [1960]).

Hoffmann, H.D., *Reform und Reformen: Untersuchungen zu einem Grundthema der deuteronomistischen Geschichtsschreibung* (ATANT, 66; Zürich: Theologischer Verlag, 1980).

Hoglund, K.G., 'Achaemenid Imperial Administration in Syria–Palestine and the Missions of Ezra and Nehemiah' (PhD dissertation, Duke University, 1989).

Horst, F., 'Die Kultusreform des Königs Josia (II. Rg. 22-23)', *ZDPV* 77 (1923), pp. 220-38.

Hyatt, J.P., 'The Deuteronomic Edition of Jeremiah', in R.C. Beatty, J.P. Hyatt and M.K. Spears (eds.), *Vanderbilt Studies in the Humanities I* (Nashville: Vanderbilt University Press, 1951), pp. 71-95.

Ihromi, 'Die Königsmutter und der Amm Ha'arez im Reich Juda', *VT* 24 (1974), pp. 421-29.

Irigaray, L., 'Sexual Difference', in T. Moi (ed.), *French Feminist Thought* (Oxford and New York: Blackwell, 1987), pp. 118-30.

Iser, W., *The Implied Reader* (Baltimore: Johns Hopkins University Press, 1974).

Ishida, T., 'Solomon who is Greater than David: Solomon's Succession in 1 Kings I–II in the Light of the Inscription of Kilamawa King of Y'dy-Sam'al', in J.A. Emerton (ed.), *Congress Volume: Salamanca 1984* (VTSup, 36; Leiden: Brill, 1985), pp. 145-53.

—'Solomon's Succession to the Throne of David: A Political Analysis', in *idem* (ed.), *Studies in the Period of David and Solomon and Other Essays* (Tokyo: Jamakawa-Shuppanska, 1979), pp. 175-87.

—'The House of Ahab', *IEJ* 25 (1975), pp. 135-37.

—*The Royal Dynasties in Ancient Israel* (BZAW, 142; Berlin: de Gruyter, 1977).

Jepsen, A., *Die Quellen des Königsbuches* (Halle: Niemeyer, 2nd edn, 1956).

Jobling, D., 'Mieke Bal on Biblical Narrative', *RSR* 17 (1991), pp. 1-10.

—*The Sense of Biblical Narrative*. II. *Structural Analyses in the Hebrew Bible* (JSOTSup, 39; Sheffield: JSOT Press, 1986).

Johnston, E.B., 'Jezebel', in G.W. Bromiley (ed.), *The International Standard Bible Encyclopedia* (Grand Rapids: Eerdmans, 1982), pp. 1057-59.

Kampman, A.A., 'Tawannamans, der Titel der hethitischen Königin', *JEOL* 2.6-7 (1939–42), pp. 432-42.

Katzenstein, H.J., 'Who were the Parents of Athalia', *IEJ* 5 (1955), pp. 194-97.

Kaufman, S.A., *The Akkadian Influences on Aramaic* (The Oriental Institute of the University of Chicago, Assyriological Studies, 19; Chicago: University of Chicago Press, 1974).

Kenik, H.A., *Design for Kingship: The Deuteronomistic Narrative Technique in 1 Kings 3.4-15* (SBLDS, 69; Chico, CA: Scholars Press, 1983).

Kent, R.G., *Old Persian: Grammar, Texts, Lexicon* (AOS, 33; New Haven: American Oriental Society, 1950).

Kittel, R., *Die Bücher der Könige* (HKAT, 1.5; Göttingen: Vandenhoeck & Ruprecht, 1900).

Klein, R.W., *1 Samuel* (WBC, 10; Waco, TX: Word Books, 1983).

Knauf, E.A., 'War Biblisch-Hebräisch eine Sprache? Empirische Gesichtspunkte zur Annäherung an die Sprache der althebräischen Literatur', *ZAH* 3 (1990), pp. 11-23.

Knight, D.A., 'Moral Values and Literary Traditions: The Case of the Succession Narrative (2 Samuel 9–20; 1 Kings 1–2)', in P.J. Haas (ed.), *Biblical Hermeneutics in Jewish Moral Discourse* (*Semeia* 34; Atlanta: Scholars Press, 1985), pp. 7-23.

Kochavi, M, 'The Land of Geshur Project', *IEJ* 39.1 (1989), pp. 1-15.

Kraeling, E.G., *The Brooklyn Museum Aramaic Papyri: New Documents of the Fifth Century BC from the Jewish Colony at Elephantine* (New Haven: Yale University Press, 1953).

Kristeva, J., *Revolution in Poetic Language* (trans. M. Waller; New York: Columbia University Press, 1975).

Laroche, E., 'Le Voeu de Puduhepa', *RA* 43 (1949), pp. 55-78.

Lasine, S., 'Jehoram and the Cannibal Mothers (2 Kings 6.24-33): Solomon's Judgment in an Inverted World', *JSOT* 50 (1991), pp. 27-53.

—'The Riddle of Solomon's Judgment and the Riddle of Human Nature in the Hebrew Bible', *JSOT* 45 (1989), pp. 61-86.

Lauretis, T. de, *Technologies of Gender: Essays on Theory, Film and Fiction* (Bloomington: Indiana University Press, 1987).

Leach, E., 'The Legitimacy of Solomon: Some Structural Aspects of Old Testament History', *European Journal of Sociology* 7 (1966), pp. 58-101, reprinted in M. Lane (ed.), *Introduction to Structuralism* (New York: Basic Books, 1970), pp. 248-92.

Lemaire, A., 'Who or What was Yahweh's Asherah?', *BARev* 10.6 (1984), pp. 42-51.

Levenson, J.D., '1 Samuel 25 as Literature and as History', *CBQ* 40 (1978), pp. 11-28.

Levenson, J.D., and B. Halpern, 'The Political Import of David's Marriages', *JBL* 99.4 (1980), pp. 507-18.

Lévi-Strauss, C., 'L'analyse morphologique des contes russes', *International Journal of Slavic Linguistics and Poetics* 3 (1966), pp. 122-49.

Levin, C., 'Joschija im deuteronomistischen Geschichtswerk', *ZAW* 96 (1984), pp. 351-71.

Lewy, H., 'Nitokris-Naqi'a', *JNES* 2 (1952), pp. 264-86.

Lichtheim, M., *Ancient Egyptian Literature* (Berkeley: University of California Press, 1975).

Lipiński, E., 'Ahat-Milki, reine d'Ugarit et la guerre du Mukiš', *OLP* 12 (1981).

—'The Wife's Right to Divorce in the Light of an Ancient Near Eastern Tradition', *Jewish Law Annual* 4 (1981), pp. 9-27.

Ljung, I., *Silence or Suppression: Attitudes toward Women in the Old Testament* (Acta Universitatis Upsaliensis; Uppsala Women's Studies, Women in Religion, 2; Stockholm: Almqvist & Wiksell, 1989).

Long, B.O., 'A Figure at the Gate: Readers, Reading, and Biblical Theologians', in G.M. Tucker, D.L. Peterson and R.R. Wilson (eds.), *Canon, Theology, and Old Testament Interpretation: Essays in Honor of Brevard S. Childs* (Philadelphia: Fortress Press, 1988), pp. 166-86.

—*1 Kings—With an Introduction to Historical Literature* (FOTL, 9; Grand Rapids: Eerdmans, 1984).

—*2 Kings* (FOTL, 10; Grand Rapids: Eerdmans, 1991).

Luckenbill, D.D., *Ancient Records of Assyria and Babylonia* (New York: Greenwood, 1968).

Lust, J., 'A Gentle Breeze or a Roaring Thunderous Sound?', *VT* 25 (1975), pp. 110-15.

Maier, W.A. III, *'Ašerah: Extrabiblical Evidence* (HSM, 37; Atlanta: Scholars Press, 1986).

Malamat, A., 'Aspects of the Foreign Policies of David and Solomon', *JNES* 22 (1963), pp. 1-17.

—'The Historical Background of the Assassination of Amon, King of Judah', *IEJ* 3 (1953).

—*Israel in Biblical Times: Historical Essays* (Hebrew; Jerusalem: Bialik Institute, 1983).

—'Comments on E. Leach: "The Legitimacy of Solomon—Some Structural Aspects of Old Testament History"', *European Journal of Sociology* 8 (1967).

Maranda, P. (ed.), *Soviet Structural Folkloristics: Texts by Meletinsky, Nekludov, Novik, and Segal with Tests of the Approach by Jilek and Jilek-Aall, Reid and Layton* (Approaches to Semiotics, 43; The Hague: Mouton, 1974).

Mayes, A.D.H., *The Story of Israel between Settlement and Exile* (London: SCM Press, 1983).

Mazar, B., 'Geshur and Maacah', *JBL* 80 (1961), pp. 16-28.

McCarter, P.K., Jr, *I Samuel* (AB, 8; Garden City, NY: Doubleday, 1980).

—'Aspects of the Religion of the Israelite Monarchy', in P.D. Miller, Jr, P. Hanson and S.D. McBride (eds.), *Ancient Israelite Religion: Essays in Honor of Frank Moore Cross* (Philadelphia: Fortress Press, 1987), pp. 137-55.

McCarthy, D.J., 'Compact and Kingship: Stimuli for Hebrew Covenant Thinking', in T. Ishida (ed.), *Studies in the Period of David and Solomon and Other Essays* (Tokyo: Yamakawa-Shuppansha, 1982).

McCown, C.C., 'City', *IDB*, I, pp. 632-38.

—'Gate', *IDB*, II, p. 355.

McDowall, H.M., *Jezebel: A Tragedy* (Oxford: Basil Blackwell, 1924).

McKenzie, S.L., *The Chronicler's Use of the Deuteronomistic History* (HSM, 33; Atlanta: Scholars Press, 1984).

Meier, S., 'Women and Communication in the Ancient Near East' (unpublished paper, presented at the 1988 International Meeting of SBL, Sheffield).

Meletinsky, E., *et al.*, 'Problems of the Structural Analysis of Fairytales', in Maranda (ed.), *Soviet Structural Folkloristics*, I, pp. 73-139.

Meshel, Z., 'Did Yahweh have a Consort?', *BARev* 5.2 (1979), pp. 24-35.

Meyers, C., 'An Ethnoarchaeological Analysis of Hannah's Sacrifice', in D.P. Wright, D.N. Freedman and A. Hurvitz (eds.), *Pomegranates and Golden Bells: Studies in Biblical, Jewish, and Near Eastern Ritual, Laws, and Literature in Honor of Jacob Milgrom* (Winona Lake, IN: Eisenbrauns, forthcoming).

—'Of Drums and Damsels—Women's Performance in Ancient Israel', *BA* 54 (1991), pp. 16-27.

—'The Creation of Patriarchy in the West: A Consideration of Judeo-Christian Tradition', in A. Zagarell (ed.), *The Foundations of Gender Inequality* (Kalamazoo: New Issues Press, forthcoming).

—'The Israelite Empire: In Defense of King Solomon', *Michigan Quarterly Review* 22 (1983).

—*Discovering Eve: Ancient Israelite Women in Context* (Oxford and New York: Oxford University Press, 1988).

Meyers, E., 'The Shelomith Seal and Aspects of the Judean Restoration: Some Additional Reconsiderations', *EI* 17 (1985), pp. 33-38.

Miller, J.M., and J.H. Hayes, *A History of Ancient Israel and Judah* (Philadelphia: Westminster Press, 1986).

Miller, N., *The Heroine's Text: Readings in the French and English Novel, 1722–1782* (New York: Columbia University Press, 1980).

Molin, G., 'Die Stellung der Gebira im Staate Juda', *TZ* 10 (1954), pp. 161-75.

Morgan, T.E., 'Is There an Intertext in this Text? Literary and Interdisciplinary Approaches to Intertextuality', *American Journal of Semiotics* 3.4 (1985), pp. 1-40.

Morgenstern, J., 'The Oldest Documents of the Hexateuch', *HUCA* 4 (1927).

Morton, P., *Disfigured Images: The Historical Assault on Afro-American Women* (New York: Greenwood, 1991).

Murphy, R.E., 'The Kerygma of the Book of Proverbs', *Int* 20 (1966), pp. 3-14.

Natanson, M., *Anonymity: A Study in the Philosophy of Alfred Schutz* (Bloomington: Indiana University Press, 1986).

—*Phenomenology, Role and Reason* (Springfield, IL: Charles C. Thomas, 1974).

Nelson, R.D., *The Double Redaction of the Deuteronomistic History* (JSOTSup, 18; Sheffield: JSOT Press, 1981).

Niditch, S., 'Portrayals of Women in the Hebrew Bible', in J.R. Baskin (ed.), *Jewish Women in Historical Perspective* (Detroit: Wayne State University Press, 1991), pp. 25-42.

Noth, M., *The Deuteronomistic History* (JSOTSup, 15; Sheffield: JSOT Press, 1981 [1943]).

—'Die Bewährung von Salomos "Göttlicher Weisheit"', in M. Noth and D. Winton Thomas (eds.), *Wisdom in Israel and in the Ancient Near East* (VTSup, 3; Leiden: Brill, 1955), pp. 225-37.

—*Die israelitischen Personennamen im Rahmen der gemeinsemitischen Namengebung* (BWANT, 3.10; Stuttgart: Kohlhammer, 1928).

O'Brien, M.A., *The Deuteronomistic History Hypothesis: A Reassessment* (OBO, 92; Freiburg: Universitätsverlag; Göttingen: Vandenhoeck & Ruprecht, 1989).

Olyan, S., *Asherah and the Cult of Yahweh in Israel* (SBLMS, 34; Atlanta: Scholars Press, 1988).

Oppenheim, A.L., 'The Family of Nabonidus', *ANET*, pp. 311-12.

Peckham, B., *The Composition of the Deuteronomistic History* (HSM, 35; Atlanta: Scholars Press, 1985).

Pedersen, J., *Israel: Its Life and Culture* (London: Oxford University Press, 1926; London: Cumberlege, new edn, 1953).

Peritz, I., 'Women in the Ancient Hebrew Cult', *JBL* 17 (1898), pp. 111-48.

Plaskow, J., *Standing again at Sinai* (San Francisco: Harper & Row, 1990).

Polzin, R., *Samuel and the Deuteronomist* (New York: Harper & Row, 1989).

Porten, B., *Archives from Elephantine: The Life of an Ancient Jewish Military Colony* (Berkeley: University of California Press, 1968).

Porten, B., and A.L. Yardeni, *Textbook of Aramaic Documents from Ancient Egypt* (2 vols.; Winona Lake, IN: Eisenbrauns, 1986, 1989).

Pritchard, J.B. (ed.), *Solomon and Sheba* (London: Phaidon, 1974).

Propp, V., *Morphology of the Folktale* (Austin: University of Texas Press, 2nd rev. edn, 1968).

Provan, I.W., *Hezekiah and the Books of Kings* (BZAW, 172; Berlin: de Gruyter, 1988).

Rad, G. von, 'The Joseph Narrative and Ancient Wisdom', in *The Problem of the Hexateuch and Other Essays* (Edinburgh: Oliver & Boyd, 1966), pp. 292-300.

—*Wisdom in Israel* (New York: Abingdon Press, 1974).

Rashkow, I., 'Daughters and Fathers in Genesis...Or, What is Wrong with This Picture?', in A. Brenner (ed.), *A Feminist Companion to Exodus–Deuteronomy* (The Feminist Companion to the Bible, 5; Sheffield: Sheffield Academic Press, 1994).

Rehm, M., *Das zweite Buch der Könige: Ein Kommentar* (Würzburg: Echter Verlag, 1982).

Reinhartz, A., 'Anonymity and Character in the Books of Samuel', *Semeia* (forthcoming).

Reviv, H., 'On the Days of Athaliah and Joash' (Hebrew), *Bet Miqra* 47 (1970–71), pp. 541-48.

Rich, A., 'Twenty-One Love Poems', in *Dream of a Common Language* (New York: Norton, 2nd edn, 1978).

Ringgren, H., *Israelite Religion* (Philadelphia: Fortress Press, 1966).

Robbins, T., *Skinny Legs and All* (New York: Bantam Press, 1990).

Rofé, A., 'The Classification of the Prophetical Stories', *JBL* 89 (1970), pp. 427-40.

Röllig, W., 'Semiramis', in *Der kleine Pauly* (Stuttgart: A. Druckenmüller, 1975).

Rose, M., 'Bemerkungen zum historischen Fundament des Josias-Bildes in II Reg 22f.', *ZAW* 89 (1977), pp. 50-63.

Rosenthal, F., 'Kilamuwa of Y'dy-Sam'al', *ANET*, pp. 654-55.

Rost, L., *Die Überlieferung von der Thronnachfolge Davids* (BWANT, 3.6; Stuttgart: Kohlhammer, 1926).

Roth, M.T., *Babylonian Marriage Agreements 7th–6th Centuries BC* (AOAT, 222; Neukirchen–Vluyn: Neukirchener Verlag, 1989).

Rudolph, W., *Jeremia* (Tübingen: Mohr [Paul Siebeck], 1985).

Ruether, R.R. (ed.), *Religion and Sexism* (New York: Simon & Schuster, 1974).

Sahlins, M., 'Exchange Value and the Diplomacy of Primitive Trade', in J. Helm, P. Bohannan and M.D. Sahlins (eds.), *Essays in Economic Anthropology Dedicated to the Memory of Karl Polanyi* (Proceedings of the 1965 Annual

Spring Meeting of the American Ethnological Society; Seattle: University of Washington Press, 1965), pp. 95-129.

—*Stone Age Economics* (Chicago: Aldine–Atherton, 1972).

Šanda, A., *Die Bücher der Könige* (EHAT, 9.2; Münster: Aschendorff, 1912).

Satir, V., *Conjoint Family Therapy* (Palo Alto, CA: Science and Behavior Books, 3rd edn, 1983).

—*The New Peoplemaking* (Mountain View, CA: Science and Behavior Books, 1988).

Savran, G., '1 and 2 Kings', in R. Alter and F. Kermode (eds.), *The Literary Guide to the Bible* (Cambridge, MA: Harvard University Press, 1987), pp. 146-64.

Sawyer, J.F.A., 'Daughter of Zion and the Servant of the Lord in Isaiah: A Comparison', *JSOT* 44 (1989), pp. 89-107.

Schramm, W., 'War Semiramis Assyrische Regentin', *Historia* 2 (Wiesbaden: F. Steiner, 1972), pp. 513-21.

Schüssler Fiorenza, E., *In Memory of Her: A Feminist Theological Reconstruction of Christian Origins* (New York: Crossroad, 1983).

—*Revelation: Vision of a Just World* (Proclamation Commentaries; Minneapolis: Fortress Press, 1991).

Schweickart, P., 'Reading Ourselves: Toward a Feminist Theory of Reading', in E.A. Flynn and P. Schweickart (eds.), *Gender and Reading: Essays on Readers, Texts and Contexts* (Baltimore and London: Johns Hopkins University Press, 1986), pp. 31-62.

Scott, R.B.Y., 'Solomon and the Beginnings of Wisdom in Israel', in M. Noth and D. Winton Thomas (eds.), *Wisdom in Israel and in the Ancient Near East* (VTSup, 3; Leiden: Brill, 1955), pp. 262-79.

Segal, M.Z., *The Books of Samuel* (Jerusalem: Kiryat Sefer, 1956).

Sellin, E., and G. Fohrer, *Introduction to the Old Testament* (Nashville: Abingdon Press, 1968).

Seow, C.L., 'The Syro-Palestinian Context of Solomon's Dream', in *SBL Abstracts 1982* (*HTR* 77.2 [1984]), pp. 141-52.

Sered, S.S., 'Conflict, Complement, and Control: Family and Religion Among Middle-Eastern Jewish Women in Jerusalem', *Gender and Society* 5 (1991), pp. 10-29.

Showalter, E., 'Feminist Criticism in the Wilderness', in *idem* (ed.), *The New Feminist Criticism: Essays on Women, Literature, and Theory* (New York: Pantheon Books, 1985).

Silverman, K., *Male Subjectivity at the Margins* (New York: Routledge, 1992).

—*The Acoustic Mirror: The Female Voice in Psychoanalysis and Cinema* (Bloomington: Indiana University Press, 1988)

—*The Subject of Semiotics* (New York: Oxford University Press, 1983)

Simon, U., 'The Story of Samuel's Birth: Structure, Genre, and Meaning', in *idem* (ed.), *Studies in the Bible and Exegesis* (Hebrew; Ramat Gan: Bar Ilan University Press, 1986), II, pp. 57-110.

Simpson, W.K. (ed.), *The Literature of Ancient Egypt: An Anthology of Stories, Instructions and Poetry* (New Haven: Yale University Press, 2nd edn, 1973).

Slotki, J.J., *Daniel, Ezra and Nehemiah* (London: Soncino, 1951).

Smith, D.L., *Religion of the Landless: The Social Context of the Babylonian Exile* (Bloomington, IN: Meyer Stone Books, 1988).

Smith, H.P., *The Books of Samuel* (ICC; Edinburgh: T. & T. Clark, 1899).

Smith, M., *The Early History of God* (New York: Harper & Row, 1987).

Soggin, J.A., *Das Königtum in Israel* (Berlin: Töpelmann, 1967).

Spieckermann, H., *Juda unter Assur in der Sargonidenzeit* (FRLANT, 129; Göttingen: Vandenhoeck & Ruprecht, 1982).

Steck, O.H., *Überlieferung und Zeitgeschichte in den Elia Erzählungen* (WMANT, 26; Neukirchen–Vluyn: Neukirchener Verlag, 1968).

Sternberg, M., *The Poetics of Biblical Narrative: Ideological Literature and the Drama of Reading* (Bloomington: Indiana University Press, 1985).

Tadmor, H., 'Autobiographical Apology in the Royal Assyrian Literature', in H. Tadmor and M. Weinfeld (eds.), *History, Historiography and Interpretation: Studies in Biblical and Cuneiform Literatures* (Jerusalem: Magnes, 1983), pp. 36-57.

Tannen, D., *You Just Don't Understand: Women and Men in Conversation* (New York: Ballantine Books, 1990).

Terrien, S., *Till the Heart Sings: A Biblical Theology of Manhood and Womanhood* (Philadelphia: Fortress Press, 1985).

—*The Elusive Presence: Toward a New Biblical Theology* (Religious Perspectives, 26; New York: Harper & Row, 1978).

Teubal, S.J., *Hagar the Egyptian: The Lost Tradition of the Matriarchs* (San Francisco: HarperCollins, 1990).

Thibault, P., *Social Semiotics as Praxis* (Minneapolis: University of Minnesota Press, 1991).

Thiel, W., *Die deuteronomistische Redaktion von Jeremia 1–25* (WMANT, 41; Neukirchen–Vluyn: Neukirchener Verlag, 1973).

—*Die deuteronomistische Redaktion von Jeremia 26–45* (WMANT, 52; Neukirchen–Vluyn: Neukirchener Verlag, 1981).

Thompson, S., *Motif-Index of Folk Literature* (Bloomington: Indiana University Press, rev. edn, 1975).

Thornton, T.C.G., 'Solomonic Apologetic in Samuel and Kings', *CQR* 169 (1968), pp. 159-66.

Timm, S., *Die Dynastie Omri: Quellen und Untersuchungen zur Geschichte Israel im 9 Jahrhundert vor Christus* (FRLANT, 124; Göttingen: Vandenhoeck & Ruprecht, 1982).

Trible, P., *God and the Rhetoric of Sexuality* (Philadelphia: Fortress Press, 1978).

—*Texts of Terror: Literary-Feminist Readings of Biblical Narratives* (Philadelphia: Fortress Press, 1984).

Turner, V., *The Ritual Process* (Chicago: Aldine, 1969).

Uffenheimer, B., 'The Stories of Elijah; the Stories of Elisha', in *Ancient Prophecy in Israel* (Hebrew; Jerusalem: Magnes, 1973), pp. 186-277.

Van Seters, J., *In Search of History* (New Haven: Yale University Press, 1983).

Vaux, R. de, *Ancient Israel: Its Life and Institutions* (trans. J. McHugh; New York: McGraw–Hill, 1961; London: Darton, Longman & Todd, 1962).

Vos, C.J., *Women in Old Testament Worship* (Delft: Judels & Brinkman, 1968).

Washington, H.C., 'The "Strange Woman" of Proverbs 1–9 and Post-Exilic Judean Society' (unpublished paper presented at SBL Annual Meeting, New Orleans, November 1990).

Weinberg, J.P., 'Die Agrarverhältnisse in der Bürger-Tempel-Gemeinde der

Achämenidenzeit', *Acta Antiqua Academiae Scientiarum Hungaricae* 22 (1974), pp. 473-85.

Weinfeld, M., 'Kuntillet 'Ajrud Inscriptions and their Significance', *SEL* 1 (1984), pp. 121-30.

—*Deuteronomy and the Deuteronomistic School* (Oxford: Clarendon Press, 1972).

Weippert, H., *Die Prosareden des Jeremiabuches* (BZAW, 132; Berlin and New York: de Gruyter, 1973).

Weisberg, D.B., 'Royal Women of the Neo-Babylonian Period', in P. Garelli (ed.), *Le Palais et la Royauté, XIXe RAI* (Paris: Geuthner, 1974).

Westendorf, W., 'Ursprung und Wesen der Maat, der altägyptischen Göttin des Rechts, der Gerechtigkeit und der Weltordnung', in S. Lauffer (ed.), *Festgabe für Dr Walter Will, Ehrensenator der Universität München zum 70. Geburtstag am 12. November 1966* (Cologne: Carl Heymanns, 1966).

Westermann, C., *Genesis 12–36: A Commentary* (trans. J.J. Scullion SJ; Minneapolis: Augsburg, 1985).

White, D.G., *Ar'n't I a Woman? Female Slaves in the Plantation South* (New York: Norton, 1985).

Whybray, R.N., *The Succession Narrative: A Study of 2 Sam. 9–20 and 1 Kings 1 and 2* (SBT, 2.9; London: SCM Press, 1968).

Williams, J.G., 'Between Reader and Text: A General Response', *Semeia* 46 (1989), pp. 169-79.

—*Women Recounted: Narrative Thinking and the God of Israel* (Sheffield: Almond Press, 1982).

Williamson, H.G.M., 'The Composition of Ezra i–vi', *JTS* NS 34 (1983), pp. 1-30.

—*Ezra, Nehemiah* (WBC, 16; Waco, TX: Word Books, 1985).

Willis, J.T., 'Cultic Elements in the Story of Samuel's Birth and Dedication', *ST* 26 (1972).

Wilson, R.R., 'Family', in P. Achtemeier (ed.), *Harper's Bible Dictionary* (San Francisco: Harper & Row, 1985), pp. 302-303.

Wiseman, D.J., *Nebuchadrezzar and Babylon* (Oxford: Oxford University Press, 1985).

Wolff, H.W., *Anthropology of the Old Testament* (trans. M. Kohl; Philadelphia: Fortress Press, 1974).

Würthwein, E., 'Die Josianische Reform und das Deuteronium', *ZTK* 73 (1976), pp. 395-423.

—*Die Erzählung von der Thronfolge Davids—theologische oder politische Geschichtsschreibung?* (Theologische Studien, 115; Zürich: Theologischer Verlag, 1974).

Yeivin, S., *Studies in the History of Israel and its Country* (Hebrew; Tel Aviv: Newman, 1960).

Zakovitch, Y., *Ruth* (Hebrew; Miqra LeYisra'el; Tel Aviv: Am Oved; Jerusalem: Magnes, 1990).

Zalevski, S., *Solomon's Ascension to the Throne* (Hebrew; Jerusalem: Marcus, 1981).

Zimbalist Rosaldo, M., 'The Use and Abuse of Anthropology: Reflections on Feminism and Cross-Cultural Understanding', *SIGNS* 5 (1980), pp. 389-417.

Zimbalist Rosaldo, M., and L. Lamphere (eds.), *Woman, Culture, and Society* (Stanford: Stanford University Press, 1974).

Zimmerli, W., *Ezechiel* (Neukirchen–Vluyn: Neukirchener Verlag, 1969).